Harvey Adelberg, Owner: Adventures Video Productions

Some day all the wisdom that lies between the two covers of "Unforgettable Bosses" will be encapsulated in a pill and transferred via injection. What a shame! We would miss the "getting there" portion of reaching our destination. Bob DeLisa has prepared a portable feast of insights, advice and practical tips that pair well with a desire to better one's management skills.

Richard Cohen, President-Waverly Markets (a ShopRite Co-Op member)

"There are certain books which, when puzzled, frustrated, or indecisive about how to handle people issues, are really helpful for any business owner or manager. This one is essential! Bob DeLisa has written a great guide to improving teamwork, understanding and productivity in any company."

Marnie Cooper, Sales and Marketing Manager-Roncari Express Valet Parking

Throw away those other tomes, UB has everything you need to know. Bob DeLisa, with heart and good humor, guides you through the steps to become a better manager.

Forget the fads and flavor of the month. Bob DeLisa has delivered a workplace handbook that you can carry with you while you and your company grow up. His insight, concern for his clients and comedic timing ALWAYS bear fruit. Unforgettable Boss is easy to read, easy to implement, impossible to ignore.

Bernie Demko, COO/CFO: Purple Communications, Inc.

The Unforgettable Boss is the most effective tool in developing critical leadership skills. After working with Bob (DeLisa) over 20 years, and implementing many of these tried and true techniques, I can say from personal experience, it works. An easy and entertaining read with valued lessons, you will find Unforgettable Boss the best leadership/management development tool yet. Bottom line, it really works.

Martha (Marty) Hunt, former President, Connecticut Economic Resource Center (CERC) and currently Executive Director, Green Mountain Horse Association

If you think your employees are your most valuable asset, then you need to be the best manager you can be to maximize their potential and run a successful organization. I have worked with Bob managing two very different organizations and not only did I do a better job as a result of his coaching, my employees were happier and the places ran better.I have found that behind just about every confrontation, disagreement or argument is some communication issue. Either there was not not enough communication or it was not clear or not understood. These techniques can improve your communication skills, help you improve others and cause immediate positive results.

Bob McCue, retired VP-GM Emhart Teknologies – North American Industrial Division (A Unit of Black & Decker)

In this superb presentation of practical advice to bosses of all stripes, we have concentrated wisdom gained through experience and deep reflection. With many anecdotes and illustrations, it's a practical how-to on interpersonal communications, team building, and personnel selection and training. Anyone who directs, manages or bosses others will benefit from its insights. A book to read and then keep handy!

Henry McNulty, former Associate Editor at The Hartford Courant

This book is that great rarity: a serious guide to better management that's fun to read. Bob DeLisa's practical, no nonsense advice garnered from his extensive business experience is lightened by dozens of often amusing true-life examples of the pitfalls all managers face ... and the ways to avoid them. The result is a how-to guide that actually works!

Stefan Morgenstern, President and CEO of MTU-Aero Engines North America

At least twice a day I find myself smiling after using Bob's fundamentals while thinking: Managing can be really easy. Reading the book is (almost) like having a coaching session with Bob: You leave with a bunch of useful tips, an appropriate portion of self-reflection and stronger than before the session.

Alan Ortner, President of Sirois Tool Company

What a fine book! A great read the first time through and a keeper to refer back to when needed. When Bob's advice is followed it really works. It has worked for me.

Stephen Schwartz, Chairman of the Board and CEO S&S Worldwide

Bob has always been honest and straightforward. His messages, like the ones in this book, are filled with common sense and delivered with a generous helping of humor. You find yourself repeatedly thinking, "Why didn't I think of that?"

Greg Wolf, President – BHS Corrugated North America, Inc.

The Unforgettable Boss is a lot like Bob himself - approachable, to the point, and full of common sense. This book talks about all the things that take years of experience to learn. It breaks down the essential tasks of management - setting goals, managing teams, communicating, and evaluating and developing talent - in an accessible, easy to understand way. These are the things that all of us as managers - highly experienced, new to the job, or somewhere in between - must learn to do better."

The Unforgettable Boss

The Seven Fundamentals of Managing and Motivating

Bob DeLisa

And Kelly McDaniel

THE UNFORGETTABLE BOSS.

Printed in the United States of America

First Printing, 2013

ISBN: 0988650967
ISBN-13: 978-0988650961

Significance Press
200 Park Avenue, 26th Floor
New York, NY 10166
www.SignificancePress.com

For my sweet mother, Rose, who even though she loved her four sons unconditionally, would sometimes ask me in private: "Bob, just what is it that you really do for a living?" Mom, this is it.

CONTENTS

Most men [and women] lead lives of quiet desperation and go to the grave with the song still in them.

-Henry David Thoreau

We teach best what we most need to learn.

-Richard Bach

Foreword

Bob DeLisa not only has a real passion for his work, but also has a very outgoing and dynamic personality, which has made me and my colleagues feel in many of our training sessions over the years like we were being entertained rather than trained. Whether learning management techniques or continuous improvement principles or participating in teambuilding exercises, we always had fun. But most importantly, we always left the sessions with a new perspective and understanding of the topic.

Bob has a way of fitting in and quickly becoming part of your team. This doesn't happen by itself; Bob spends hours with you prior to the actual training session preparing and understanding your corporate culture. While you're prepping, you don't realize how well he's listening and his remarkable attention to detail until later, during the training session, when he makes a comment or recalls an anecdote about the staff that you had told him weeks earlier. This is impressive to witness.

I've learned a lot from Bob and over the years have used many of the techniques described in this book almost every day. I also realize there are a few techniques I should use more often, especially when dealing with delicate employee situations. So I plan to keep a copy of this book near me to help guide me in my day-to-day management responsibilities.

About halfway through The Unforgettable Boss, I knew that we would be purchasing enough copies for our entire management team. I knew it would be the perfect refresher for some of our long-time managers, and a great tool for newer managers.

I've attended many management training sessions in my career and have read numerous management books, but this book is unique. Not only does it describe management principles, but it also gives you tools to effectively implement those principles. Furthermore, though he has aimed his messages at the smaller business enterprises, I feel the management techniques and tenets Bob instructs us in are applicable to a wide spectrum of organizations, both large and small.
I urge you to read The Unforgettable Boss and share it with your entire management team. Bob and his team have done a lot to help strengthen my company's management, and now with this book, he has given you the same opportunity.

Tony Barillari
Vice President-Administration
Connecticut Business and Industry Association

Acknowledgements

Writing this book was a little like traveling around a Monopoly® game board (in the automobile token, of course) with all its associated moments of elation and frustration, where at certain stops along the way some pretty amazing people offered me guidance, moral support, critical comments, and sometimes all three. Their contributions, next after being blessed with three terrific and loving kids, are recalled here as some of the best moments of my life.

My thanks to Harvey Adelberg and Mike Watt for their friendship and continuing support. I first met Harvey Adelberg, owner of AdVentures Video Productions, and Mike Watt, Executive Producer at American Audio Visual Center, as clients when they were members of the executive management team at a Connecticut TV station back in the mid-1980s. The three of us formed a close friendship and would meet several times a year over dinner to offer each other advice and counsel on our respective life and work challenges. I had been keeping a file folder of client experience notes, and Harvey and Mike regularly pushed me to get busy writing the *definitive management book* I often talked about during our dinners together. But I kept putting them off with the excuse that I needed to engage with people as I did in my live seminars in order to be effective; that writing about my client adventures wouldn't work for me. These guys didn't buy my excuse, and they finally embarrassed me enough to roll the dice and get off *Oriental Avenue* toward better *properties*.

My thanks also goes to Lise Dondy, who, as she was re-
tiring from her presidency of The Connecticut Clean Energy
Fund (CCEF), logged several hours listening to and commenting on the different ways I wanted to present the subject matter of this book. In addition to Lise's enthusiastic encouragement, she offered to buy me dinner upon completion
of the book. Lise, get out your AMEX card.

I then began working on an outline for the manuscript,
but got stalled in a space reserved for procrastinators in *Free
Parking* for a couple of months until Bob McCue came along.
Bob is retired VP-GM of Emhart Teknologies – North American Industrial Division (a unit of Stanley Black & Decker),
and a former client who became a friend. My thanks to Bob
for being instrumental in prompting me to get back to writing and for being a tough, honest, but supportive critic of the
manuscript.

In addition to Bob McCue, my thanks go to 12 other jun-
ior editors: Rich Cohen, President-Waverly Markets (a
ShopRite Co-Op member); Marnie Cooper, Sales and Mar-
keting Manager at Roncari Express Valet Parking; Bernie
Demko, COO/CFO Purple Communications, Inc.; Juergen
Eschenbacher, Managing Director of The MTRI Consortium
in Munich, Germany; Marc Giles, Executive Director, Gerber
Scientific, Inc.; Martha "Marty" Hunt, former President,
Connecticut Economic Resource Center (CERC) and current-
ly Executive Director, Green Mountain Horse Association;
Roger Kern, Editor and Publisher, EDM Today Magazine
and consultant at International Technology Professionals;
Stephen Schwartz, Chairman of the Board and CEO, S&S
Worldwide; Mark Soycher, Human Resource Counsel at the
Connecticut Business and Industry Association (CBIA); and

Greg Wolf, President, BHS Corrugated North America, Inc. They took valuable time from their busy lives to offer moral support and editing suggestions. I was singularly touched by how they all enthusiastically agreed to provide their valuable assistance. More than anything, it was their positive and constructive feedback that drove me to hustle toward *Park Place* and finish the manuscript. Particular thanks also go to Alan Ortner, President of Sirois Tool Company, and Stefan Morgenstern, President and CEO of MTU-Aero Engines North America, for their extremely valuable critiques and statements of support. Their reinforcement was just what I needed to come out from under the bed and really home in on the book's *Part Two: The Manual.* Saying that you have my heartfelt thanks doesn't do justice to my sense of gratitude.

My appreciation also goes to Joe Tessitore, Patrick Malone, Nate Adams and Jim Zebora at Significance Press. Their help was easily worth the rent for landing on *Atlantic Avenue.*

Further gratitude goes to Henry McNulty, a former Associate Editor at the Hartford Courant and currently a consultant, who was an immense help in hacking through what I was calling *The Gordian Knot* of trying to sort out *The Seven Fundamentals.* In addition, his guidance, incredible insights and gentle demeanor made Henry an invaluable co-pilot. Henry got the motor in my little automobile game piece revved up, and I took a sharp right past the *Go To Jail* corner and sped toward *Pennsylvania Avenue.* Many thanks to Henry, who I'm lucky to have as a colleague and friend.

I would also like to thank Stan Cohen, a mentor as well as a client, who willingly read and made suggestions on the first few chapters and graciously let me identify him as a central character in a couple of what I think are the best stories in the book. Kelly McDaniel, my business partner and contributing author, not only wrote most of Chapter Five in *The Unforgettable Boss*, she also was holding up the walls of our management consulting practice, DeLisaGroup. My thanks to Kelly for allowing me to dedicate the time needed to work on this book and always cheerleading.

While I was having an engine tune-up at *Park Place*, Tony Barillari, VP of Administration at CBIA, graciously agreed to write the Foreword of *The Unforgettable Boss*. Not only do I thank Tony for his effort, but having his name connected to this book is an honor.

I was also fortunate enough to enlist the services of Dr. Paul Lupia, General Educational Consultant in Dallas, who reviewed the final manuscript. My deep appreciation goes to Paul.

Finally, and maybe most importantly, I want to thank darling Wendy, my spouse and navigator on this trip around the Monopoly Board, always at my side and with her gentle spirit and sweet grace helping me to keep on keeping on. Through it all, Wendy got me to *Boardwalk.*

Authors Note

The.

There, I finally wrote it.

When I first considered I had enough miles on my career as a management consultant and was ready to share with the world my extensive knowledge about managing people, I sought counsel on writing discipline from a good friend, Hal who wasn't a writer himself, but had more self-control and ability to focus on a mission than anyone I had ever known. Hal invented board games, which is probably as lonely a vocation as writing, as I've come to find out. To give you an idea of just how disciplined he was, early in his game invention career, he set a goal to come up with one new game concept a month and sell one each year. And that's exactly what he did!

Hal's advice to me to get over the hump of starting to write this book was to simply type the word, "The," then go from there. So, some 15 years later, I just did. But hey, enough about Hal. This book isn't about him. Mostly, it's about you, and maybe me a little.

There is no question that the messages in The Unforgettable Boss speak to a universal audience of managers and leaders in all sizes and shapes of organizations. Colleagues and clients who have read early versions of the manuscript have affirmed this. However, this book is especially for the people who own and/or manage in the smaller companies or organizations, or what I'll frequently refer to as "enterprises." Whether it's a family-owned manufacturing company or job shop, doctor's office or healthcare facility, wholesale distributor or service company, not-for-profit organization or association, retail, insurance, media or finance-based organization – my associates at DeLisaGroup and I worked in them all. We understand more than just about anybody the mindset and experiences of the people who manage small enterprises, many of which were begun in a garage, in a basement or on a kitchen table. We understand the limited physical resources and bench strength, the really short line between profit and loss, the sense of family that develops in small enterprises and how this characteristic can help and hinder growth and decision-making, and the limited opportunities there are to promote good people. I understand the absolute joy of small successes, and the abject fear that if one mistake is made, the whole world will hear about it and the phone will never ring again.

I've enjoyed a nice career consulting to hundreds of smaller enterprises over a 35-year period; a career that's been rewarding in the sense of the wonderful clients I've worked with whose beliefs, experiences, courage and moral fiber have inspired me. Before the consulting career, and except for two years of teaching junior high right out of college, I spent about 12 years starting and running my own small businesses, including restaurants, direct sales and advertising. Over that period of time, I learned along the way as much about what not to do as what to do. The management consulting practice was built over time largely through referral. And our drive in building our business has always been along the lines of: *Is what we're recommending really in the client's best interest, or too much in ours? Do they really need us to do this, or should we be teaching them to fish?*

When I was in consulting school – there actually is a school for what we do – I was one of those who believed it when the textbook said: *As a consultant, your job is to work yourself out of a job – to essentially help the client become self-reliant.* On the other hand, we built relationships with clients that have endured for years, even to succeeding generations of management or ownership. In all that time, and through hundreds of jobs, we've never not been paid – even though most of our work over the years was contracted with a simple handshake.

A major reason for writing this book is that my head is bursting with terrific client stories: how, with our help, they managed conflict, re-arranged their enterprise's structure to suit the times, and built or disbanded teams. We helped them hire good people, and coached them on how to manage people up, sideways, or sometimes, out. We've helped write policy manuals, and lit the match to burn them when clients tried to use them to replace good judgment. We trained scores of newly minted managers on the basics of supervision, and re-trained experienced managers who were caught in a rut. We helped an ambulance company during their management team retreat when the team was struggling with trying to decide who to promote to the top position. Partly from exhaustion, and partly from the owner's entrepreneurial spirit, they followed our suggestion to hold an election, based on the notion that employees wouldn't vote for a jerk as their boss. The election was held, and the person worked out just fine.

I once read an interesting book of poetry by James Kavanaugh entitled *There Are Men Too Gentle To Live Among Wolves* (E.P. Dutton; 1972). The title poem was, in its time, written as a slam against the stereotypic politics of life in larger corporations; the infighting, backstabbing, posturing, playing both sides against the middle and general win-at-all-costs behavior indicative of such environments. The poem makes the point that some people not only don't fit well in such environments, but get eaten alive in them, because their senses of ethics and right and wrong won't allow them to play by those rules. We have tended to be drawn to, and work very well with, such clients: people whose moral fiber has them wanting to do the right thing versus the easy thing.

Don't get me wrong. Our clients aren't meek little namby-pambies afraid of their own shadows. Far from it. Our clients are typically heroic, tough, passionate, enterprising risk-takers and decision-makers with the courage to question and challenge themselves and the status quo at appropriate intervals. If I had to describe them succinctly, I'd quote the High Priest in legendary Shangri-La in James Hilton's book Lost Horizons, who said to the Englishman whom he wanted to take his place when he died: "We live by a simple principle. Be kind." This is the sort of men and women with whom we've worked so closely and so admired for their ability and preference to be fearless and yet be kind. The work world of these people is not one of political intrigue. Their biggest concerns are adjusting to their ever-changing cultures. These people play it and tell it like it is, with no hidden agendas, just straight plain talk and behaviors. What they struggle with quite often is why things can't be the way they used to be when they had just one milling machine, phone, desk, or blue suit for calling on customers.

As a side point, and after so many years of working in many different environments, I'd say there is a high correlation between the size of an organization and its tendency toward political behavior. You need lots of scorecards and road maps to get through the political maze of larger organizations. To be sure, lots of conflict and dysfunctional behavior goes on within the walls of smaller enterprises, but it generally gets played out more in the open with fewer hidden agendas afoot. Furthermore, we have found within smaller enterprises a greater willingness to get at the problems in a forthright way, resolve them, and move on.

On a recent client visit to a health care company with about 350 employees, I brought along with me Paul, an industrial psychologist whose company we often partner with when we need profile and feedback surveys. Paul's company has for years usually worked with Fortune 500 companies, and he came with me to explain to my client's management team the values and nuances of a particular personnel selection tool we felt would be helpful as they worked toward recruiting a high-level manager. As Paul and I were driving back from the meeting, he turned to me and said, "You know, Bob, I just love your clients! They're so real and upfront with their thoughts, questions and disagreements." Paul went on to say that he never feels he has to be careful in choosing his words with our clients, or wonder whether there are messages within messages in their comments or questions. In essence, with our clients, what you see is what you get, and that makes it so easy to work with them. In short, we've always been more comfortable and operated more fluidly in the trenches than in the boardroom.

Thoreau's observation about quiet desperation is so *not* true of our smaller enterprise clients, who every day face down the failure demons and do the right thing (sometimes rather than doing things right). While a number of clients we've served have been classical entrepreneurs – visionaries who started their own companies, often on a shoestring – many more of them either took over from the founder or rose through the (small) ranks to take the organization to the next level. In all cases, though, our clients represented in this book have been people who always strived to do the best for the enterprise as well as its people. They had the wisdom to seek counsel from people like us (even though they sometimes didn't follow it or agree with it), sometimes after problems occurred, and sometimes operating ahead of the curve and using us to pre-empt problems, but always being humble enough to know they didn't know it all. They are the ones who actually wrote a lot of this book. I mostly just took notes. And those notes, once reviewed, began to take the shape of a series of consistent dos and don'ts messages about managing people.

Therefore, this book is designed to be a manual of practical tips for pretty much any situation that you might be presented with in managing an enterprise, from hiring, to training, to coaching, to counseling, to firing, to teamwork, and lots of stuff in between. The first four chapters set the tone and parameters for what makes *Unforgettable Bosses* who and what they are. Each subsequent chapter is designed as a stand-alone treatment of a given subject. We've tried in all cases to prescribe not just what to do, but how to do it; to provide the actual script and/or steps in a process. This feature, I think, differentiates this book from others on the subject of managing people-especially in the smaller enterprise.

As I began to actually write, I relied on some collected wisdom that seemed to be consistent with most "How-To" books. They are all under 300 pages long and usually have a number in the title (Twelve Ways to Tie Your Shoes, The Six Rules of Being a Road Hog, etc.). Three hundred pages, I'm advised, is about the tolerance level for busy people who want to learn new stuff quickly, and it seems people like numbers because numbers refer to a list, and lists are relatively easy to commit to memory and recall, especially when you want to sound brilliant in front of the troops ("The five reasons for our success are..."). A third bit of wisdom I encountered came from a number of clients who have said to me that reading any business "How-To" book is worthwhile if they could get one good idea or message from it. I covered the first two pieces of wisdom (around 300 pages and a number in the title), but hope I missed on the third. It would be great if you get several really good ideas, rather than just the one, from reading these lessons on how to be an *Unforgettable Boss*.

All the client stories are true, but names are disguised, and sometimes the stories are a composite of two or more events – all in the interest of maintaining anonymity for these terrific, *Unforgettable Bosses* who have touched and enriched our lives as we hope we have touched and enriched theirs.

Organization

Part One of this book, or the first four chapters, deals with the building blocks or understandings that all bosses should have when it comes to leading the enterprise and the people in it. Part Two is what I call "The Manual," with three chapters examining the functions of management during the life cycle of people at work, beginning with recruiting and hiring.

The idea is that once the basic building blocks are embraced and practiced, they become what you stand on to apply to all the possible boss-employee relation situations.

More specifically:

PART ONE: THE BUILDING BLOCKS

Chapter 1: Physician, Heal Thyself is about the importance of self-examination of your motives and drives as a boss, and the fairness factor of knowing that the employee and you both play a part in the success or failure of the relationship. It still takes two to tango.

Chapter 2: The Seven Fundamentals is a compendium of tried and true theories, beliefs and practices of *Unforgettable Bosses*. It covers the buttons to push and those to avoid to get optimum performance out of people – because optimum performance is what it should be all about, not making people feel good just for the sake of making them feel good.

Chapter 3: The Basic Objectives in Managing Others. A popular definition of a manager or management is: *Getting work done through others*. This chapter boils this responsibility down into three basic objectives: being clear about goals and expectations; creating an environment where people can be fully successful, and finding out about people's willingness or ability to do a job.

Chapter 4: The Art and Science of Communication. To be sure, electronic communication (e-mails, tweets, blogs, etc.) is a rapid way to get information out, but it's a poor substitute for resolving problems or clarifying issues and directions. This chapter focuses on the key communication skills bosses need to master: *presenting your thoughts, ideas and wishes, and listening to the thoughts, ideas and wishes of others.*

PART TWO: THE MANUAL

Chapter 5: Interviewing, Selecting and Orienting Good People. Those who own or manage in smaller enterprises are at a distinct disadvantage when it comes to finding good people because they are too busy running things and usually aren't big enough to have a human resources professional on board to help them in these critical functions. This chapter provides some simple but useful steps and tools to help you hire better – and with your head, not your heart.

Chapter 6: Identifying and Developing Talent. "There's no room to grow here" is a long-standing myth within small enterprises. Growth can go sideways as well as vertically. This chapter lays out the BOSS-2000 model that walks you through a step-by-step process to help you give your best people their best shot at success, and they'll love you for it.

Chapter 7: The Toughest Part of the Job – Counseling and Terminating. If I guess right, you are tempted to jump ahead and read this chapter first, but don't. If you do everything outlined in all the preceding chapters, you might not need to read this one at all, even though it's got some great advice in it.

PART ONE:
THE BUILDING BLOCKS

1

PHYSICIAN, HEAL THYSELF

What if Shirley MacLaine is wrong?

W hat if we don't get to come back again and again, rounding out our experiences until we've tasted all the wines and sampled all the fruits? What if there is no "do-over," and this is our only chance to get it right? Instead of leading a life of "quiet desperation," being pulled instead of doing the pulling, or accepting anything less than what is optimal for you, wouldn't it be gratifying to get the most out of this life? You've already been told countless times in books and articles that if you want the way your life works – at the office or anywhere – to be more fulfilling, you're the one who has to make it happen.

Let's see how you can go about doing so.

The best place to start in becoming an *Unforgettable Boss* is with taking a trip into your own psyche. If you're like most managers/owners I know who work in smaller enterprises, you probably never went to an official "Management School." Most likely you either set up shop one day to do a thing you knew a lot about and wanted to take a chance on being successful at; or you rose through some very small ranks to a power position because you were recognized as being very good at your core job, and it was assumed that if you were good at designing widgets, you must be good at managing the other people who designed those widgets; or you had the same last name as the owner of the company, and it was assumed you'd take over one day and morph into the personality and skill set of the founder.

I've often wondered about this tendency to have people manage other people and provide them with little or no formal training beforehand. Think, for instance, about how much training time is needed even for jobs requiring the most limited skills. At one point, L. L. Bean, in its hugely successful mail order business, spent 40 hours training customer service personnel before they were allowed to take their first phone order (this, in the days before the Internet). If you've ever ordered anything from L.L. Bean, you now know why it was such a positive experience.

How about in your own organization? A machine operator? A data entry person? A receptionist? A retail sales clerk? A food packager? How much time is devoted to training a newbie at any of these jobs? Certainly, at least 5 to 10 hours of training to at least be able to wade into the water, and substantially more hours to become proficient and swim on their own. How about the time required to be trained in higher-skilled jobs? Programmers, researchers, lathe operators, bookkeepers…weeks, months, even years. And yet, we regularly put people in charge of other people (the most complex of all machines) with *maybe* sending them out to attend a one-day, public registration seminar for $100. That's six hours of training, discounting the hour for lunch. Don't get me started on how ridiculous this habit is. What potential and real damage we can do to subordinates and ourselves by not getting some formal training to perform the people-management work!

Don't get caught bagging groceries, or – better yet – should you even be a boss?

Being a boss requires a certain mindset. For some people, the preference is to take direction from others and generally restrict your focus to doing your job well, and not have to be responsible for others doing their jobs and/or a broader range of decision-making responsibilities. That's perfectly fine. The world needs both Indians and Chiefs. But, the boss needs to be more the "Chief."

Early in my career, Stan Cohen (actual person) was all at the same time a boss, mentor, partner and pain in the butt. Stan was president of a supermarket chain of some 26 stores, and I was hired by him to establish a human resources training and development function for the company, as well as serve as his executive coach (before the term was even invented). Stan was a unique guy. He had a somewhat intimidating presence: tall, with a deep baritone radio-announcer voice, and glasses resting toward the end of his nose so that when he looked at you, you had the sense of being looked down upon. At the same time, he had an acute awareness about the function of management and the negative and positive payoffs of having either poorly or well-trained supervisors in place. For his time, and in that industry, he was a pioneer in his commitment to training. I had the (management) science in my pocket, and he had the experience in his, and together we made a good team, although there were a lot of disagreements along the way. There will be a few Stan Cohen-based stories in this book. This one fits well here.

Stan took the shaken manager up to the office, retracted the termination and told him he was hired to manage situations, not bag groceries...and that while he was flailing away stuffing paper and plastic sacks, the store was going to hell. From then on, "bagging groceries" became my term for whenever a manager was doing and not managing.

As his executive coach, I would occasionally accompany Stan on his visits to individual stores in order to check on store conditions, managers' concerns, etc. On this particular trip, it was a very busy pre-holiday Friday afternoon, and this store was absolutely wall-to-wall with customers. As we walked in, the store manager was at one of the registers frantically bagging groceries (He must have come up through the ranks, because he was quite good at loading those bags to just the right amount of content a customer could handle). Stan took the manager aside and fired him on the spot. I was flabbergasted. After all, here was a poor guy doing the best he could, trying to plug a hole during a peak period, breaking a sweat while doing so, and his reward was immediate termination? This was early in my work with Stan, and for the moment, I thought I had hired on with a bully for a client. A few minutes later, Stan took the shaken manager up to the office, retracted the termination and told the manager that he was hired to manage situations, and that while he was flailing away stuffing paper and plastic sacks, the store was going to hell. It's an experience I've never forgotten (I'm sure the store manager didn't either). From then on, "bagging groceries" became my term for whenever a manager was *doing* and not managing.

In a similar but more dramatic example of a person avoiding the management function, I'm reminded of a VP of Operations for a distribution company with about 250 employees who was charged with overseeing the building of a new warehouse facility. This VP took the term "oversee" to mean "manage," and he proceeded to become the general contractor (GC) for the new building, ostensibly to save the money that would have to be paid to an outside GC. Well, to be sure, this VP did save the company about $100,000 from the original quotes, but at the same time, the company lost out on a new business opportunity and suffered increases in operational expense that more than off-set the $100,000 "savings" while he was *bagging groceries.*

> *It's OK and normal for managers to want to occasionally go and hide out from the day-to-day ambiguities of managing people and things. We all need those kinds of escapes to keep ourselves sane.*

Now, I knew both guys – the store manager and the VP of Operations – and I will tell you truthfully that the store manager really wanted to manage, but simply lacked the tools and training. However, the VP of Operations, who had a strong financial background, was, in my view, always more interested (and capable) in managing numbers than he was people. You might ask how, then, he got to be a VP of Operations? He happened to be one of those people who was there when the company was formed, grew up with it, was smart with the financials and loyal, so it was *assumed* he'd be good at operations … it happens all the time. Please understand, it's OK and normal for managers to want to occasionally go and hide out from the day-to-day ambiguities of managing people and things by having their mini-games of golf (opening the mail, running an errand others would normally do, writing checks, or even bagging groceries). We all need those kinds of escapes to keep ourselves sane. Just be sure you are doing these tasks as *"want* tos" not *"need* tos."* It's OK to bury yourself in analyzing the financials because you want to, rather than having *the talk* with Marlon because you need to. Just be sure, also, that these interruptions are the exception and not the rule of how you work your day. Otherwise, think again about whether or not you really should be a manager. OK?

This management job is serious business. Even in the smaller enterprise, once that first layer of new people comes on board – the ones who weren't there to share the original vision or dream – managing becomes more and more a full-time job requiring a lot of energy, focus and dedication. Leaders in most enterprises that deliver excellent customer service will tell you that if you take care of your employees, they'll automatically take care of your customers – and very well. Unfortunately, the opposite also holds true .

Now, let's examine…

How we form our management styles

Even without formal training, we do get our management styles from somewhere. Possibly, it's the imitation of a style we admired in a former boss. For instance, she could have been trustworthy, honest, supportive and nurturing.

A number of years ago, in conducting management training courses, I would regularly ask the group of trainees which words came to mind when they thought about the best boss they ever had. I began to compile their answers over time, and this is the distilled list of responses in no specific order:

- Supportive; interested in my development
- Fair in distributing work
- Approachable
- Non-judgmental
- Gives feedback; positive and negative
- Shows confidence in her/himself
- Holds people accountable
- Coaches and mentors; empowers
- Sets clear expectations
- Shows sincere concern; takes a personal interest

Keep in mind these were spontaneous responses to the "Best Boss I Ever Had" question that was asked at the *beginning* of the seminar, before any teaching or learning occurred.

On the other hand, maybe your style is the practiced antithesis of a former boss whom you couldn't get away from fast enough – that boss who was self-serving, autocratic and harsh, or AWOL when you needed guidance and left you hanging out to dry when a crisis hit. I didn't have to ask management training seminar participants to compile a "Worst Boss" list, as pretty much everyone agreed it would comprise the opposite of the "Best Boss" one, or:

- Self-serving; showed little or no interest in my development

- Unfair distribution of work; played favorites

- Unapproachable; harsh and critical

- Judgmental (see "Unapproachable")

- Doesn't give feedback, or only recognizes faults and failures. One of the most common complaints I hear from subordinates about bosses is: "They always tell me when I've done something wrong, never when I've done something right." Sound familiar? (If you're a boss who holds strongly to the belief: "Why should I commend a person for just doing what's expected?" or "If I praise them, they'll want more money or get a big head and start to slack off," please hang in there with me. I'm hoping to change your mind. Besides, do you really want to feel and act this way?) When we do management feedback surveys where the troops anonymously rate their bosses, consistently the lowest rating is about the lack of any kind of feedback at all from the boss!

- Not confident; tentative and indecisive

- Doesn't hold people accountable; avoids confrontation or is un-aware of what's going on – "clueless."

- Poor coach and mentor; either uninvolved and *laissez-faire* ("I'm busy, you figure it out"), or autocratic and controlling ("my way or the highway")

- Has a fuzzy or changeable vision (however, usually enjoys being a Monday morning quarterback)

- Lacks concern for the person; cares only about getting the job done ("It's only a flesh wound, suck it up and get back in there.")

A third way that your style may be formed has to do with your genetic makeup. Think parents and other relatives. For instance, my father lived with the firm belief that toilet paper should be placed in the "over-the-roll" position on the holder, and that lawns should be mowed in a concentric pattern, never up and down. Family legend has it that in later life my dad would flip the roll in other people's homes, kind of becoming known as the toilet paper Johnny Appleseed of New England. As a result of his idiosyncrasies, part of *my* belief system is that there's only one way to slice a tomato: on its side, holding the stem end. Also, that peanut butter goes on one slice of bread and jelly on the other – never mixing the two together on the same slice! Or, if you're doing clean-up work in the kitchen, you should always have a dish towel handily draped over your shoulder. Is there any other way? In short, you don't want to work with me in the kitchen (think control freak).

My Aunt Jo was a special person. She never minced words and always told you what she thought, *if you asked her.* Unless really provoked by some outlandish remark or behavior, she usually kept her opinions to herself. She might disagree with you, but she never judged, and she always accepted you for who you were. You knew she loved you, but if you went out of bounds – which were clearly defined before the fact – there was a penalty. And she enforced it.

One summer at around age 14, my cousin Carol and I – without the required permission – took a boat trip across the Sound from Connecticut to Long Island with four other kids in three very small boats. We figured we could get there and back with no one finding out. It all would have been cool, except that a storm came up, and hours later we just barely made it back to our shore. There was Aunt Jo standing at the dock, looking stern with her arms folded (think George Patton) and my mom, in tears. Without raising her voice, Aunt Jo made it clear that Carol and I were to be grounded, in our respective bedrooms, for a week, coming out only for meals. Imagine, two 14-year-old kids on summer vacation spending a whole week in their rooms! Of course, my mom, sweetheart that she was, often sneaked up chicken and other vittles to us, but that was small solace.

Aunt Jo raised four kids, and to my knowledge she never worked at a regular job except when she was quite young and unmarried. But had she worked, she would have been one of the best managers you could ever work for. Clear rules, unemotional, fair…why go on? Just re-read the Best Boss list. I'd like to think some of Aunt Jo rubbed off on me in my management style. I certainly know she keeps coming back to mind whenever I read books and articles about effective managers, or when I see one in action, or when I teach about management practices.

Think about your own parents or other close relatives. Which of them was more allowing, controlling, supportive, judgmental, permissive, rule-setting, nurturing, demanding, risk-oriented, risk-averse, fun-loving, serious, organized or easy going? Which one was more sequential in their thinking patterns (B follows A and precedes C), and which one was more creative and imaginative? Which one are you more like? The answer is you likely have bits and pieces of several of these traits from more than one relative, but a few dominate and – as much as you'd like to think so – you're probably not at the midpoint on a scale of any of the opposites. For instance, you may have behavioral elements of being both *allowing* (letting people do their own thing) and *controlling* (telling people what to do), but you lean, or even leap, left or right of the center line. C'mon, you know you do. How about when it comes to being either highly organized or loose and easy going? Or being more reserved than outgoing? Once again, if you step out there where the rest of us see you, you'll find you're most likely tilting more to one side than the other.

I do an informal exercise in seminars to determine the basic management style of each participant. I draw a horizontal line on the flipchart and write the words "Autocratic style" at one end, and "Laissez-faire style" at the other.

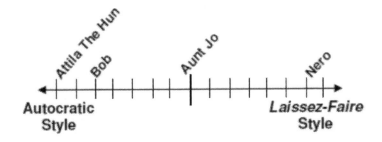

Then I briefly explain what is meant by both: The auto-cratic management style – at its extreme, is highly control-ling, with the autocrat suffering lots of discomfort in accept-ing methodology other than his or her own. The *laissez-faire* management style essentially means "hands-off," do it your way, with a preference for me not to have to give directions. Just so they more fully understand these style opposites, I explain to the class that autocratic managers are not neces-sarily aggressive, mean-spirited, loud or tough. They just simply prefer things be done their way and can often be very subtle about getting there ("Don't you think it would be bet-ter if we did it this way?"). Nor is it a fact the *laissez-faire* managers are necessarily "lazy." In fact, quite often they are hard workers and because of this, are just plain unavailable to provide direction. Nor are the *laissez-faire* managers nec-essarily quiet or shy.

Then I ask the group, by show of hands, to demonstrate on which side of the scale's center line they fall. A number of us autocrats raise our hands when I point to the left side of the scale; then a number of *laissez-faire* types raise theirs when I point to the other end. There are, however, a few remaining twits who claim they are a perfect mixture of both, at the same time probably wondering why they got stuck in this class of less-than-perfect people. If it's a management class of peers from the same company, the "middle-of-the-road types" are outed by the rest of the class with friendly hoots and boos. If it's a group where participants don't know each other, then I'm the one with the friendly hoots and boos. The point that needs to be stressed here is that if we think about it a bit, we all pretty much know where we fall on scales of any of these opposite behaviors. On some of the behaviors, we're slightly left or right of the middle. On others, we're way off to one side. But, once again, we're pretty much never exactly in the middle!

As an aside, the management style we espouse for managers to learn or strive for is commonly called the "participative style," and is a combination of autocratic and laissez-faire. We'll examine this style more closely in Chapter 5 on identifying and developing talent where we review our *BOSS 2000* model.

"The unexamined life is not worth living"

- Socrates

As an executive coach, a continuing message I give to managers is to always take time to consider the part you play in any relationship with peers, bosses or subordinates. The business of managing others gets a whole lot easier once we have a good idea how our own behavior positively or negatively impacts the people with whom we work. Sometimes I wish we walked around with a mini-cam on our foreheads so we could record our interactions with others throughout the work day. Then, with a good, single-malt scotch handy that evening, we could watch the video. Wow!

What insights we could have. We could actually see the reactions of others to our verbal and body language actions.
We could see the smiles or cringes, the pulling back or lean-
ing in, the animation or deflation, the look of empowerment
or giving up, and the laughter or anger.

I first got to thinking about how much we miss by not seeing ourselves as we appear to others a number of years ago
when I had the good fortune to attend the Boston Red Sox
fantasy baseball camp. This is a week in February, in the
warm climes of Florida, where about 80 over-the-hill, mostly
middle-aged baseball player wannabes gather under the
watchful, critical eyes of a bunch of retired pros who actually played this wonderful game. These camps have become
very popular over the years and most professional sports
teams sponsor them. The retired pros serve as coaches for
the "campers," teams are formed, and you practice and play
a game every day, assuming you have any feeling left in
your body after the second day.

All the games are videotaped and you can select – for
purchase, of course – a souvenir video of any of the games,
especially the ones where you felt you had your best pro
moments, or as in my case, the one, single pro moment.
(Stupidly, there were actually times during that week when I
believe all the campers had this remote thought of being discovered as a true, albeit a tad old, talent and signed up for
one glorious year as a professional ball player.) Anyway,
the video I chose to purchase was of the game where I had
smashed a solid base hit to right field. Taking a slight lead
off first base, I was ready to take off as the next batter, a fur-
niture company executive from Worcester, Massachusetts,
hit one down the first base line and into right field (not quite

the stinging liner I hit, but a good shot nevertheless). So, being the superb and canny athlete I was, I took off at the crack of the bat with third base as my only destination. Moving like the Road Runner, I flew past second base, and as I headed for third I saw the third base coach signaling me to slide, meaning it was going to be a close play at the bag. Now, all this was going on during the era of Pete Rose, aka Charlie Hustle, who was renowned for his prowess as a base runner and would do whatever it took to reach a base; dive, leap, scratch, kick or bite. So, now I'm nearing third and see the third baseman getting ready to receive the throw from right field. About 10 feet from the bag I dive forward – at least four feet in the air – with outstretched arms, looking, I was sure, like a freestyle swimmer lunging off the starting blocks. In my mind's eye, I saw myself in super-slow motion as I finally landed chest-first and grabbed the bag, bouncing once or twice. Safe! I stood up, dusted off, patted dry the blood from my elbow and yelled: "Pete Rose, eat your heart out!" Our next batter hit a fly ball to center, and I scored easily with the

I'm a firm believer that – except for the psychotics among us – people do not deliberately act in a nasty, mean-spirited or evil manner; that all these behaviors are either unintended or rationalized. For instance, if I habitually interrupt you, even if you're in mid-sentence, I'm either unaware (or unconscious) that I'm doing it, or it may be that I think I have something very important to add and need to do it at that moment or the thought will be lost.

winning run. I was on cloud nine for the rest of the camp and with all due modesty couldn't wait to get home and treat my family to what I knew would be a thrilling video record of my camp highlight.

So here's what we actually saw. This rather paunchy guy hits a dribbler that gets past the even paunchier first base-man, and he kind of rumbles to first base. I had forgotten how strained my upper leg muscles were from being so out of shape (Who knew you needed to be in shape to play baseball?), so I looked more like the Frankenstein monster stiff-legging it down the line. Mercifully, the camera pans back to the next batter, so I wasn't seen bending at the waist trying to catch my breath. The camera pans back toward me again after my teammate hits the ball to right, a long hit by the way, and I'm seen taking off – well more like fast walk-ing – toward second on my way to third and the famous slide. By now, my so-called loyal family is laughing their collective heads off, but I'm expecting redemption any se-cond. Long story short: Instead of this flying gazelle-like, graceful head-first slide into third, what we all see looks more like a whale beaching itself. More laughter...More humiliation. So much for us being able to see ourselves as we think we are. The image we think we're projecting quite often is far off the perspective of the one others see – or even more importantly - *experience* on the receiving end of our be-havior. So, we really need to work with techniques and tools to help us see ourselves in a truer light.

I'm a firm believer that – except for the psychotics among us – people do not *deliberately* act in a nasty, mean-spirited or evil manner; that all these behaviors are either unintended or rationalized. For instance, if I habitually interrupt you, even if you're in mid-sentence, I'm either unaware (or un-conscious) that I'm doing it, or it may be that I think I have something very important to add and need to do it at that moment or the thought will be lost. Or, if you sent me an email I interpret as hostile, I might send you a nasty one back – and even copy the world – as what I *rationalize* as due retribution for what you did to me...also known as revenge. Think about it. No one I know gets up in the morning and decides:

I think I'll yell and bang the table at this morning's meeting just to see what reactions I get from others; or: I think I'll hijack Mary Jane's conversation when she starts talking about her week-end just to irk her.

No one deliberately decides to act like a know-it-all, or to disagree just for the sake of disagreement, or to show dis-gust with other's ideas, or to bore you to death with a lecture on how to live your life, or even to annoy you by snapping their gum (Oh? You're a gum snapper yourself? So I guess it's not annoying).

Even though I never met this person, I was once told about a hiring manager who used to sit behind his desk with a soccer ball hidden on his lap. Then, during the job inter-view, when the person least expected it, he would snap toss the ball at the interviewee. What was his rationale for doing this? To see how the person would function under condi-tions of surprising, unexpected circumstances. All of a sud-den I'm imagining some readers thinking: *What a cool idea! I'll have to try that.* If you're one of those people, stop read-ing this book. I can't help you. But imagine, this hiring manager probably thought this was a helpful tool and the interviewee would hold him in awe. I'm pretty certain he didn't *deliberately intend* to come off looking like a jerk.

I recently got derailed while on my way to becoming the world's most perfect human being. I was playing golf with three other guys, and we partnered up in a match. As often happens in these events, there was some good-natured ribbing going on as we played for the high stakes of a dollar. I sank a long birdie putt to win one hole and gave it the old Tiger Woods fist-pump in triumph. I must confess, I exaggerated the fist-pump a bit, but did it in what I saw as good fun. A few days later, my playing partner told me that one of our opponents, Marty, was quite offended by my display. It turns out he was a natural fist-pumper and felt I was directly mocking him. Now, did I deliberately mean to offend him? Of course not. Was he being a bit too sensitive? Maybe. But what matters is that he *was* offended. Did I come across as a jerk to him and maybe the others? Probably. The fact that Marty didn't tell me directly about the offending behavior raises another problem we'll address later on in the book, but for now let's realize that's how negative legends grow. Here I am thinking I'm a pretty funny, cool guy, but seen in a very different and less desirable way by others.

Now, let's go back to the drawing board.

As a postscript to the story, I had to deal with the problem of how to apologize to Marty. After all, he never said anything to me about the offense, and I didn't want to betray my playing partner's sharing the information with me. So I wrote myself a script for talking to Marty (script writing is an activity I strongly recommend for situations like this where you might feel a bit awkward or at risk, or where there's a concern about you getting too defensive, argumentative, preachy or aggressive: "Why are you making such a big deal of so small a thing, Marty? Don't be so touchy."). My script, pretty much as I presented it to Marty was: "Marty, I got to thinking about the golf match and that I probably went overboard on the ribbing business, especially my exaggerated fist-pump. If that offended you in any way, I'm sorry." As you would guess, Marty claimed it was no big deal and said he hardly had given my behavior a second thought. Whether or not Marty was being completely honest with me is beside the point. The important thing was that I apologized, so my part was done. Aunt Jo would have been proud.

Go back to the "Worst Boss" list and consider that kind of boss actually deciding each morning deliberately to do some of the things on this list. My strong belief is that even the worst of the worst of bosses is either unaware of the impact of his behavior, rationalizes it, or does it in retribution for something the other person did that deserved a sort of punishment. Whatever impression you *intend* to create in others really doesn't matter if the intention doesn't match up to the perception held by others. As you probably have heard, *perception is the only reality*. Perceptions of our intentions get formed based on our behavior, and our behavior is a result of our style.

Management styles get formed over time through *nature*, from genetic imprinting and the way our parents and relatives behaved, and *nurture*, from learning and value models we've been exposed to or read about. Think, for instance, about the classroom environment in which you were raised. Was it high control, with desks screwed to the floor and assigned seating (thus keeping you away from anyone whose company you might enjoy), or was it more fluid, allowing more freedom of movement? If your family had meals together (a dying tradition, I'm afraid), were the children to be seen and not heard? Or was your situation more like the dinner table of Judge Learned Hand, where the thoughts and ideas of the children were not only cultivated, but considered to be as valued as those of the adults in the family? Think a bit about how growing up in these various environments might have had an influence on how you manage others.

Let's agree that, like it or not – and especially as bosses – our behavior impacts the behavior (that is, the *performance*) of others. We are such a presence in the lives of those who report to us that it can't be any other way. Many people spend more work time in the company of their boss than doing anything else. No wonder there's such a push for more work-from-home hours! In short, we, as bosses, have an incredible influence on and set the tone for how others will behave at work; or more accurately, how they will *react*.

We recently worked with a guy, Desi, who owned a small distribution company with a total workforce of seven people. Desi had for years worked as a general manager in a large international manufacturing company and decided in his early 40s to follow his bliss and strike out on his own. Desi was an engineer by training, and he wanted to get back to the joy he once felt in spending time working directly with customers, helping them solve their unique problems. In his plan, he hired a couple of reliable self-starters who could manage the finances, warehouse and distribution. Desi would be available for minimal direction, but otherwise they all functioned quite well as independent people in an interdependent unit. The company thrived with this group of three, and Desi was indeed blissful. As he explained to us when he brought us in for a problem he was facing, the last thing he wanted to do was function as a day-to-day manager of people. For him, at this point in his life, it was more fun *doing* than it was *managing*.

As the business grew, Desi had to add another layer or two of people, and he did so assuming the new folks would mesh well with the original group. They'd all learn the words to "Kumbaya," would perform their pants off, and he could continue on as before, spending his time working directly with customers. Silly man. Desi was perplexed that seemingly all of a sudden, his work unit of seven was becoming a snake pit of conflict. He would come back from the road and be bombarded with complaints from almost everyone about almost everyone else. This person was leaving work behind for others to do. That person wasn't completing paper work in the required format. Another person was grunting his way through the day about how ungrateful everyone was towards him. Desi was finding himself acting like Solomon, trying to sort out truth from fiction, the good guys from the bad. This was clearly not the vision he had in starting his own business!

In trying to help Desi figure all this out, we did one-on-one interviews with his employees and learned some interesting stuff. While not intentionally trying to do so, Desi had fallen into the role of becoming the *parent* to a group of children. As the employees saw it, Desi would listen to each person's complaint, than make a pronouncement on how the matter should be fixed – quite often doing the fixing himself. For example, if Brian was having a tough time getting Mary to help him on a project, Desi would become the go-between and deal with Mary on Brian's behalf. Or, Desi might listen (which in all cases he was willing to do) to a complaint from Mary about John goofing off and do nothing at all about it. In short, people were dropping plops at Desi's feet, and he was picking them up!

Now, there are a lot of angles to this story that would be interesting to analyze (e.g. the importance of clarifying roles and responsibilities for new hires) but for the purposes of the point being made here, we made it clear to Desi that, unwittingly, he was acting as the classic *parent*, entertaining complaints and taking on finding the remedy himself. That brought out the petulant *child* in his employees. To be sure, there were a couple of genuine interpersonal conflicts that required mediation, but he was making it worse by playing this role. Essentially, he was *setting the tone for how others would behave.* His motives were honorable – trying to keep the peace. He was simply unaware of the negative impact his choice of leadership was having on the troops. Part of the remedy of the situation was for Desi to not only clarify roles and responsibilities, but also to remove himself from playing Solomon. His new approach was: "From now on, if you have a complaint about a fellow worker, I suggest you take it up with that person, because if you bring it to me, I'm going to call for a meeting among the three of us to help *you* arrive at a solution." Guess what? The problem behavior stopped after a couple of test runs on Desi by an employee or two.

Let's further agree that if we are to be truly successful at this management game we need to conduct a rigorous exam-ination of our own current style and motives, and build on our strengths and improve our weaknesses. And it *is* a game. Why not, then, play it by learning healthy rules that advance everyone's cause – what we know as win-win. If, as some believe, all behavior is a manipulation of one form or another (think Pavlov's dogs), why not manipulate people toward happiness instead of misery? By the way, Socrates also said: "Do not do to others what angers you if done to you by others."

A number of years ago, I was working with a client co-designing training for first-line supervisors at her bank. We wanted to illustrate the impact of positive, negative and neutral reinforcement (aka "manipulation") according to the theories of B.F. Skinner, the renowned psychologist who was among the first to put forth theories about behavior modification. Skinner can be a tough read, and quite often his theories can appear to be contradictory. In fact, if you're an insomniac, I recommend reading *Walden Two* by Skinner(1948). You'll be asleep in no time. Essentially, Skinner's research indicated that we are all pretty much manipulating or modifying the behavior of each other – by design or not – most of the time, by using certain inputs that re-shape a person's environment, therefore their behavior. A simple for instance is that by significantly raising the temperature in a room, I can make people feel uncomfortable and likely perspire. More to the point, if you've demonstrated a behavior I like, such as getting a report in to me ahead of time, and I'd like more of the same kind of what Skinner called "desirable" behavior, then all I have to do is say something *positive* to you like: "Thanks. I really appreciate you getting this done so quickly." According to Skinner, you would then likely repeat this kind of behavior because it was positively reinforced. Likewise – and here is where Skinner can appear to be confusing – if I say something *negative* to you like: "I see you finished the report ahead of time, obviously you're not as busy as I thought, so I should give you more work to do," you would probably demonstrate *more* of the *same* behavior, simply because you were getting attention. And Skinner preached that any attention, positive or negative, is better than none at all (or, *neutral* reinforcement). In other words, Skinner was saying that if I ignore or neutralize your early completion of the report, you won't repeat more of that desirable behavior because it didn't get recognized at all.

Confused? So were my client and I. But read on.

The client and I wanted to have the trainees go through an exercise where they could have a first-hand experience of Skinner's theories. So we designed an exercise called *Crazy Eights*, and here's how it worked: There were about 20 participants in the training class, and we divided them into three roughly equally sized groups. We gave all three groups the same assignment: First, select a group leader. Then draw a picture on flipchart paper that illustrates what they had learned in the earlier part of the day's session – which, as I recall, was about teamwork and collaboration. Once the exercise was finished, they would be presenting the interpretations of their drawings to the other two groups. A prize would be awarded to the group with the best drawing. The three groups were sent to different parts of the training room so they could complete their assignments in relative privacy. No further direction was given except a 30-minute time limit to complete the task. The design my client and I put together called for me, as the trainer, to visit with two of the groups and ignore the third as they worked on completing their drawings. I had pre-determined that the group to my left would be dealt with positively, the one to my right negatively, and the one in the middle ignored (or dealt with neutrally). Unknown to the participants, the client was going to act as observer and take notes on what she saw during the exercise. Having had that baseball fantasy camp experience, I certainly wasn't going to rely on *my* ability to recollect objectively!

After the group leader selection was made, I went to the group on my left and praised them for the wise selection they made; that the person they chose to lead them illustrated both their good sense and wisdom (I actually had no idea how good the person was whom they selected). I assured them they would do well in completing their drawing. I then skipped past the middle group and went directly to the group on my right. There, I nit-picked at their leader selection process ("It looks like you were rather hasty in choosing your leader."), and the person they chose ("I hope you know what you're doing in choosing him."). Once again, I had no idea of the qualifications of the leader they chose, as my goal was to be negative in my comments. I could sense how stung the group and their leader were by my behavior, but I stayed within my role. Once again, I ignored the middle group and went to the front of the room and shuffled around some papers, occasionally smiling toward the group on the left, kind of coldly staring at the group on my right, and ignoring the one in the middle as if they weren't in the room.

After a few more minutes, I visited my "favorite" group and gave them glowing reviews of their drawing: "Boy, it's obvious you guys get it...this drawing is really intriguing...nice job...I can't wait to hear how you'll present your interpretation." The actual drawing could have been absolute trash, but my job was to praise it to the high heavens. The group was almost giddy in their joy and enthusiasm. Next, I again walked past the middle group, which by now was getting more than a little irritated by my lack of attention. Interestingly, as my client/observer said later during the debriefing of the exercise, some of the middle group members began to drift from the task, holding side conversations. iPhones weren't invented yet. I then re-visited the "negative" group. I was actually a bit reluctant to do so as I was beginning to feel their heat from across the room...but into the Valley of Death I rode.... I again found lots of fault with what they were doing ("Is this all you have to show for your efforts? I'm really disappointed with the quality of this...I don't know if you'll be able to present your interpretation."). Their anger toward me was conspicuous, bordering on open hostility. It was all I could do to keep from apologizing to them for being such a creep, but I had to stick with the mission and hope the outcome would be OK.

As an aside, please note that I never raised my voice in my visits to this group. Being negative doesn't have to be loud to be damaging.

I then went back to the center of the room, doing one final skip of the middle group which by now seemed to be completely unfocused and depressed (I was pretty sure at least two people were sucking their thumbs). The client/observer said later they were beginning to grumble and to no one in particular, as if they were giving up.

The final phase of the exercise called for the group presentations. I let my "favorite" group go first, and of course made it clear to everyone in the room that their drawing was the gold standard and that I was extremely pleased and impressed by both the way they were led and their productivity as a group. It was so sugary, it was almost icky. No, it *was* icky. The group to my right went next, and of course I continued the negative criticism, but now more in public. Truly, I can't recall ever feeling so much like a heel, but hoped they would forgive me later. I can best describe them as being stunned and completely embarrassed. Now came the ignored group's turn, and here is where the client and I felt we were geniuses in our design. I looked at my watch and said something like: "Gee, it's getting rather late, so I'm sure it's OK with you guys if we just skip your presentation and go on with the rest of our training." You could have cut the silence with a knife. Their collective jaws dropped – at least those of the few group members who had remained with the task. Their anger was conspicuous and showed all over their bodies. I was just grateful the end of the exercise was near at hand.

Before anyone could say anything or gather their strength to physically attack the trainer, I said: "OK, here's what I want you all to do. Without any discussion among yourselves, on a piece of note paper, please write the number '8' as many times as you can in the next 60 seconds. Ready? Go." With varying degrees of effort, people began writing their 8s. After the 60 seconds, pencils were put down, and everyone was asked to total up the number of 8s they each wrote. We then compiled the numbers by group, with the client and I hoping the experiment would come out as we guessed it would. When all the totals were in, here's what we found: The positively reinforced group had written the largest number of 8s. No surprise there. However, the negatively reinforced group came in second; a very close second.

The ignored or neutrally reinforced group came in a distant third.

We had proven at least one thing in our anecdotal, single-event experiment: When people or groups are positively reinforced, they become more productive. We were a bit confused, though, by the high score of the negatively reinforced group. As we debriefed the exercise in open forum with all the groups, we learned that the relative high productivity of the negatively reinforced group was driven by what became (in only 30 minutes, mind you) intense anger toward the trainer (aka boss!). We further surmised that while an angry group can be quite productive — driven by an I'll-show-you-you-S.O.B. motive — as a boss you wouldn't want to rely on that sort of reinforcement over time; that angry people will eventually burn out and either become complacent, or – as applies to the really good employees – leave.

> *Positive reinforcement has little to do with being nice. It's just a smart way to improve performance and productivity*

Before summarizing this story, I'd like to share a couple of other insights about this experiment. First of all, I learned that bad feelings die hard. Once the client and I explained what our motive was in doing the exercise, *everyone* became angry with us, especially with me as the perpetrator and purposeful manipulator. The team leader and members of the positive group wondered now if I really liked them and their work or not. Was my praise completely phony? Some members of the ignored group were so depressed by the experience, they were lost for the rest of the day. Strangely, the negatively reinforced group became closer, united in their anger toward the common enemy...the trainer/boss. I kept thinking to myself:

Wow, all this emotion produced in 30 minutes. Think how damaging some bosses can be by acting this way regularly!

As difficult as this exercise is to lead as a trainer and experience as a participant, I've done it a number of times since that day, and the results have been the same every time: The positively reinforced group always wins the *Crazy Eights* exercise, the negatively reinforced group comes in a very close second, and the ignored (neutrally reinforced) group always comes in a distant third. And they all place in that order for the same reasons every time: The positive group is highly productive because they feel appreciated and recognized by their boss and therefore good about themselves. The negatively reinforced group is also quite productive, but for all the wrong reasons (anger bordering on hatred). And the ignored group is so bummed out by being completely erased by the boss that they cannot perform to any reasonable or acceptable standard.

So B. F. Skinner was right all along when he postulated that both positive and negative reinforcements will likely get behavior to repeat itself, but that neutrally reinforced behavior will extinguish itself because people need to be recognized – even in a bad way – in order to produce at high levels.

There is a footnote to the *Crazy Eights* story. Over the years, I have run into people who have participated in this experiment with me, and they have consistently said it was the most powerful classroom learning experience they ever had. Hopefully, they all became better bosses as a result. And hopefully, this story reinforces in you, the reader, the significance of the notion that if life is one grand manipulation, then why not manipulate in a healthy, respectful way. It takes the same amount of energy to do it well than it does not to. Are you still uncomfortable about giving praise? Look at it this way. Positive reinforcement has little to do with being nice. It's just a smart way to improve performance and productivity.

So, back to our premise, that step one is to develop a healthy curiosity about self, then use that curiosity to find out more about what makes you tick and why. The next chapter will add in the beliefs and practices we should work on to improve our managerial behavior, but for now let's look at ways to conduct the self-discovery journey.

It's all about you

There are numerous so-called personality profile surveys available to you to help provide an accurate image of your individual style and the effects it might have on others. The Myers-Briggs Type Indicator (Briggs and Myers, 1998) is the grandmother of these style instruments and has been used for decades to help people get a handle on how they relate to others, process information, think through problems and make decisions. Our consulting firm quite often uses the MBTI as a team-building tool, to help management teams get a better sense of what makes them tick as individuals, so they can hopefully work better together as a high-performance unit. In larger organizations, most managers have taken the MBTI in one form or another early in their careers, but managers in smaller organizations quite likely haven't been exposed to this helpful tool. The MBTI is a great place to start on the style-discovery trip. There are other very good *style indicators* on the market. Two popular ones are the DISC Behavioral Style Indicator (Wikipedia, 2012) and the Enneagram (Enneagram Worldwide, 2012). An Internet search will show you even more. Whichever one you decide to use, we urge you to find and use a coach certified in that instrument. These coaches can help you more accurately interpret your scores. Doing it on your own is OK, but it's a little like kissing your sister; it's a kiss, but it's not very interesting.

There are more in-depth profile instruments you should also look at. An executive coaching tool that our firm has used – as well as a *job fit* measurement when doing recruiting for our clients – is called the Hogan Personality Inventory (HPI) and (its sister instrument) the Hogan Development Survey (HDS). The HPI and HDS (Hogan Assessments, 2012) are harder-hitting than the MBTI and other *style* instruments in terms of helping respondents learn about personal assets and liabilities. What I explain to clients when debriefing their HPI results is that there is no such thing as a perfect personality, sorry to say. (This is a good thing for people like me who would be out of business if perfect personalities became achievable.) All aspects of our personalities have an asset *and* liability built in. For instance, people who score as being very ambitious will usually be good at taking charge and getting things done in a self-confident way, but at the same time could be overly competitive, difficult to coach, and think their way is the best way. Conversely, people who score as being low on the *ambitious* scale can usually be very good team players and will take constructive feedback well. At the same time, they may lack necessary initiative and drive.

Another example of the asset/liability aspect of our personality traits is that a so-called *multitasker* tends to think around corners. This is a good thing if you're looking for someone to manage a dynamic, complex process, but not so great if you expect that person to be able to be a research chemist, for instance, where staying focused is the need. In this case, you'd want a *single-tasker* who, of course, would likely not perform as well in a crisis leadership situation.

The HDS is used to help you get a better feel for how you act when under stress. Usually, people will spike high on two or more of the 11 HDS dimensions, thus showing the participant and coach those areas of caution for when – under stress – the person might get overly aggressive or retreat and hide. Interestingly, some people score very low on all the stress measurements on the HDS. Initially you would think this is a good thing, as it seems that remaining calm, cool and collected no matter the situation appears to be an admirable trait. Sometimes, though, it can backfire. As an example, I remember an IT guy – let's call him Bill – at a mid-sized manufacturing company, whose job was to help operations people manage key projects. Now, Bill was a very bright, friendly guy, certainly not within the evil, heartless Dilbert stereotype of IT. However, Bill had developed a wide reputation among operations types for lacking a sense of urgency when it came to meeting deadlines. He gave off this casual, "no-big-deal" response to the frustration and anxiousness his *internal* customers were conveying to him. The negative feedback was piling up on Bill's boss. "Bill doesn't seem to care about my priorities." "Bill's dragging his feet in helping me on my project." "Bill is totally non-responsive."

I met with Bill in a coaching session, and he expressed genuine, sincere concern about how he was letting people down. His plate was pretty full, and he was running as fast as he could to keep up with his assignments (He also had a problem delegating, but that's another story). In short, Bill didn't convey to me any of the signs of not caring or dragging his feet that his peers were alleging. As part of my coaching work with him, Bill completed the HPI and HDS. In examining the results of the HDS, I saw that Bill had exceptionally low stress ratings on *all* of the survey dimensions, a quite unusual condition, because as mentioned above, most people will *spike high* on at least two or three of the eleven dimensions measured on the HDS and at moderate levels on several of the others. This meant that while Bill was able to verbally *express* a sense of anxiety and concern – in this case, for others' issues and frustrations – he was not the kind of person who could *show* it. He, therefore, gave the impression of being casual and not caring. In other words, if Bill was more within the norms of stress responses, he would have shown more anxiety and sense of urgency, so people would feel he at least shared their pain. Poor Bill. Here was a guy whom you'd think would be envied by others as great at managing stress, but instead was resented because people couldn't identify with his stress management personality type. Sometimes you just can't win. By the way, Bill and his colleagues got along a lot better once he shared the rationale of his HDS results with them...and after he got better at delegating.

The MBTI is like arriving at Vermont Avenue on the self-discovery Monopoly board, but the HPI/HDS gets you more toward Marvin Gardens. Additionally, what you learn from instruments like the HPI and HDS is that while our person-alities aren't likely to change, we can modify our behaviors or environments so as to keep ourselves or others out of harm's way. Recall what I said earlier about my controlling the kitchen environment; you know, the slicing tomato thing. Knowing that a dimension of my personality tends toward being more controlling than passive, if I want to have someone else take charge, I will actually leave the room while that person establishes her or his territory. At work, during times when I would be developing a subordinate in, for instance, her skills as a trainer, I have found that it's best for me to leave the room for the first several minutes of her presentation, so I will be less likely to take over the class. I'm not deliberately trying to act like a control freak. There's a significant part of me that feels the presentation will fail without my brilliant intervention, but another part of me that knows that's baloney. It's not easy being me, and some-times less easy being *with* me.

The power of feedback

Let's now look at the third, and maybe best, way to learn about your style and motivational drives; how others receive and feel about you and your actions through the process of behavioral feedback.

Behavioral feedback is letting a person know whether or not his or her behavior is having the desired effect, and it comes in two varieties: unsolicited and solicited. Unsolicited feedback, while it might be welcomed, isn't invited. Quite often, it comes from friends and family members, and can be either positive (letting the person know his or her behavior *is* having the desired effect): "I really like the way you listen"; or constructive (letting the person know the behavior *is not* having the desired effect): "It would really be more helpful to me if you could listen more and comment less." The amount of unsolicited feedback is usually commensurate with the amount of trust the presenter has in how healthy a way you will receive the feedback. For instance, in responding to the above comment about listening more and commenting less, if you were to say something like: "Well, if you weren't such a blabbermouth, maybe I would enjoy listening more to what you have to say," you could pretty much figure you won't be getting a lot of new constructive feedback in the near future. Of course, that may be precisely what you want.

In a boss-subordinate relationship, you can probably imagine that unsolicited feedback doesn't occur a whole lot, and for the obvious reasons that employees usually see bosses as being in charge of the purse and promotion strings, and would be fearful of putting themselves in harm's way by giving unsolicited feedback. Although, if you are blessed with employees who give you unsolicited, constructive feedback, tie them to a desk, because such a person is a keeper, and you never want them to leave. So, while it should be every manager's aspiration to have an open work environment where feedback flows back and forth between people like water in a waterbed, we're not quite that evolved yet. What's needed then is a programmed system for the giving and receiving of feedback, and that's where solicited feedback comes in.

Solicited feedback occurs when we directly ask one or more people – either subordinates or peers – to respond to one or more specific questions about our performance or behavior. For instance, we've worked with managers who include subordinate-to-boss questions on performance appraisal forms (more thoughts about the value – or lack thereof – of formal performance appraisals later). We call them "Stop/Start/Continue" questions. They usually appear on the last page of the appraisal form and look something like [Stop] "Tell me one thing you'd like me to stop doing in order to make your work life easier/better;" [Start] "Tell me one thing you'd like me to start doing in order to make your work life easier/better;" and [Continue] "Tell me one thing I do that you'd like me to continue doing that makes your work life easier/better." Employees are asked to respond to each of these questions either in writing or orally, and then the boss is expected to listen non-defensively, finally agreeing to work on improving or maintaining the discussed behaviors.

There are some real virtues to this process. It promotes open dialogue and a better relationship between boss and subordinate. It also formulates a specific plan for improvement for the boss that can be referred to over the course of coming weeks and months. At the same time, there are a few obvious drawbacks. For instance, the chances of the boss getting defensive and dismissing the feedback as unfounded are pretty high. Also, and unfortunately, it's not a general workplace norm for bosses and subordinates to have the level of trust (no retribution) that's required for this process to work effectively. Remember the purse and promotion strings point made earlier. What we've often seen happen is that the first time the feedback-to-the-boss process is used in a performance appraisal, the subordinate usually tosses a puff ball and says something like: "I want you to stop working so hard and take more time off," perhaps actually interpreted as: "Get off my back so I can do my job."

It takes a while for the appropriate trust levels to get set in place for this feedback method to work, but once it does, the benefits to the relationship with the subordinate are huge.

As an example, one morning several years ago, I was conducting performance appraisal sessions (actually we refer to it as *performance planning*) with the three people who directly reported to me. The format called for me to ask each person to tell me one thing he or she would like to see me do differently to help them do their jobs. Assuming they would have very little to say, or at least be somewhat at a loss for words (after all, I teach this stuff, so I must be a pretty good boss), I was quite surprised to be told by all three – at separate meetings, mind you – that I frequently interrupted them at their work with questions during the course of the day, causing them to lose concentration and productivity. It was the word *productivity* that really got my attention. Now, keep in mind that these were *separate meetings* with each person, and yet the feedback message was consistent. I momentarily wondered if they might have had a meeting-before-the-meeting to plan their assault. Our performance planning procedure calls for an action plan for improvement as part of the boss feedback step. So, while I wasn't fully convinced that my so-called interruptions were such a big deal, I held a joint meeting with them and at their suggestion made an agreement with all three that I would begin to write down my questions and batch them into two or three interruptions per person, per day. The fair assumption here was that almost all of my questions were of the non-urgent variety and could wait to be asked during the two or three *touch-point* meetings. The deal was struck at around 11 a.m., and I began to write down my questions, all the while assuming it was a rather wasteful exercise, but honoring their right to the request and its validity. Well, to make a long story short, by 2 p.m. I had written an average of seven questions for each person, which amounted to about 21 interruptions that I would have made during a three-hour period, and I even took a half-hour off for lunch! Needless to say, I was astonished by the results and humbled by the lesson learned.

I have never forgotten the impact of that episode, and while I'm sure I still interrupt people's work more often than either they or I would like, I know it happens a whole lot less. This story is also a good example of the earlier point made about there being no such thing as a perfect personality, and that all facets of our personality have an asset *and* liability built onto them. The part of me that annoyingly interrupts people with minor questions is the *liability* side of the same coin as my *asset* for being a good planner, because of a heightened awareness I have of things going on in my environment.

Other forms of solicited feedback

Perhaps the best way to get reliable and honest solicited feedback is through the tool commonly called 360 degree feedback surveys, or 360s. The term comes from the fact that each person going through a 360 process gets feedback from a full circle (360 degrees) of respondents – the boss (from above), peers (from each side), and subordinates/direct reports (from below). Most 360s include the participant being reviewed completing the same survey on "*Self.*" The survey will usually contain 20 or more questions about your management and/or leadership prowess. A typical survey item (question) might be: "This person makes his/her expectations clear." A five-point scale allows the survey respondent to check off the appropriate *score* for each item. If it's a survey filled out strictly by your peers, then the questions are aimed at how well you play in the sandbox with others. So a typical question might be: "This person collaborates well on projects we work on together." Most of these surveys have a *stop/start/continue* section at the end of the survey for the respondent to offer narrative comments.

But here's what makes the information more *reliable and honest.* All responses in a 360 are anonymous, so the person being reviewed doesn't know who scored or said what. We usually require four or more respondents for each person being surveyed in order to enhance their anonymity.

'Fifty Million Frenchmen Can't be Wrong'

The line is a song title that inspired an old Cole Porter musical, but the implication here is that in a 360 survey, when you see a feedback theme forming, you'd better pay attention to it. For instance, if you averaged a 2.50 rating (on a five-point scale) on *making your expectations clear*, and the rest of your ratings are at 3.50 and above, you'd better take a look at what barriers exist for you when it comes to this area. Perhaps you assume that everyone gets it and knows what has to be done without a lot of what you might think is hand-holding. Perhaps your organization is growing and some of the newer people are in the dark – unlike the original small crew who could read your mind – when it comes to knowing the culture and how you like things done. Whatever the case, it's important to act on the feedback and craft an action plan for improvement.

To help you better understand the feedback from the 360, you might review your results with a trusted colleague – perhaps one of those members of the *original small crew* – and ask for additional feedback from them. Or you might want to hire an executive coach, where people like me come in to help you analyze the data and get a plan going. Good executive coaches should also be able to help design or select a reliable 360 survey and fully explain its nuances.

A few final words on the use of 360s:

- *Initiate the process only if you're fully committed to acting on the information you get back.* As a general rule, it's always a good idea to go back to the people who complete any kind of a survey – even employee attitude surveys – and let them know what you've learned and what you intend to do about it. If you don't correspond with your raters, you've taken a step backward.

- *Leave your emotions at the door, and don't overreact.* "OK, so they rated me a 2.50 on making expectations clear. If they want clarity, I'll give them clarity. From now on, all assignments will be written, emailed and copied to everyone in the entire organization just so there is no ambiguity."

- *Look at the forest, not the trees.* All too often when we're debriefing 360 results with a client and looking at the written comments on the *stop/start/continue* narrative section of the report, they become Sherlock Holmes wannabes, trying to figure out who said what, then invalidating the feedback. "I'll bet Tim wrote that. It looks like something he'd say. I give him plenty of direction, but he's one of the lazy ones and needs lots of hand-holding. I should have gotten rid of him a long time ago. Next?"

Try New Haven before going to Broadway.

Years ago, the way a stage play or musical got to Broadway was to scrub it in New Haven. After each performance, and based on audience response and the producer's and director's observations, script parts and/or songs were often added, deleted or changed. In a similar fashion, when it comes to embarking on the self-discovery journey, you might want to do a dry run on the feedback circuit by trying it out in a safer setting.

A simple way to do this is to take the Best Boss list home and check it out with your spouse or (soon-to-be-ex) loved ones. Now, you may feel that most of the items on the Best Boss list are too work-related for a spouse or loved ones to be able to fairly comment on, but I would make a case that the person you are at work is not too distant from the person you are outside of work. If you're a Type A or Type B person at work, I'm sure there's plenty of supporting evidence of the same behaviors away from work. If you're a planner at work, you're a planner at home, and so on. Over coffee or cocktails (or both), ask these folks to what extent they think you are approachable, non-judgmental, supportive, etc. Now, don't stock the stream by, for instance, dangling the car keys in front of a teen-age son before asking the questions.

It won't be an easy conversation to have, but handled the right way, it will be very rewarding. At the beginning of my management consulting career – and before I had any other associates in the firm – I wanted to experiment with this feedback idea. I decided to ask my oldest daughter, Janine, a teen at the time, for feedback as a dad (the Best Boss list hadn't been developed yet). I must confess to stocking the stream a bit by taking her to lunch. After a bit of small talk, I set up the feedback session by saying something like: "Honey (a good lead-in, I thought), I really want to be a good dad to you, so tell me at least one thing you'd like me to do differently that would help improve our relationship." Notice, I was smart enough to ask for only one thing.

Well, you might think Janine had been waiting for years to be asked this question, because the answer came spilling out almost before I finished asking it. She said, "Dad, you really don't listen very well. When I start to tell you something, you sometimes cut me off and begin lecturing." Calling on my best listening skills, I waited for about three seconds and said back: "Janine (no more "Honey" for her!), you know, in my profession, I have to listen to people all day, they load me up from all sides and when I get home I need a break, blah, blah, blah..." By the time I got to the third "blah," I realized how incredibly easily I fell into the very pattern she was talking about, and we both started laughing...so much to learn, so little time.

Now, if you don't have a spouse from whom to ask for feedback, then ask your kids, as I did with Janine. If you don't have a spouse or kids, then ask other family members. If you don't have a spouse, kids or other family members, then ask friends. If you don't have any of the above, then this problem is bigger than we both thought!

I've mentioned *Coach/Executive Coach* as a term several times in this chapter as a role I've played with numerous clients. Hiring an executive coach is a great way to help you put together all the pieces of the *me* puzzle. She or he can keep you honest with yourself about the things you need to recognize as the road blocks keeping you from becoming and remaining an *Unforgettable Boss*. Just be sure you use his or her services in the best way. Press the coach to not just listen, but guide you with good, objective counsel. A good coach should help you stretch, but not beyond your talent range.

I had one very short-term client with whom I met twice. At our first session, she spent almost two hours regaling me with all the terrific things she was doing as a manager in a decent-sized tech company. I didn't consider her droning on and on about her accomplishments to be too unusual, chalking it up to her probable need to establish herself as a basically successful leader. Our second meeting started out in precisely the same way – her telling me about her most recent tall building she leapt in a single bound. And, every time I tried to inject a question or offer a comment, she would go faster and get louder. It couldn't have been more obvious that all she wanted was to talk, while all I was allowed to do was listen (throwing in an occasional head nod). After about 20 minutes of trying to get into this double-dutch jump roping game, I finally put my hand on her arm and said, "Joanie, I get that you have lots to tell me, and I really want to know these things, but if I'm to be an effective coach for you, you should be seeking input and feedback from me on areas where you can improve. Up to this point, I've been more like your audience than a participant." Joanie seemed a bit stunned and generally disagreed with my assessment, claiming she felt she had shared a lot with me about herself and her needs. The meeting ended shortly after that, and I never heard from Joanie again. I did, however, hear from one of Joanie's colleagues a few weeks later, telling me Joanie was glad she had me as her executive coach and that my counsel was extremely helpful. Go figure.

One last – and perhaps disturbing – thought on *healing thyself.* It's been said: "We dislike most in others that which we most dislike in ourselves." I've always wrestled with the validity of this assertion, shuddering at even the remotest possibility that some of the *jerk* behavior I experience or witness in others can be assessed to me. Interrupting others, not listening, bragging, being condescending, *poor me*, victim language – none of these traits could possibly be me. Or, could they?

Summary: Here's what I hope you learned in this chapter.

- Management is a full-time job that's not for everyone. Just because you *arrived* at it doesn't necessarily mean you should stay in it. If it's not a fit for you – even if you're a family member – go find your bliss somewhere else. It'll be much better for you (and everyone else) rather than continuing to climb that mountain made of ice.

- We all have a style that we use to manage relationships at work, whether boss-to- subordinate or peer-to-peer.

- Our style has formed over time through a combination of nature (genetic) and nurture (learned/taught) influences.

- We can't likely change our style to any great degree, but we can practice new behaviors that can soften or strengthen style parts that need it.

- There is no such thing as a perfect personality. Each facet of our personality has an upside and downside built in.

- Our style has positive and negative impacts on the people around us, and most of the time we are unaware of what that impact is.

- Positive reinforcement makes people more productive, and while negative reinforcement can produce similar results, they are short term at best because of the destructive nature of this type of reinforcement. Neutral reinforcement (ignoring) is worst of all and deflates performance.

- To learn more about our styles and their impacts on others, it's helpful for us to use psychological profile tools and (solicited) feedback surveys, the combination of which tells us what we do in the eyes of others and why we do it.

- It's not easy to take this kind of look at ourselves, but if we don't start here, we're less likely to become successful managers.

2

THE SEVEN FUNDAMENTALS

Marnie Cooper is a long-time and valued colleague who interned and then worked with our consulting firm for a number of years. During her internship we would often travel together to clients where she could sit at the foot of the master (that would be me) and observe and learn. One day, as we were driving back to our office from a client visit she said, "You know, Bob, I've heard you say several times to different clients, 'You really only need to know a few fundamental things in order to effectively manage the people in your enterprise.'"

Marnie went on to say, "Then, you would mention a couple of these 'fundamental things' as a way to help that client understand a particular point you were trying to make. The only thing is you never seem to mention the same fundamentals to any of these different clients, and I was wondering, is there an actual *list of fundamentals*, and have you ever attempted to codify it, or are you just making it up as you go along?" *Very funny, Marnie*, I thought, at first bristling a bit at her unsought observation, but then realizing that one of Marnie's gifts is that she never hesitates to venture into the provocative comments arena.

Giving her comment a bit more thought, I then realized that while I truly *did* have a list of *management fundamentals* in my mind at all times, and that I would draw on them as the situation presented itself with a client, there was no actual *list* of them that I had pinned to a wall somewhere. So I set about sorting out the list of what has come to be called "The Fundamentals." At first, it was a bit like trying to gather a bunch of stainless steel ball bearings rolling around on a marble-top table. Just when I thought I had this neat, logical list all together, another *fundamental* would turn up, and in an attempt to grab that one and fit it into my hand, several others would roll away. Over time, though, through reordering and refining, I can finally declare the list of *fundamentals* complete (except perhaps for that one over there just about to roll off the table). There are seven of them.

The Seven Fundamentals (sounds a little like a '60's rock group, doesn't it) constitute what I see as the tenets of a healthy work environment where an employee's successful completion of any task is optimized. They are the essentials the *Unforgettable Boss* needs to learn, embrace, and then practice.

If you can find a way to understand and make these seven principles a part of your everyday habits and culture, you'll have enormous success in your career. Statues will be built honoring you as an enlightened leader. The opposite sex will tear their clothes off at your arrival on the scene. You will be hosted on the red carpet. Guaranteed.

So, with a bow toward Marnie (whom I hope will now get off my back!), ladies and gentlemen, put your hands together and please welcome...*THE SEVEN FUNDAMENTALS!* Ta-Da!

FUNDAMENTAL No. 1:
Always the Boss, Never the Parent

Picture the world of work as being made up of two giant sandboxes. One is for children, where rules and regulations are written to ensure obedience and strict adherence. The children's sandbox is for people who can't or won't take responsibility for their actions, need lots of guidance and direction, and are loophole finders. ("The handbook says I'm allowed to be tardy once a month, but this month has five weeks in it, so I should be allowed an extra late day.")

If the enterprise you own or the place where you work has more than 20 people, you probably have an employee handbook. In the first years of your enterprise, when there were only a handful of you, a handbook wasn't necessary, because everyone knew the "rules" and what was expected on a day-to-day basis. As you grew and added a few "strangers" to the original crew, you noticed that not everyone understood or practiced the so-called rules in the same way. Some people came in later or left earlier than others, some needed more definition about things like time off, smoking, productivity expectations and the like. And so, the Employee Handbook was born. Now, there's essentially nothing wrong with a list of dos and don'ts (We've helped many clients design employee handbooks.), but when the list is used to run the company and takes the place of conversation, mutual fairness and common sense, then you've drifted toward becoming the parent to the children. You've essentially built a good-sized children's sandbox that will probably get a lot bigger. Think about the handbook in terms similar to the list of dos and don'ts parents put on the refrigerator in a silly attempt to catalog or document what constitutes acceptable behavior in the household.

We talk to managers and business owners all the time who tell us that if they don't have the handbook to fall back on, lawsuits or unions or both would be lurking around the next corner. Handbooks, they say, protect the company and level the playing field so that everyone is treated equally. We agree. Everyone should be treated equally, as an adult! It's even more important for everyone to be treated *fairly*. Here's one of my favorite examples to make the point that handbooks can easily become a blunt instrument and lead to a widening gap of mistrust and dislike between employer and employee:

Most employee handbooks have a bereavement leave policy, one that's probably been edited and honed over the years (because of some loophole twits who tried to beat the system) to say something like: "Up to three days of bereavement pay compensates employees who lose work time due to the death and funeral of an immediate family member. 'Immediate family' includes spouse, parent, child, sister, brother, grandparent, father-in-law, mother-in-law, and same-sex domestic partner." So now, let's say we have Mary in payroll, who was raised by her aunt because her parents died at an early age. The aunt died recently. Let's check that good old policy manual for Mary. "Hmmm. Sorry Mary, but aunts don't qualify. We'd like to make an exception for you, but then other people would come up with a dead aunt who raised them and soon we'd have chaos. You'll have to take unpaid time – with the permission of your supervisor, of course – or not go." An exaggeration? Not really. Just ask most HR professionals who (because managers like to hide behind them) often become the queens and kings of the Land of Don't, Can't and Won't (as in: "Don't do that." "You can't do that." And: "We won't do that."). They'll tell you how much of their time is spent (or wasted) in having to interpret policy.

Here's the point. Employee policy manuals are actually written for the few people (about 11 percent, and more on this later) who work in your organization and can't function or fit as an adult. They are the ones who are always complaining about "how things are done around here," feeling mistreated, looking for loopholes in the system, goofing off on the Internet, pushing the envelope on time and attendance, acting miserable with customers...and on and on. Quite often, they see themselves as victims, caught in someone else's trap and never responsible for anything that goes wrong with their jobs or themselves, and living in the world of "If only..." (*If only I had a better childhood, more accepting spouse, more grateful kids, better job, more money*). What's that old chestnut? "If *ifs* were horses, beggars would ride."

These are the people I call The White Knuckle Group (WKG). As you're driving to work Monday morning, just the sheer anticipation of having to see and deal with these people one more day makes your knuckles go white on the steering wheel. You want to rip the wheel off the steering column, crash the car and even accept the possibility of serious injury just so you won't have to see or deal with them even one day longer. You get to work, and either here they come or you just know you're going to hear yet another tale about them from someone else on their continuing saga of lament and hard times. Nowhere to run. Nowhere to hide.

An interesting, unscientific, but pretty reliable, experiment I do when discussing the WKG in a supervisory skills seminar or workshop is to ask a couple of the attendees who have 10 or more people reporting to them to volunteer for the experiment. Let's say I get three such volunteers. I will then describe to them, in detail similar to above, the WKG (without having yet mentioned the 11 percent number). Next, I'll ask them to think about their entire work group and freeze-frame a mental picture in their minds on the number of people who make up their WKG without saying the number out loud. I then – in my best Carnac the Magnificent imitation – turn to a couple of other attendees seated close to where I'm standing, and in a whispered aside tell them that the number each of the volunteers has in mind will equal roughly 11 percent of the whole work group. Sure enough, as each volunteer offers his or her number, it equates to roughly 11 percent almost every time. Occasionally, one of the volunteers pulls a Pollyanna routine claiming he or she has no WKG members, but that person is living in self-denial La-La Land. Or, there will usually be one joker who will claim that the company's entire 11 percent is in his or her department.

The trap most bosses fall into is to respond to these 11 percenters as if they were their parents. The boss begins giving advice, setting up rules and limits, and generally taking responsibility for the person's situation and/or choices – in essence, building a nice, square, children's sandbox with substantial, protective sides.

We were working with a group of supervisors in a customer service department at a mid-sized HMO on a continuing performance problem involving employee time and at-

tendance. The supervisors were complaining about an ir-
regularly high number of absences. Staff would call in the
morning before their scheduled start time to say they had an
illness or family emergency and *ask* the supervisor if they
could miss work that day. The supervisor would then say,
"Yes, you may stay home," or words to that effect. This situation had been repeating itself for some time and almost always followed the same pattern: A request to miss work followed by a grant of permission.

The supervisors said, in essence, that they felt as if they
were dealing with a bunch of adolescent kids. Small wonder, since that's precisely how they were treating the staff –
as kids. They were setting up a classic parent-child interaction (or as Eric Berne described in his fascinating book,
Games People Play (1964), a parent-child *transaction*). What
was happening in the client's customer service department
was the staffer would function as a "child" in asking for
permission to miss work (children ask permission, adults
don't), thus avoiding taking any responsibility for the decision to do so. The supervisor then would fall right into the
trap of becoming the "parent" by taking on the decision-
making responsibility and granting the request, "By all
means, if you don't feel well, you should stay home and get
better." Pretty subtle, huh?

At the risk of splitting hairs, but to clarify the point, there
is a difference between an employee saying to the boss: "I
don't feel well and I plan on staying home. Is that OK with
you?"…and saying: "I don't feel well. May I stay home?" In
the first instance, the employee is taking the "adult" route in
making the decision to stay home, then checking that decision out with the boss, more as a courtesy than anything

else. While in the second instance, the entire decision is put on the boss. In scenario one, the employee presents the problem *and* supplies the solution ("I'm sick and will be taking time off."). In scenario two, the employee presents the problem for the boss to solve. Most bosses I know prefer the first scenario, but they forget they have the power to create that scenario, forcing adultness, if you will, onto the employee.

As most of us should know by now, part of being a child is to avoid responsibility, and part of being a parent is to assume responsibility...and carry it around on one's shoulders like a huge boulder. Eric Berne, in *Games People Play*, theorized that there resides in each of us a Parent, Child, and Adult, and depending on the vehicle one uses to communicate to another, a certain "transaction," as Berne calls it, will occur. If someone acts or speaks as a "Parent," that action or communication will appeal to the "Child" in the other person and create a Parent-Child transaction, or vice-versa.

> *As most of us should know by now, part of being a child is to avoid responsibility, and part of being a parent is to assume responsibility...and carry it around on one's shoulders like a huge boulder.*

Here's a list of examples of each of the three delivery systems:

The Parent Function...
- Sets limits
- Gives (un-asked for) advice

- Disciplines others

- Protects

- Makes rules and regulations about how life should be: the dos, don'ts, always, nevers, shoulds, shouldn'ts, musts, ought-tos, have-tos, can'ts, goods and bads, and who wins and loses.

- Keeps traditions

- Nurtures

- Judges

- Criticizes

The Child Function…

- Acts angry, rebellious and frightened

- Conforms (to please the Parent)

- Acts in a natural, spontaneous and loving way

- Is adventurous, curious, trusting and joyful

- Will often use words like: "Wow, Gee, I can, I can't, I won't, If only, Please"

The Adult function…

- Acts rationally and with little or no emotion

- Seeks results

- Computes; what fits and is most expedient

- Is descriptive versus prescriptive

- Helps others make choices and decisions; what's the best way to get there

If you're like most people who first see these lists, you must be thinking: "As good bosses, aren't we supposed to be doing a bunch of the things that fall on the "Parent" list? I mean, isn't our job to 'set limits,' 'discipline others,' and make 'rules and regulations'?" Boy, are you in for a surprise!

But I digress. Back to our story of the HMO. We talked at length with the group of supervisors about how they inadvertently – but often – played the parent role with their subordinates. We recommended a subtle but distinctly different response approach to the supervisors. In the future, when a person calls to ask to take time off for things like illness or family emergencies, they were to say: "If you don't feel well, *you* need to decide whether or not you plan on coming in to work. So, just tell me if you're planning on coming in or not." In other words, they were to force the decision-making back on the customer service representative staff, thereby transferring the boulder. The supervisors were at first skeptical that this tactic would work, but willing to give it a try.

A couple of weeks later, we met again with the supervisors to get a progress check. We heard that when they put the onus on the employee to make the decision about staying home or coming in to work, the first reaction they got was one of silence; the employees were caught flat-footed and didn't know what to say. (We had cautioned the supervisors in advance to wait for an answer as long as it took and not jump in with more verbiage on their part until the employee spoke first. This advice was based on the theory of: *The first person who talks loses.*) In other words, if the supervisors jumped in too soon to make or help make the employee's decision, they would lose. In almost every instance, the employee finally made the decision, in some cases choosing to come in and in others choosing to stay home. Over a brief period, the absenteeism began to ebb with fewer people calling in sick, and less often. As we anticipated, with the decision-making function regarding showing up to work shifted from the supervisor to the employee, the employees became more responsible (and grown up).

A sad postscript to this story was that two or three of the supervisors had a really difficult time letting go of the parenting role and continued to take on the responsibility of choosing for the employee. They also continued to complain about the employees acting like children. It showed me that even a perfectly sound theory is sometimes difficult to put into practice; especially, as in this instance, if one really likes being the parent.

In sum, among the first actions you need to take in *creating an environment where the person's successful completion of the task is optimized* is to avoid or eliminate all vestiges of children's sandboxes and make the determination that everyone who works with you will be treated as an adult – by other adults. You'll see how this works more in subsequent chapters in this book, especially those that deal with developing talent, and counseling and termination. For now, know that every time you establish a sweeping, draconian edict or policy to close a loophole, or get too involved in the personal lives of employees, or get all bent out of shape and take personally what you see as acts of insubordination or disobedience, you're probably cutting up the two-by-fours and buying the nails and glue you'll need to assemble the sandbox. Netflix, an extremely successful and well-run company that makes most "companies-I-want-to-work-for" lists, says in its website section on *Working at Netflix:* "Rules annoy us...Rules are developed to create boundaries and dictate behavior."

For those of you who are still having a tough time accepting this because you're so focused on and preoccupied with the few who make up the White Knuckle Group, hang on. More advice on this topic will be here before you know it.

FUNDAMENTAL No. 2:
Be Curious

When my kids were growing into their teen years, they were given a wider berth in which to make their own decisions and more latitude on things like curfew time. Occasionally, they would get home later than the permissible hour. In my worry and consternation, the typical question I would ask – but really didn't want to know the answer to – was, "Where the heck (okay, maybe not "heck") have you been?" Another of these don't-want-to-know-the-answer-to questions might have been: "Well, young lady, did you have a good time?" In either case, the kids were smart enough not to offer an answer because they knew it was a setup, and any answer they might give would only get them in more trouble. I'll devote more time to what I call the "bag job" questions later, but for now suffice it to say any of us who are parents – or had parents – are quite familiar with this sort of rite-of-passage dance that parents and children engage in: asking questions to which there is no safe answer, with both sides knowing that no answer is expected.

Along my way, I've often wondered not only why we sometimes ask such stupid questions, but what's behind our hesitancy to want to know the answer. I mean, shouldn't information be pretty harmless in and of itself? And wouldn't having more information actually be more helpful for all of us? A very popular and productive practice in industry today is referred to as getting to the "root cause" of a problem, so that it can be fixed, hopefully forever. You would think that getting at the root cause of a problem would be something we would do naturally and not something we'd have to go out and spend thousands of dollars being trained to do. Somewhere in our evolution as humans, we learned *not* to be curious, especially when it comes to interacting with other humans, and moreover, interacting on a level playing field.

> *Perhaps more than anything else, the one factor that keeps folks like me in business is people's – especially managers' and parents' – underdeveloped sense of curiosity when it comes to understanding why people think what they think or do what they do*

Perhaps more than anything else, the one factor that keeps folks like me in business is people's – especially managers' and parents' – underdeveloped sense of curiosity when it comes to understanding why people think what they think or do what they do. What's the motivation behind their thoughts or actions? In our consulting firm, we make a very good living by acting as the curious one, often on management's behalf, conducting interviews and employee surveys, for example. I'm not completely sure what's behind this "underdeveloped sense of curiosity," but it definitely is a prevalent mode of functionality (or should I say *dys*-functionality) among the ranks of most bosses I know. Bosses usually do get upset, or at the least, disappointed when mistakes are made, and even more so when they get repeated. However, too many bosses we've known either work around the mistake or the person committing it, or go into preaching lecture mode, often asking one of those unanswerable bag job questions: "How many times do we have to go over this?" Or scolding: "You know, these parts cost lots of money, so I expect this not to happen again." In both these instances, the speaker has no interest at all in getting to the root cause of the problem, and yet when asked about these kinds of comments most managers will claim they've done their jobs with the preaching lecture. Not by a long shot have they done their jobs.

A supervisor's hesitancy or inability to ask *root-cause* questions is largely the reason we aren't big fans of Written Warning forms. The only way we will design or support such a system with our clients is if the form includes a section that says: "The employee's reason for why the situation occurred." The form will not be accepted by management or HR unless this section is completed. It's amazing to us and our clients how responding to this simple statement dramatically and quickly improves not only the problem, but the relationship between the supervisor and the employee.

The best guess I can make about a manager's hesitancy or inability to *Be Curious* is an unconscious fear that they won't be able to handle the information, meaning having an answer as to how to fix the problem. Pay attention here because this may be the most important thing you'll learn in reading this book: *It's not necessarily your job to solve every-one's problems...It's mostly your job to help people fearlessly disclose the information that drove their thoughts or actions!* Let me say this again. *It's not necessarily your job to solve everyone's problems...It's mostly your job to help people fearlessly disclose the information that drove their thoughts or actions.* "Fearlessly" is the operational term here, and we'll discuss the factors of how to help people be fearless a little farther on.

One of the better *Be Curious* examples I know of had to do with one of the most dynamic, and as you'll see, courageous, managers I've ever coached. Sam, an engineer by training, led a work group of some 80 people in a small company that did engine repair. He had a management team of six people, all of whom had small groups of subordinates. Sam also had working under him a young guy named Dave, who was a project manager for the company and, while not a supervisor, had shown a real talent for getting things done and being able to effectively anticipate events, or what I like to commonly call: *think around corners.* Sam and his boss Martina (who also had recognized Dave's talents) had been looking for an opportunity to take better advantage of Dave's abilities, and at the same time give Dave the recognition he should have in order to stay motivated – a classic win-win. As it happened, an opportunity opened with the company's second-biggest customer for someone to be a dedicated, full-time liaison between Sam's company and the customer. This was certainly in anyone's view a high-profile position, and in the minds of Sam and Martina a perfect fit for Dave's talents.

A few days before our scheduled coaching session, Sam met with Dave to make the offer. When I met with Sam he reported a certain disappointment with the outcome of his conversation with Dave. Apparently, when Sam made the offer of the new position, Dave responded with something like: "You know, I kind of like what I'm doing right now, but if that's where you need me, I'll do it." On the one hand, Sam was greatly relieved that even in this lukewarm manner Dave accepted the position, because there frankly was no one else on board who could really handle this important assignment. But, on the other hand, he was far from pleased about the lack of enthusiasm on Dave's part.

Something didn't seem right to Sam. As we talked about it, I shared with him my thoughts about *Be Curious*, essentially stating that as Dave's boss, Sam could easily walk away from any further discussion with Dave about what appeared to Sam as a flat response and just assume that over time, whatever might be bothering Dave about this new assignment would work itself out. Exaggerating, I went on further to say, "After all, Sam you're the boss and Dave really has to do what he's told (Remember line #7 on the job description: 'All other duties as assigned?')." Toning it down a bit, I then suggested to Sam that unless he managed the ambiguity of Dave's response, he'd be running a longer term risk of a lose-lose-lose situation, where Dave fails at the new job, the customer becomes disgruntled, and Sam and Martina have to go back to square one.

We reviewed the rules of *Be Curious* and, with a bit of a groan, Sam (and here's where the courage comes in) went off to meet with Dave and – following the script we wrote together – expressed his concern to Dave that he appeared less than enthusiastic about the job offer, and asked if there was anything behind the tepid response. The two of them talked about it for a while, and I wish I could report here that there was some sort of incredible "Aha" moment that came out of their interaction. There wasn't. However, simply by *Being Curious*, Sam came to realize that Dave would have been moved way out of his comfort zone by taking the new job. He was much better suited to managing projects. Sam reported his disappointment to me a few days later, groaning that he still had a major hole to fill, but also agreeing that everyone was much better off with this resolution. Dave was certainly relieved. Two weeks later, Sam and Martina found another good internal candidate for the customer liaison job. Win-win-win.

Another more humorous example and positive payoff of the *Be Curious* belief occurred a number of years earlier when I was conducting a supervisory skills seminar for a group of super market chain store managers. In a previous session, we had discussed the *Be Curious* principle and the store managers were given an assignment to try it out in the intervening weeks between training sessions.

Walter was a grizzled and well-seasoned manager who had been running stores for the chain for about 20 years. The company had recently adopted a Pack-Out Rate measurement system that calculated how many items a clerk in a given department should be able to put on the shelves in a given hour. Walter had a grocery clerk, Adam, who worked the paper aisle. The pack out rate for that aisle, as I recall, was 25 cases per hour; meaning that Adam should be putting at least that amount of cases of toilet tissue, paper towels, plastic wrap and the like on the shelves each hour he worked. Adam's pack out rate had usually hovered around 18-19 cases per hour. At this point, Walter was ready to "pack out" Adam under the claim that some people just aren't cut out for this kind of work.

Walter, like many of his fellow store managers, was skeptical that the *Be Curious* idea would actually work. He came from the school that preached: "Do what you're told and don't ask questions. I'm the boss. You're the clerk." To his credit, though, Walter was willing to give it a try. He reported to me and his colleagues at the next seminar that he sat with Adam and expressed his "curiosity" as to why he wasn't reaching the 25-case-per-hour goal. Adam simply explained that on the three days he works, the delivery truck from the New Jersey warehouse dropped about six pallets of groceries in front of his paper goods in the back room. Adam went on to explain to Walter that as a result, before he could begin packing out product, he had to move these pallets, which could take almost an hour. Walter, trying hard to mask his consternation over this response, then said to Adam: "How come you never said anything about this before?" Adam's response – you guessed it – "No one ever asked me." Flabbergasted, Walter thanked Adam, arranged to have the pallets dropped in another section of the back room, and watched as Adam reached not 25 cases per hour, but 30! Ya think maybe Adam got a little extra motivated because his boss treated him kinda special by *being Curious* and asking about Adam's dilemma? I do.

FUNDAMENTAL No. 3:
It's Strictly Business – Nothing Personal

It has been said that all of life's lessons are contained in the *Godfather* films (e.g. "Make him an offer he can't refuse"). Throughout *Godfather I* (Paramount,1972) and spilling over to *Godfather II* (Paramount, 1974), there are numerous times when an expression like "nothing personal" is used and in all instances they are meant to convey that the action taken or about to be taken had no emotional element to it; it was simply what had to be done under the circumstances. Many recall the scene where Michael Corleone suggests to his brother Sonny and Tom Hagen that he be the one to kill the police captain who was instrumental in the attempted assassination of Don Corleone. At first, Sonny scoffs at the idea of up-to-now innocent Michael doing such a deed. They go back and forth until Michael, in what may be the most transformative moment of his life (and certainly the movie), coldly says "It's not personal, Sonny. It's strictly business."

Another scene more at the end of the movie is when Sal is confronted with the fact that Michael and The Family know that Sal betrayed The Don. Sal says simply to Tom Hagen, "Tell Mike it was only business. I always liked him." Then Sal is led away to what we all know is an unpleasant end. For me, and as befits this *Fundamental*, the power of that scene is that both Tom and Sal recognize the situation for what it is; no tempers flare, no emotion is displayed, and no blame is assessed. Rather, it's a mutual understanding of: "We agree with each other there was a transgression and that a consequence has to occur." How simple. How clean. In its rather grim way, how adult.

I'm also recalling a line from a song that Dave Mason recorded back in the 70's called: *We Just Disagree* (Columbia 1977). It's about a divorce and has an intriguing line in it that goes: "There ain't no good guys. There ain't no bad guys. There's only you and me, and we just disagree." The premise is that the marriage has failed, and let's not get into who did what. We both acknowledge it's a sad situation. No tempers flare, no emotions are displayed, and no blame is assessed. How simple. How clean. How adult.

For owners or managers of small businesses – and especially for people who run family businesses – keeping things between them and employees on a nothing-personal-simply-business basis is probably the most difficult belief to embrace and practice. But, it's so necessary to do so. Why? Because the more emotionally based your decisions become, the less likely you are to make good ones, either for you or the other people involved.

Families have parents and parents make lousy bosses. Only adults make good bosses.

Here are some of the reasons why it's so difficult to keep things on a "strictly business" basis. As mentioned earlier, smaller and/or family businesses quite often began on someone's kitchen table, in the garage or basement. These businesses usually have rich, entertaining histories; chronicles of people-driven events that shaped the company's success and certainly its culture. "Remember when Dan and Janice worked all night to bail out the flood we had in the basement of our first store?" Or: "How about that day when the guy from the bank came to get a mortgage check, and Jerry told him I was down with the flu, but I was actually in the broom closet hiding!" Or: "It seems like yesterday that little Billy came into the office for the first time and kept swiveling around and around in my desk chair until he got so dizzy he couldn't walk. I remember thinking: 'I can't wait until he's old enough to run this whole place from that same chair!'"

It's not just sagas like these that bring wistful smiles to the faces of these owners or managers. It's also that after a while, everyone in the company becomes part of what is often called "a family," and it's even claimed with pride. Family businesses or businesses that see themselves as a family are actually caldrons of emotion; emotions that really have no place in trying to run an efficient, excellent enterprise. Families have parents and parents make lousy bosses. Only *adults* make good bosses. (By the way, Netflix very clearly states in their organizational culture description: "We're a team, not a family.")

Let's connect the dots a bit. Remember that in the "adult function" section under *Fundamental No. 1: Always the Boss, Never the Parent,* we noted that adults "act rationally with little or no emotion." So what's wrong with a little emotion mixed in, you might ask? After all, we aren't robots, and neither are the people who work for us or with us. If we're anywhere near normal, we have feelings for people, especially when their lives are stalled or might be going a bit in reverse. I agree it's good to *care* about the welfare of others, but it's a very bad idea to become *responsible* for the welfare of others. And that's what happens all too often in these kinds of businesses. The minute you move from caring to becoming responsible, you create an imbalance in the relationship. You move from boss to parent and only bad things can happen from there.

You might pose the notion that it's natural and normal for there to be an imbalance between a boss and subordinate, and I would agree to this extent: As a boss, you have a broader range of responsibility for the enterprise and can make more unilateral decisions than any subordinate is allowed to make (except for that old curmudgeon in Quality Control who can bring to a screeching halt anything she wants to). What I'm talking about here has more to do with the adult-to-adult *balance* of each person ultimately being responsible for their own actions and welfare. As bosses or enterprise owners, you do indeed contribute to the welfare of your employees through direct compensation and benefits, but after all is said and done, you are clearly not responsible for the choices others make on how they spend their earnings, who they marry, what they eat, how they raise their children or generally live their lives. We know way too many bosses who know way too much about the trials and troubles of their employees: Marge in customer service who misses a lot of work because she's raising two of her grandchildren; or Jimmy who's having "girlfriend problems" and is on the phone with her constantly. None of this is your business – or responsibility. The adult-to-adult balance means each party has the right – moreover, the obligation – to make his or her own choices, and neither party has the right to judge or evaluate the choices made by the other.

Let's look at this last claim more closely. A few years ago while presenting a communication skills seminar, I picked up a theory sheet (left behind by the previous presenter) titled, "The Cornerstones of Trust." The document went something like:

"In order to build or maintain a trusting relationship between you and anyone else, the following 'Cornerstone' elements must be in place and continually practiced:

- *Never betray a confidence*

- *Keep all commitments, and*

- *Never judge or evaluate <u>anything</u> a person says, thinks or feels.*

Now, the first two generally make good sense, and seem unarguable as cornerstones of a trusting relationship. After all, we probably all know how disappointing or betrayed it feels to find out that information we shared in confidence with another person was in turn shared with yet another or others. We also all know how difficult it sometimes is to maintain silence about information shared with us in confidence ("This is juicy stuff and I really wanna tell somebody!").

"Keeping all commitments" is also easily understood and embraced by most as a good second cornerstone of trust. Nothing builds trust better between you and someone else than that person's following through on a promise. Think about the employees you trust most. It's likely that a key reason is they always follow through on assignments, and on time. Also, consider the reverse: A key reason for an employee to trust a boss or not is the extent to which the boss follows through on commitments made to the employee. Like the promise you made to meet with Muriel last Thursday to go over her expanded responsibilities and commensurate compensation. What? You mean you postponed the meeting? Well, Muriel will understand, won't she? After all, she should recognize how busy a person you can be.

Don't get me started on this major boss-failing. Let me just say this: If you want to buy a whole bunch of high performance and morale from your employees, start keeping all the commitments you've made to them. If there is an unfortunate time when you have cause to break one of those commitments, it's only fair that you ask for permission to do so. Assuming you are granted this permission, offer thanks and apologize without excuse. That's what adults do with one another, regardless of their station in life, or more pertinently, at work. Wouldn't you do that if you had to break a commitment with someone superior in rank to you? Tell me then, what's the difference between that person and your employee? Oh, I see. It relates to that stupid line 7 insertion on the job description about all other duties... In essence, employees don't have choices. Hogwash!

Look at the beauty of this scenario:

Muriel is an excellent performer. Her work is pretty much always acceptable without the need for edits, and she handles relationships with her peers well. She knows the people to notify when help is needed, and when to notify them. She goes the extra mile and usually makes your job a lot easier. You've decided that Muriel is ready to go to the next level of responsibility and that a salary increase would be appropriate, along with her expanded duties. When you asked her to meet with you this Friday, you hinted to her that you'd like to talk about this expanded role. Good so far.

If you want to buy a whole bunch of high performance and morale from your employees, start keeping all the commitments you've made to them.

As it turns out, on Wednesday you find out that an important customer wants to visit your company on Friday at the same time you were supposed to meet with Muriel. You visit with Muriel in her cubicle and say, "Muriel, I've got a problem. Mr. Gage from Joliet Electronics wants to visit me at the same time we were supposed to meet to talk about your new job. (Here's where it gets really good.) Would you mind if we postponed our meeting until Monday?"

Now, what's Muriel going to say? "No?" Of course not! She's going to tell you it's fine. Then, you thank her and simply apologize for possibly messing up her expectations.

OK, let's make it a little tougher. Muriel, as part of why you like her, is also assertive and says back to you, "Gee, boss, I'm disappointed. I was really counting on the meeting this Friday and wanted to share the news with my husband over a bottle of wine Friday night."

What do you do now? You accommodate both the customer AND Muriel by moving your Friday schedule around. What's the big deal? The point is that in either case, you've let Muriel know she's an important part of the success of your company. Moreover, by adapting to her preference, you *bought* that future "bunch of high performance and morale" mentioned above. Now, if your next thought after having read this mini-case is, "Oh sure, cater to Muriel like this and she'll ask for the whole farm when we meet on Friday," you're being ridiculous.

Well, maybe you weren't thinking about Muriel taking advantage of the situation, because she's a top player to begin with. But how about Marginal Marty? Same scenario:

Marty has been with you for six years and possesses some unique IT skills, but is by no means the be-all and end-all he walks around acting like he is. In fact, if you had to do it over again, you would hire someone a bit younger (Did I write that out loud?) who had more up-to-date training, plus a more cooperative personality. You've asked Marty to meet you this Friday to go over the plan for a software conversion and want to emphasize to him how important it is that he cooperates fully with the software vendors to keep the installation costs as low as possible. You're obviously worried he won't.

The same customer visit on Friday comes into play and you need to let Marty know. I'm saying you'd have the same conversation you would have had with Muriel. And I think you'd be saying, "Are you kidding? Why would I treat this guy with this much deference when he's mostly a thorn in my side? It's hard for me to imagine *asking* Marginal Marty if it's OK with him to postpone the meeting."

Let's put it this way. If you'd do the request thing with Muriel, but not Marty, then you've essentially created two sandboxes (see *Fundamental No. 1: Always the Boss, Never the Parent*), one for adults and one for children, and we've already proven that it won't work well for you in the long run as you struggle to become the *Unforgettable Boss*.

Marginal Marty will show up again as "Ronnie" in Chapter 7.

The third leg of The Cornerstones of Trust stool is: *Never judge or evaluate anything a person says, thinks or feels.* Ever since I discovered (or appropriated) this theory sheet and used its content in training sessions, this third leg has been the most difficult to both explain and defend. But it's also probably the most profound of the three. In its fullest, this statement clearly points out that no matter how silly, outrageous, off-putting or crazy the person's position, statement or idea seems, we can only disagree with it, but not judge or evaluate it in any way.

This means all of the following have to be accepted as another person's right to think, act or feel (as long as they don't tread on the same rights for others):

- Ultra-conservative political remarks or positions
- Ultra-liberal political remarks of positions
- People spending their money on "frivolous" things
- Children being treated like the "center of the universe"
- Everyone getting a trophy, or everyone _not_ getting a trophy
- Pets being treated like people
- People not recycling

And not only do we have to accept it, we cannot give off any signals – verbal or non-verbal – that show in any way we think this person is bonkers! No jaw clenching. No making fists. No raised eyebrows. No audible sighing.

Remember, I said you are free to _disagree_ (As in: "Interesting, but I don't see it the same way you do."); you just can't judge or evaluate ("I can't imagine anyone thinking in that twisted way").

But, you might ask, if you disagree, aren't you really evaluating? No. You're simply disagreeing (remember Dave Mason: "There's only you and me, and we just disagree"). By not judging or evaluating, you open the door to _fearless_ two-way communication, and the more you accept without judging or evaluating, the wider the door opens; and the wider the door opens, more and more options to resolving a problem become available. As you read later on about the elements of "participative management," you'll better see how this third leg of the Cornerstones of Trust comes into vital play.

For now, imagine what would have happened between Sam and Dave when they met to discuss the Customer Liaison job had Sam begun lecturing (that is, judging) Dave about how wrong he was not to accept this opportunity. Or, what about how things would have gone for Walter and Adam if Walter had taken Adam's head off for not opening his mouth about the pallets sooner. Both conversations would have come to a screeching halt, and further communication would have been rocky or guarded at best.

Some bosses have said to me: "This is all well and good, and I can see where being non-evaluative and non-judgmental can move the needle in a positive direction. But, what do I do about the frustration I feel when someone acts in what I see as a really stupid manner?" My short answer?... Go to the gym. The longer answer is to look at the conversation as an *exploration,* an opportunity to learn more about the reasoning, rationale and even idiosyncrasies of the other person. And for those of you wondering about it being part of your job to do employee *evaluations,* of course it is. However, in that case you are evaluating *performance,* not motives or beliefs.

Let's start stringing together a few "Fundamentals" beads:

- First, you declare henceforth and forever that at work you will no longer function as anyone's father or mother (or both).

- Second, focus on becoming more courageous in your curiosity about the motives and ideas of others. Don't be afraid of the information you'll get, and if you don't like what you hear, remember, you're still the boss and can do whatever you want..

- Third, while playing the *Be Curious* card, keep in mind that you should never judge or evaluate the information you're getting, otherwise the faucet of communication gets shut off and you're left alone with the problem, probably making things worse.

How simple. How clean. How adult.

Consider the list of emotionally based decisions you have made that have only served to erode the important balanced relationship, and how these decisions only led to more trouble. When you lent an employee money, you became the parent with subtle, assumed rights over them (*How could she be going to Las Vegas with her husband when she owes me $1,000?*). Or how about that time when you got involved in hearing all about Bill's marital woes and how his wife is an emotional abuser and how you suggested he see a lawyer and how he now blames you for his impending divorce? Or how about Mary who hasn't put in a full week's work for months and when she's here is often on the phone, but you can't let her go because she has shared so much with you about her husband who blows his weekly paycheck at the casino, and she needs the money from this job just to put food on the table?

Once again, I'm not saying you shouldn't be compassionate or caring about the personal welfare of your employees. But at some early point in the dialogue (right around where you first hear about the need for $1,000, or the abusive wife, or the husband's gambling problem), back away by saying something like: "I'm really sorry you're in such a situation. You might want to seek some help to get it taken care of." You might then refer the person to your Employee Assistance Plan provider, if you have one. In any case, after this, walk away, at least emotionally. As heartless as it may seem to some of you who place a high premium on loyalty and *family feeling* at your workplace, the rest of their story is really none of your business!

When we're teaching managers a new skill, such as delegating tasks to others, we employ a technique we call *Exaggerated Learning*, and what that means is that if you are trying to learn a new skill, it's best to *exaggerate* the effort by trying to go 100 percent of the way there. The theory is that when you first try something new, you'll only get about 50 percent of the way there. So, by exaggerating the learning you get closer to the ideal, sooner. As applied here, regarding *Strictly Business, Nothing Personal,* trying to be 100 percent arm's length and dispassionate when it comes to the personal lives of employees will likely get you halfway there. And that's good enough…for now.

FUNDAMENTAL No. 4:
Authorship Leads to Ownership

The Parable of the Shrub. Back in the days when I had the energy and the time to do family yard work, it was always very clear that my wife was management and I was labor. On a typical Saturday morning I would stand at slouched attention while we reviewed the directions for the day. [Her] "Get the shovel." [Me] "Which one?" [Her] "The long-handled one ('stupid,' implied). [Me] "OK." And so on...

The yard and gardens were, in my mind at least, essentially hers. She owned them by the fact that she controlled pretty much everything that went on there. One of those mornings when I was standing there with the wheel barrow at my feet and shovel in hand she directed me to dig up a yew that apparently had died, although it looked fine to me, but what did I know? My next question: "How deep?" was met with a harsh: "As deep as it needs to be to get the shrub out of the ground ('stupid' implied)."

I growled and grumbled, to myself, of course, and removed the shrub, roots and all. I then stood and waited for additional instruction. (How often do you think does this kind of boss-subordinate relationship develop at work?) She left and eventually returned from whatever *important* thing she was doing and said: "What are you standing around for?" And then, not waiting for the answer, because she hadn't honed her *Be Curious* skill, finished me off with: "Toss it in the woods!" ('stupid,' implied). Task completed. Next job!

She then, somewhat sweetly now, asked (not told) me if I wouldn't mind going to the nursery to buy a new yew. I finally agreed and took off for the nursery, curiously, with a sense of heightened energy. At the nursery, I took extra time to select just the right yew and gently placed it in the back of the SUV. If she were the one in the nursery, I'd probably be sitting in the car looking at my watch, wishing a baseball game were on the radio. You see what's going on here, don't you? This isn't *her* yew, it's *my* yew – and a whole new sense of *ownership* is emerging.

Let me put the planting process this way: You could have done a slide show of what I did and sold it to the American Yew Association for their website. Everything was perfect, from widening the hole to tamping down the dirt. From that day forth, the only plant in the whole garden that I cared about was that yew, watering it three times a week and admiring its beauty every day right up until we sold the house — as part of our divorce.

So, that's my long-winded, only slightly exaggerated, example of the *Authorship-Leads-to-Ownership* Fundamental. You all have had similar experiences where once you have crafted something – be it painting a bedroom, preparing a meal for the first time, or buying and planting a yew – it becomes yours; your bedroom, your meal, or your yew (which, by the way can easily be said 10 times, fast). For sure, other people might offer words of admiration for what you've done, but no one can quite feel the same sense of pride you do.

Your job as a boss, then, is to find every opportunity you can to let people *author* ideas, projects and processes. As we've stated before, it's not to make them feel good; it's to be more productive, not to mention what their input can do in helping *you* solve longstanding problems.

Tell me and I'll forget; show me and I may remember; but involve me and I'll understand   -Chinese Proverb

Another way to look at the *Authorship Leads to Ownership* Fundamental is as a grid. The more a person gets involved in a learning activity, or "authorship," the more she will take on this new way of doing things as her own.

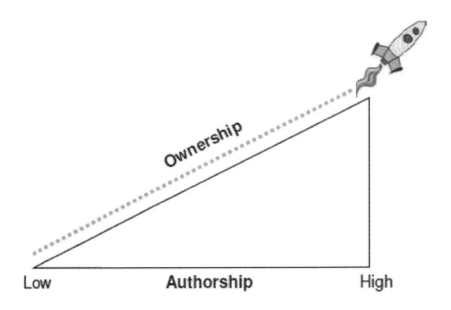

Low   **Authorship**   **High**

In recent times, countless businesses have become involved in what is called *Lean Manufacturing*, which essentially is aimed at reducing waste by continuously improving key processes. In even more recent times, the concept is being applied to all other forms of businesses, from health care to law firms to retail operations, and even to government agencies (no kidding). It's more informal nickname is *Lean*. The notion of *Lean* has its roots in what many of you either remember or read about as *Total Quality Management (TQM)*, which relies on *continuous improvement* of everything that an organization does that might hinder the highest levels of customer satisfaction. There was even a time from the 1960s into the '70s when a concept called *Quality Circles* – small groups of volunteer employees sitting together to discuss issues of workplace life (sounds like something from the 60s, doesn't it?) – was implemented by usually non-manufacturing organizations. I remember working with several health care institutions on their *Quality Circles* efforts. *Quality Circles* didn't get very far, largely because they were unfortunately looked upon by management as a way to make employees feel good by letting them meet and come up with ideas, but not to necessarily take these ideas seriously.

So, even though the names and abbreviations have changed over the years, the thrust of all these efforts has been to attack workplace problems and inefficiencies, but with employee involvement, because – it says here in fine print – *It's the employees who do the work every day who know what the problems are and how to fix them.* This has always been a shaky belief at best on the part of management, as you will see in this next story.

Our firm climbed on board the TQM bandwagon in its heyday of the 1980s into the '90s. Even though the Japanese had learned (from an American, for crying out loud) and had been practicing TQM since just after World War II, we in the U.S. pretty much went along our merry way until we looked up one day and saw that the Japanese might have lost the war, but they were kicking our butts all over the place when it came to building quality automobiles — and cars were just the beginning. The Japanese learned the principles of TQM well and had developed a passion for delivering top level customer satisfaction through relentless efforts to improve quality.

Out of necessity, because the United States began to lose market share to the Japanese, not just in automobile manufacturing but in electronics and appliance manufacturing as well, American companies were finally getting the message that they needed to sharpen their own focus on quality and customer satisfaction – and fast!   Among these companies was Pratt & Whitney Aircraft, builder of airplane engines and at that time my home state of Connecticut's largest employer. "Pratt," as the company is called, put out the word to all its suppliers that they were becoming fully immersed in TQM education and practice and expected all of them to do so as well if they wanted to continue to do business with the mother ship. The forming of employee teams within each company was a key ingredient for the TQM philosophy to work. TQM preached that first-line employees were the ones who held the key to ideas and energy that needed to be tapped into in order to truly achieve quality improvement. TQM also preached the idea of synergy: a group of employees working together to solve a problem would produce a result far superior to that group working as individuals. In other words, the whole is greater than the sum of its parts. The value of *Synergy* gets reviewed in more detail in Chapter 6.

Recognizing an opportunity when we see one, our company at the same time was building quite a reputation for being good at understanding the essence of TQM and training TQM teams and team leaders (facilitators) within smaller companies like the ones that supplied Pratt. One day I got a call from Ron, a down-to-earth, hardworking guy who, along with two of his daughters, owned a small job shop (started in his garage) of about 45 people, with Pratt as his top customer. He needed our help right away because Pratt was giving him just a few months to get up and running with TQM or they would drop his company as a vendor/supplier. Pratt's directive included the forming and functioning of two or more employee teams in all vendor/supplier companies.

At my first meeting with Ron, his opening lines went something like: "Pratt's flavor-of-the-month is TQM, and we've got to show their buyers that we're in compliance. It's just another *program* they've come up with to get in the way of our getting things done. I've already had a nice banner made that says 'Our Company is a Big Fan of TQM' that we'll put up whenever they come to visit" ("visit" being a euphemism for *snooping*).

So early on, and without a whole lot of mental effort on my part, I'm getting a pretty good sense of where Ron is coming from. What he wanted from me, of course, was to get a couple of teams up and running so the Pratt dog-and-pony show would be complete.

Ron continued: "Bob, I want you to have one team work on a safety goggles policy and the other to work on a no-smoking policy." I asked Ron: "Do you already have a safety goggles policy?"

"Sure," Ron said. "Safety goggles have to be worn on the shop floor at all times."

"Uh huh," says I. "And Ron, do you already have a no-smoking policy?"

"Yup," says Ron. "People can only smoke outside the back of the building, and during lunch and work breaks."

I ask Ron: "Do you want either of these two policies changed?"

"Of course not!" says Ron.

Then with just a touch of exasperation, I say to Ron: "If you are happy with the existing policy, why don't we have the teams work on different issues, where they can have a real and valuable influence on the outcome?"

"Are you kidding?" asked Ron. "If I did that, how would I be able to get what I wanted?" Long pause. Exhale. And I thought *I* was a control freak.

Ron was clearly going through the motions of TQM, and while a real nice guy to work for, he placed little value on – and really didn't understand – the potential positive payoffs of the authorship-ownership continuum. Eventually, Ron and I reached détente on the subject of which policies the TQM teams should work on. And he actually got some good mileage from the process. But after all was said and done, Ron was who he was and continued to figuratively put up the TQM banner when Pratt was visiting and take it down when they left the building.

The bottom line here is that the more people become involved in the brainstorming, planning and decision-making process (all elements of *authorship*), the more they will see to it that it all works and works well (*ownership*).

FUNDAMENTAL No. 5:
Freedom and Commitment Go Hand in Hand.

Wouldn't it be great if a husband and wife could have a relationship based on the following example of a spousal interaction:

The (husband or wife) calls the spouse from work and says: "Hi, Hon. I just got a call from an old college pal whom I haven't seen for years, and the two of us are planning to meet right after work for a couple of drinks and maybe a bite to eat. I hope that's not a problem."

The spouse replies: "That's great, dear! It's not a problem at all. Have a good time and I'll see you when you get home."

All right, so it does look a little Ozzie and Harriet, but what a neat interchange between two people, especially being married to each other. Notice how spouse No. 1 is courteously honoring the relationship by checking with spouse No. 2 to see if there's a problem. Notice too that spouse No. 1 isn't going with any mealy-mouthed comments like: "Gee, I wish I didn't have to go out, but I feel obligated." Or: "Please, can I go?" No. Spouse No. 1 is acting like a real adult and going with a straightforward statement of a situation. How simple. How clean.

More important, though, notice that spouse No. 2 isn't putting spouse No. 1 in a restricted position with a comment like: "Just be sure you get home by 8:00!" If this were to happen, my theory is that spouse No. 1 is likely going to want to transgress and become more pre-occupied than necessary with wanting to stay out later than 8:00. At the least – and especially if spouse No. 1 is a bit of a wuss-bunny – there will be a lot of squirming clock-watching during the drinks and the bite to eat. Whereas, in the *adult* conversation, my theory is that spouse No. 1 is more likely to look forward to coming home to spouse No. 2…and might even get home by 8:00!

Hence, the notion that the more *freedom* a person perceives he or she has in any relationship, the more likely that person is to *commit* more deeply to that relationship.

Going back to that spouse No. 1 and spouse No. 2 after-work-drink-and-bite-to-eat scenario, I've often spiced it up in seminars by continuing the fictitious conversation as follows, mostly for entertainment purposes. First, I'll select a female attendee to play the part of my *wife* where I'm spouse No. 1 calling her. I'll do the first part of the dialogue about wanting to go out after work and hoping it's not a problem. Most often, my volunteer *wife* will say – with just a touch of suspicious reluctance – that it's OK for me to go. Then I'll follow up with a line like: "Gee thanks, Hon, because, as I said, Cheryl and I haven't seen each other for years and it sure will be good to get together with her and reminisce."

It's funny how quickly adultness can disappear at the mention of "Cheryl," and be replaced by a harpy-like screeching or bellowing like an elephant.

Even between parents and their children, if the kid is on his way out to hang out with a school chum and the parent says: "Be sure you get home by 10:00," the more likely the kid is to whine and moan about the restriction and want to transgress. On the other hand, if the parent were to say: "What time do you think you'll be home?," the bet here is that the kid will probably name the time as 10:00, or even earlier. "Aha!," you might say. "What if the kid says 12:00? Then what, smart guy?" Go back and re-read Fundamental No. 2: *Be Curious* for the answer.

How, then, does this *Freedom Leads to Commitment* fundamental play out at work? While it's not as prevalent as in the past, many small business owners still often adopt the *Not-Invented-Here Syndrome*, meaning that if we didn't think of it, it can't be very good. Freedom to choose is further restricted in *paternalistic* organizations where the mantra often is, "I'm the dad and I'll protect you forever as long as you do what you're told and color within the lines." Finally, people who own or manage in smaller enterprises tend to want to keep their talented people barefoot and ignorant for fear that if they become too enlightened, they might leave the *farm*.

When you batch all these representations together, you get a picture of repressed *freedom* where all employees get robotized and just kind of go along to get along. Strangely, a lot of bosses who foster this kind of environment are at the same time confounded by the fact that "no one here seems to be able to have a creative thought or solution." Fortunately, in more recent times – and especially in small companies founded and run by young entrepreneurs – we see much more advocacy, stimulation and cultivation of creative thinking. These bosses turn their people loose to do their best by giving them the freedom (and resources) to take risks and make unilateral decisions, or at least make major contributions to the decision-making process. Huge companies like GE, for instance, make it a habit and practice to give top performers the opportunity (*freedom*) to grow, with the full expectation that some of these folks will leave and go on to other companies. Of course, in a company the size of GE, one could rightly argue that it's easy for them to offer this kind of freedom, because the talent pool is so large. Fair enough. But look at it this way. While it's true that smaller enterprises usually don't have the wherewithal to offer their best people *vertical* growth opportunities, they certainly can entice the best people to stay by offering *horizontal* growth opportunities like subject matter courses (whether job related or not), working on a new project that's outside of their normal responsibilities, cross-training them in a skill or other job they'd like to learn, or even doing volunteer work they'd enjoy and on company time! Expensive? Only if they're really good and they leave over the frustration of being stifled or restricted.

What do you think of this example of playing the *freedom* card? One day, employee Bill comes to you and says: "Boss, I just got a call from my wife, Mary, telling me our daycare person is ill. Mary took the morning off but needs to go in to work at 2:30 to take care of a couple of important reports. Do you mind if I leave around 2:00 so I can relieve her at home?" Being the good and caring boss you are, what would you do? If you're like most people by whom I've run this scenario, you'd likely tell Bill it was fine to go. And if you're a real sweetheart, you might tell Bill to give their child a little tickle for you. I've had a few bosses temper their permission with a mild admonition to Bill that he could go if he saw to it first that his work got done either by Bill or others. But in pretty much all cases, bosses I've put this situation to would let Bill go home.

So far, not too bad. Now, let's say Beth Marie comes up to you a few days later, in a semi-frantic state, saying that she just got an email from her friend and that tickets for a Twisted Sister reunion concert next month are going on sale at 3:00 PM today, that Twisted Sister (a group whose signature song by the way is "Burn in Hell") is her most favorite heavy metal band, that she'll be miserable if she misses out on getting a good seat, and could she leave early to get in line to be sure she can get tickets. Being the good and caring boss that you are, what would you do in this case? A little different reaction, here, eh? When I've posed these dual situations to a seminar group, I've gotten a whole spectrum of responses. The super-enlightened will say, "Let them both go without judging or evaluating their reasons (Remember the Cornerstones of Trust written about under Fundamental No. 3: *It's Strictly Business – Nothing Personal*)). Their reasons are valid to them, so they should be valid to us, as the boss." Or, at the other end of the spectrum, I'll get the Stone Age responses like: "I'd let Bill go because his reasons are based on a family need which is a good thing, but Beth Marie's request to see a rock band that represents the antithesis of family life is not valid and therefore unacceptable."

A lively discussion ensues, but eventually the point gets made that of course you should let them both go – without stipulations like: "Be sure your work is done first (see Fundamental No. 1: *Always the Adult, Never the Parent*)." If you can't trust them to do the adult thing, like ensuring their important work is done, then they shouldn't be working for you in the first place.

The lesson is even stronger when I muddy the waters more by posing: "What if Bill is a problem employee and Mary Beth is a superstar?" It's around here that migraine headaches set in. Even though the discussion about handling performance issues doesn't come up in depth in this book until Chapters 5 & 6, for the record and while we're on this subject of Bill being a problem employee and Beth Marie being a superstar, the simple answer to this question is to treat the requests to leave early and good/poor performance as separate issues. One really has nothing to do with the other. If you address performance problems in real time, as they occur, you won't run into this clogged drain of irritation you feel toward an employee, thus you'll be more able to keep requests and performance issues separate. I've actually had managers report to me that in situations similar to these examples, where employees ask for permission to take care of a personal situation, and the boss gives them carte blanche to do whatever they need to do, the employee will either make up the missed work time on their own, or take extra work home. It really happens. A lot.

By the way, as this is being written, Netflix's vacation policy reads something like: "If you need time off, take it."

To sum it up, the way you should look at the *Freedom and Commitment Go Hand in Hand* Fundamental is *the more you provide employees with the freedom to participate in choosing or designing their own daily and future lives within your enterprise, the more likely they are to commit to staying and performing at a high level.* In the long run, a basic underpinning of what can make you an *Unforgettable Boss* is to try to help all who work with you achieve their highest potential…which, by the way, might *not* be in *your* enterprise, but somewhere else..

You may ask, "I should help everyone? What about the few who are driving me and others crazy?" Funny you should ask. Here's the next Fundamental you need to know.

FUNDAMENTAL No. 6:
The 11 Percent Solution

Back under Fundamental No. 1: *Always the Boss, Never the Parent*, I mentioned the group of people for whom we write our policy manuals and who otherwise drive us loony; also referred to as the White Knuckle Group (WKG). I want to hit that point a little harder here.

Fundamental No. 6 is probably the one that is most difficult for my clients to grapple with. After I explain the concept and its implications, they understand it and even agree with it, but implementing a Fundamental No. 6 action plan is real tough for them, as I'm sure it would be for most of you.

Jack Welch, the legendary CEO of GE for many years beginning in the early 1980s, is credited with developing and
implementing the assertion that was at times called *The Bottom Ten*, which means that each year, every manager has to
terminate the poorest performers, which Welch figured to be
the bottom 10 percent of their workforce. I first heard of this
concept in 1983, not from Jack Welch, but from the head of a
small management consulting firm for which I did some
contract work. This company termed the idea as *The 11 Percent Solution.*

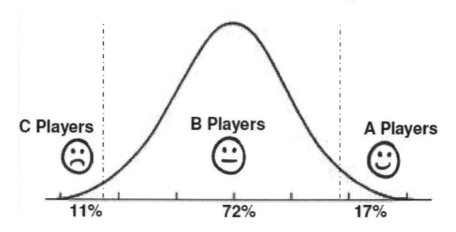

C Players   B Players   A Players

11%   72%   17%

In essence, here's what it means. In all organizations,
roughly 11 % of the population doesn't belong there. It is
not always an issue of competence, but quite often one of *fit*.
For instance, an employee who was with you in the glory
days and who was a gifted bookkeeper and hard worker and
was crucial in getting you *here* (where you are now) may not
have the skill set or temperament to take you *there* (where
you need or want to be). It could be a situation where the
person is more suited to a company of a different culture or
size. Quite often we have seen employees who thrived for
years in a larger, more bureaucratic company decide to go

with a smaller company and fail miserably in what is usually a less-structured environment that has fewer resources. The opposite phenomenon occurs when an employee goes from a small to a large organization.

The problem of *fit* would also apply to those employees who worked well under an autocratic leadership style, but falter when a more open, participative one became the way of work. We often saw this played out when companies began *employee involvement* initiatives where either as individuals or through team effort, employees were being asked to take on more problem-solving and decision-making responsibilities. An interesting phenomenon occurred in some cases, because employees who might have heretofore been seen as loyal soldiers who followed orders to the letter were suddenly out of their element and buckled under what they saw as added pressure. I was a witness to this when a mid-level manager in my client company who had been a high performer under her previous boss suddenly fell from grace when a new boss cycled in from another location (equally adept as a manager as the one he replaced, by the way). Same employee. New boss. Different expectations. Weaker performance.

Conversely, and even more interestingly, employees who might have been classed as part of the 11 percent under the previous autocratic style of leadership (perhaps demonstrating too much *maverick* behavior) suddenly became part of the 17 percent (the other end of the bell-shaped curve) and highly valued for their creative, thinking-out-of-the-box capacity.

We'll call the third class that fits the 11 percent profile the *prima donnas* who somewhere along the line developed – or had reinforced by management – the notion that the company couldn't live without them, that they are a rare breed, and in this capacity have management at least fearful, if not in full retreat of them. Think toolmakers or programmers as two examples. In my own example of dealing with *prima donna* behaviors (and a career-long bit of valuable advice I received), my very first entrepreneurial venture was with two of my brothers in the restaurant business. My oldest brother, Peter, had developed a huge following as an entertainer in the Frank Sinatra style. His good looks, coupled with an extraordinary talent as a musician, were packing them in all over Hartford County. Peter and my brother Tom, who up to this point was pressing pants and doing the books for our father's dry cleaning business, invited me to join them in a restaurant venture – better known then as a "supper club," offering dining and dancing. At the time I was teaching junior-high English and going to law school at night. To make a long story short, we all went into hock to venture into an enterprise that none of us had any idea how to run. Peter was an entertainer, and what do they know? All we wanted him to do was look handsome, sing, and pack the place. Tom had the most closely aligned talent to the business in that he held a two-year accounting degree. And I, at age 25, was mostly along for the ride, fortunate enough to have two big brothers putting their arms around me, and being willing to do whatever it took to learn the business.

One of the wisest first moves we made was to hire Ralph, a long-time restaurant manager, as a consultant, so we wouldn't make too much of a mess of things. As it turned out, the restaurant we bought already had a built-in chef named Mario who the year before had been named "Chef of the Year" in Hartford County. What a great deal, we thought: Mario to feed them and Peter to entertain them. How could we miss?

There was just one small problem, as we discovered. Mario, it proved, had a bit of a temper and was known to occasionally throw knives at the wait staff if he was unhappy with just about anything. He was sometimes whimsical in deciding when he would strike next, thus creating an unacceptable level of fear among the people who had to work with him. This all occurred, of course, in the days before the words *hostile work environment* ever got strung together in the same sentence. We turned to Ralph to help us figure out what to do. We didn't want to lose such a valuable resource as Mario, especially on top of the fact that none of us knew anything about being a chef. We feared we'd be lost without this guy, scary and intimidating as he was. At the same time, something really bad could happen by keeping him, which could seriously jeopardize our future in the business. Ralph, a bald Clint Eastwood type, softly said to us the words I've never forgotten either in running my own businesses, or counseling my clients in theirs: "If you're going to keep him (Mario), then you might as well give him the keys to the front door, because he'll own you." Bam! That was it. Long story short: We said goodbye to Mario and were still hugely successful from then on.

A similar situation occurs on a regular basis with so many of our clients, especially those managing smaller enterprises: "This person is killing me, but she is too valuable for me to let go." One of my favorite clients is Albert, who runs a small job shop of about 40 employees. Among the reasons I admire Albert is that he tries as hard as anyone I've ever worked with to provide and cultivate an environment where people are treated fairly, provided plenty of information about the status of the company, given timely feedback about their performance, and are generally treated as adults. Albert loved coming to work, except for this major thorn in his side.

Albert had been complaining about the same toolmaker for about three years. Roman, we'll call him, was a Class A *prima donna* who treated everyone the same – miserably. He pretty much did what he wanted, when he wanted, and considered his supervisor as just another nuisance getting in the way of how he wanted to do his work. At the same time, Roman was also a Class A toolmaker and had unique skills that helped Albert keep a couple of his key customers. Roman's name and his latest adventure in defiance was brought up about every other time Albert and I met. His name also surfaced pretty much every time I met with Albert and his management team to talk about current strengths and weaknesses of the company and plans to address them. In short, Roman was consuming an enormous amount of time and energy not only with Albert, but his team as well...and probably eating up the energy and morale of a number of other shop personnel.

Albert and I began to talk about the amount of actual dollars that all this time and energy equated to, and began to realize that the real cost of keeping Roman and his negative attitude on board was huge. I threw in my story about Mario, and Albert decided he had had enough – in spite of his real and legitimate fears of how he could do without Roman. We wrote an action plan and a script for Albert to use with Roman, and within two weeks Roman was gone. Albert's business? Doing just fine, thank you (it turned out there were other shop people who had the talent but not the opportunity). Albert's management team? Enjoying a new lease on life. Shop morale? Priceless! In fact, as happens in almost every one of these instances, a number of employees came up to Albert asking why it took so long to make the move.

The fourth sub-group making up the11 percent is what we'll call the *Victims Unit*, or VU for short. Now, the *Victims Unit* is a very special group and probably causes even more *agita* than the *prima donnas*. I'm not really sure how these people actually get into organizations, but they have a staying power that's truly awesome. Earlier in this book, when talking about the *White Knuckle Group*, I was probably thinking mostly about VU people. In brief, they are pretty much unhappy about everything that goes on within your enterprise. And they accept absolutely no responsibility for anything that goes on in their lives. In essence, every problem they have, all their life's ills, are caused by others, or circumstances beyond their control. Hence, the term, *victim*.

In business literature, I've seen VUs referred to as the "I've-got-a-wooden-leg-so-what-can-I-do" people. They might have been a good hire initially, but something just went wrong for them, and they turned sour. Or they gave a good first impression that hid their VU membership. All I know is they serve as a drain on the company energy and are the daily subject of angst among most employees. They are the ones we rewrite employee policy manuals for because they spend so much of their time looking for the loopholes in the system. ("The manual only says I have to wear safety goggles. It doesn't say they have to be worn to cover my eyes."). They complain about everything ("How come this year's [free] Thanksgiving turkey was only 10 pounds?"). They always feel shorted ("I should have gotten that promotion. Mary has always been the boss' favorite.").

Get this straight. YOU WILL NEVER MAKE MEMBERS OF THE VU HAPPY, SO STOP TRYING! Trying to please members of the VU is like holding a balloon half-filled with water. You squeeze it in one place and the water disperses to another, creating another about-to-burst bubble.

Worse yet, anecdotal research suggests that the tolerance of the energy draining behavior of the 11percent – whether they are a poor fit, not competent, prima donnas or victims can be a key factor in you losing your best people, the 17 percent at the other end of the scale. For a long time, it was felt that if we tolerated the 11 percent group, then everyone else would begin to think "the heck with it" and become less productive, adopting the behaviors of the 11 percenters. This would only hold true for those who are just above the 11 percent line and could go either way. However, it's logically not in the nature of the 17 percenters to dumb down and perform at a level less than their optimum. So what do they do? They leave and go to work at a place where 11 percent behavior isn't tolerated.

In any case, and no matter how you define or subcategorize it, the number holds true; about 11 percent of the people in a given enterprise should be somewhere else. In order to get our clients to more deeply think about this unpleasant subject, we point out that this small group of people is not only making the boss and others unhappy by their continued presence, but they are miserable themselves. Let's face it. If you and the person's supervisor and/or peers are unhappy with their performance, don't think for a minute that the 11 percenters don't know it and feel a sense of failure every day. As long as these people are around, everybody loses, including them.

In *all* cases, it's this group – the 11 percent – who rule way too much of our clients' time. Whether we're doing a seminar, off-site retreat, one-on-one coaching, or exercises in organization renewal; the names of the people who constitute this group constantly come up as being either a speed bump, pothole or Jersey barrier. And yet, the response I get most often from clients when I ask why they are still there is: "Well, maybe one day they'll leave." But, they don't leave, and never will. You know it and I know it.

I'm aware that my words may appear a bit harsh and seemingly coming from a cold heart. Hopefully, you will realize that's not true, and that you'll see my message having more to do with my empathy, tinged with frustration, for my clients' tendency to rule with their hearts rather than their heads on the matter of the 11 percent population – and by acting in this manner they still have a resultant atmosphere of failure for all involved.

Even though we'll be looking at ways to administer the 11 Percent Solution in the fairest manner in Chapter 7, here's an example of how the 11 percent concept can play itself out. I'd like to share an experiment I conducted a number of years ago while teaching a graduate-level course called Human Factors in Management.

One of the course concepts was *Adult Learning Theory*, which is that people learn best when they control the pace, environment, and even the content of the learning experience (*Authorship-Ownership*). This model is sometimes called a *Learner Controlled environment*. Another facet of this model held that the fewer the external controls or restrictions (by a boss or teacher, for instance), the freer the *learner* is to learn (*Freedom-Commitment Continuum*). The role of the *boss* or teacher thus becomes one of facilitator or coach, whose job is to find out what the learner needs to learn (*Be Curious*), then access and administer those resources to the learner. All of this, by the way, got business leaders to begin thinking about the *Inverted Pyramid* management model, where instead of the boss being at the top and served by his or her minions, the order was reversed, with the boss at the bottom, whose sole job was to provide the resources and environment where people could reach optimum performance. Hmmm. I'm thinking this whole book could pretty much be wrapped up in this paragraph.

At any rate, here I was teaching this course all about this open system, Adult Learning Model, but doing it in a traditional environment of a top-down hierarchy. For example, *I* would assign grades to people based on how well *I* thought they contributed in class or by the score they achieved on tests that *I* developed. They would also have to follow a syllabus *I* wrote up based on what *I* thought they needed to learn. After one semester of *teaching* in what I was beginning to feel was a contradictory environment, I decided to try out an idea that I'm sure was not totally original, but unheard of at the college.

I met with the 23 graduate students on the first evening of classes (they were mostly part-time students with day jobs and families), and discussed the problem I had in *teaching* an Adult Learning Model against a traditional hierarchy classroom backdrop. I offered the following as ways for us to best imitate an open system, Adult Learning Model:

- *I will not take attendance.* "How will you know if we are here," they asked? "I won't," I replied. "You will know if you are here" (a little Buddhism thrown in there).

- *There will be no tests.* "How will you know if we are learning?" "I won't. You will."

- *Everyone gets a "B" grade to satisfy the university requirement for a letter grade.* "What if we want an 'A'?" *"If you want an 'A' you will be turning more control over to me, and I will design a test based on the learning material, and be the sole judge of whether or not you earn the 'A'."*

- *The class will help me design the syllabus by discussing their course-related needs, based on life- or work-based issues you face.* We used the first class session to do this. Then, based on our joint input, I designed the syllabus for presentation at the next session.

That was essentially it. I can almost see some of you twitching at the thought of all this lack of control and structure, but what a positive and extraordinary experience it was for all of us. With all the control pressures off, we were all able to have a very rich learning opportunity with lots of give and take among all of us; at least for those of us who showed up. Okay, I admit, not all 23 people showed up for every class. However, about 90 percent did! Now, because I only did head counts and didn't take attendance, I can't be sure that the same 11percent were no-shows every week, but there was always between 19 and 21 students at each class. And this number held for the three successive semesters I ran this course. Oh, and by the way, the number of students who opted to take a test to get an "A"? Always about 17 percent (or in Jack Welch terminology, the top 20 percent).

As we debriefed the class at the end of each of these semesters, comparing it to a workplace situation, we invariably discussed this bell-shaped curve (11 percent at the bottom end, 17 percent at the top end; and 72 percent dispersed between the two) and how to best manage these populations on the job. What we generally agreed to was that even though the 11 percent self-selected themselves out of the class, it would be management's job to actively counsel them and move them up or out (more on this in Chapter 7). It would also be management's duty to work to ensure the 72 percent got better and better and that the 17 percent never left the building (more on the techniques of how to keep your best people in Chapter 6).

I mentioned above that managers should look for *the fairest manner* possible to administer *The 11 Percent Solution*. And I just went over how it was experimented within a classroom situation. Here's a very good example of how it can be done in a true workplace setting.

Barney was a VP of a good-sized financial division of an even larger corporation, but his operation was quite independent of the larger operation. So for all intents and purposes he was running his own small company of about 75 people. I had worked with Barney on a number of training and development initiatives for him and his staff. He was always one of the most forward thinking of all my clients when it came to continually improving his organization culture and its people. He invested a lot of time and dollars in these what is too often and unfairly called *soft skills*. Among the investments he made was to re-form his group of 8 managers, who in the past operated as individual contributors, into a high-performing, *intradependent* team.

As part of the team development and team maintenance process, Barney and his team and I would go off into the woods twice a year on a team retreat to work on improving team performance and develop action plans for departmental initiatives and problems. On this one particular retreat – and I don't clearly recall what led to it – a couple of Barney's team members were grousing about employees who were driving them to distraction with their poor work habits, habitual absenteeism and general lousy attitude. I pointed out to the team that I had noticed these complaints about certain employees came up in conversation just about every time we met and that it seemed to consume a lot of air time and energy – time and energy we could be otherwise expending on more positive, worthwhile efforts. They agreed, and we talked a while longer about the need to finally take some action with this group because, as it was noted by a few of the team members, none of these people were leaving the company on their own.

I then asked the team members to privately make a list of the names of the people throughout the entire department whom they thought fit this profile of employees who were serving to suck all the energy out of the department. Once they made their lists, and before we went on to the next step, I asked the team members to promise themselves they would keep the rest of our discussion confidential and within the confines of this room. I especially asked Barney, who was a man of action, to participate in the rest of our discussion without getting too far ahead or asking a lot of "Why is this person still here?" questions. All agreed.

Everyone then disclosed their list of names, and a couple of extraordinary things were noted. All the lists contained somewhere between seven and nine names (roughly 11 percent of the department), and except for an odd one here or there, all the lists had the same names! Having done exercises similar to this before, I was less amazed by these outcomes than were the team members. A few of them were a bit embarrassed by the fact that employees in their own department were seen as non-performers by their peers heading other departments. In a few instances, managers attempted to defend a couple of the people whose names were listed from their departments. But this team had learned to be good at giving each other feedback and they forthrightly challenged each other as appropriate.

Next, I asked the team to begin, through dialogue, to list the reasons why people made what we were now calling the "11 Percent List," disallowing words like "attitude" or "temper" (because no one knows what an *attitude* or *temper* looks like). They were required to use *behaviorally specific* terms (e.g. *usually turns in assignments late, frequently complains about work load)* instead. All of the reasons for making the list fell pretty much along the lines of the four categories outlined above: *poor fit, incompetence, prima donna behavior,* and/or *Victim Unit membership.* Eventually, the team agreed on a final group of nine staff members who comprised the "11 percent ."

This was a pioneering event for the team, so they needed time at each step of the way to determine what to do next and how to do it. Barney, in his enlightened boss role, made the steps easy by prompting and contributing to an open discussion, using at least two of Cornerstones of Trust (from Fundamental No. 3: *Strictly Business, Nothing Personal*) as ground rules: *Never betray a confidence* and *never judge or evaluate anything anyone [on the team] says, thinks or feels.* After a couple of hours of open debate, here's what they decided to do:

- Each team member/manager would meet one-on-one with each of their direct reports and informally review the person's performance on an A-B-C Player basis. The "A" Players were the ones whom the boss felt were really valuable to the department (the 17 percent); the "B" Players were the ones in the middle (the 72 percent) who needed some coaching and maybe a little prodding to improve in certain areas of performance; and the "C" Players were, of course, the 11 percent who needed this meeting as a last stop on the train. The decision to meet with all staff members was partly driven by the concern that if the managers met only with the 11 percenters, people would soon start to figure out what was going on and the process would be counterproductive ("Hmmm. I see Joel going into Kathy's office. I'll bet he's the next one who's in trouble.").

- Each team member paired up with another team member as a *study buddy* to help each other write scripts for the A-B-C Player meetings. The scripts followed a model more fully explained in Chapters 5 and 6, but essentially were built on the principles of the Fundamentals: *being curious, building owner-ship, nothing personal, etc.*

- The "C" Players were essentially to be told they were on thin ice and the reasons why. They were then to be asked if they understood the message, whether or not they agreed with the perception, what the reasons were behind the behavior, and – perhaps most important – if they really wanted to stay in the department or company by improving in the ways discussed during the meeting. Finally, they were told to think over their answer and come back in two days (very specific on the number of days) and tell their boss either "Yes, I want to stay and am willing to do what was asked of me," or "No, I can't agree with what you want and there-fore choose to leave." (How simple. How clean. How adult.)

- The "A" and "B" players were to be coached for im-provement or praised as the situation called for, and again following a script outline similar to the ones in Chapter 5.

A few of the managers confessed to feeling quite uncom-fortable with what called for a more confrontive approach than they had used before with the so-called 11 percenters. In the past, they often relied on the compensation system to do their dirty work for them – giving the 11 percenters only a 1 percent wage increase at review time and never really discussing performance (more on the ridiculousness of this compensation distribution philosophy in Chapter 7). Or, they lived with the hope the 11 percenters would leave on their own – which as an actual matter never happens. To help them build up their courage to do these scripts, I offered the following thoughts:

When it comes to staying or leaving, especially after having given the employee time to think things over, the following guidelines should hold:

- You can stay and abide by the *Rules of Play* as outlined in the meeting with the boss, or

- You can leave because you feel you cannot abide by the *Rules of Play*, but

- You can't stay and continue to fight with the *Rules of Play*.

Similarly, and while on the subject of the *Rules of Play*, here's another angle you should always keep in mind on your way to becoming an *Unforgettable Boss*. In order to maintain the healthiest possible relationship between you and all the folks who work with you, you should always promote the right of everyone to question and/or complain about any portion of the status quo they neither like nor understand. The notion is that if we don't continually challenge ourselves, we can't get better. For instance, let's say you've had an ongoing policy that doesn't permit flexible work schedules where people can sometimes work from home. But under your guiding principle of *challenging the status quo* Billy Bob and Janie have approached you with the idea of allowing people flextime under certain conditions that won't, in their view, have a negative impact on the operations of the enterprise. They feel that Friday, being the slowest day of the week in your business in terms of customer contact, would be an ideal day to have a third of the work force work electronically from home. You see the idea as having some merit and would gladly give it more consideration if you hadn't already invested in some new software aimed at, among other initiatives, picking up Friday business.

You explain this to Billy Bob and Janie, and thank them for coming up with the idea, but your answer – at least for the mid-term – is "no." Janie accepts the answer and its rationale, but Billy Bob grouses about it, essentially saying you're not giving the idea a fair chance of working. He may be right, and you tell him so, but that you're going to stick with your original answer. As an aside, it's to your credit that you've fostered an environment where the Billy Bobs of the world can openly disagree without fear of retribution. It's to Billy Bob's credit as well that he has the courage to directly disagree. OK so far.

A few weeks go by, and Billy Bob is still grousing and complaining that you and the company are not being fair or open-minded, and so on. Pretty much the same *Rules of Play* get applied. Billy Bob can:

- Stay and live with the decision, or he can

- Leave because the decision is just too unfair for him to live with, but he can't

- Stay and continue complaining. That would not only be unfair, but the way I look at it, hard-ass that I am, is that Billy Bob's staying on and complaining while collecting a paycheck is actually unethical behavior on his part.

Going back to Barney and his management team and their mission to meet with and give feedback to all staff members, but most particularly to work on the 11 percent problem, here are the results of the meetings with the nine people: After the "two days" to think it over…

- Two of these employees decided to leave the company, realizing their job satisfaction would have to be realized elsewhere.

- Two did a 180-degree reversal and began to perform at a much more acceptable level. The word I got from the managers on these two employees was that they really didn't know about how poorly they were seen in the eyes of their bosses, and decided to get it together with one of them asking for and getting more training and the other taking care of some personal issues affecting job performance.

- The other six pledged to improve, but really couldn't make the changes and improvements called for and over the course of the next two months their employment was terminated.

At the next management retreat, some six months later, the management team shared their experiences with this process, disclosing that while the meetings with the 11 percent were probably the most difficult people-related task they had ever performed in their careers, the upbeat results they got from the "A" and "B" player meetings made the entire effort worthwhile. Several of the managers also said they wished they had acted much sooner, and that coming to work was now much more pleasant for everyone.

FUNDAMENTAL No. 7:
Life is Just One Big Cost/Benefit Analysis

This Fundamental is a logical next item on our agenda since it not only picks up where we just left off with our friend Billy Bob, but it also prompts us to start thinking about hard choices we need to make, such as dealing with the 11 percenters, and how to make those choices with as little emotion as possible. Borrowing a bit from "Nothing personal...," the Cost/Benefit Analysis (CBA) as it applies to being an *Unforgettable Boss* is a methodical process we ask our clients to follow whenever faced with a tough decision; especially relating to their own career, personnel issues with employees or possible confrontations with either peers or their own bosses. It's a real simple play.

The key question to ask yourself whenever facing one of these decisions is:

Does the benefit of acting outweigh the cost of acting?

Or turned the other way:

Does the benefit of not acting outweigh the cost of not acting?

For example, back with our friend Albert in trying to decide what to do about Roman. In doing his CBA, Albert essentially tipped the scale toward acting when asking Roman to take a hike. He decided that the ongoing *cost* of keeping Roman wasn't worth it, and he'd rather focus on the long-term *benefit* of living without Roman's services.

In another application of CBA, for instance, accepting a promotion or a new job opportunity outside your current enterprise, you would ask yourself what's the cost and benefit of each choice? The CBA is a simple, emotion-free tool for helping you. As you think the process through, try also to assess a weight factor to each element of the choice. In thinking about accepting a promotion, you might see as benefits such things as having a higher profile within your company, developing new relationships with a new group of people who report to you, or learning a new skill. At the same time, however, another person might see these very same *benefits* as costs.

Do I really want to stick my neck out any more than it already is? I really like my current group; we've worked through some difficult issues together. Do I really want to leave them and start over with a new bunch? Is learning a new skill really that important to me at this point in my life?

Applying weight factors to the process can be of real value, as in:

This new company is offering to double my salary. However, does the weight of that single but huge benefit offset or outweigh the multiple costs of moving the kids out of a school they love, leaving friends and family behind, and the added travel the new job includes?

Finally, you might want to consider the benefits of confronting that guy on your management team who always tries to show you up by hiding important information you need and then dumping it on the table at the meeting right in front of the boss. Is the benefit of confronting him (possibly getting an apology and pledge not to do it again) worth the cost of confronting him (the possibility he may see you as a cry baby)? A factor to keep in mind when you are doing this kind of CBA is what I call *the importance of the relationship*. In other words, if the guy who delivers your fuel oil is a crotchety crank who is always complaining about how miserable his job is, but you're getting a terrific price from his company, you're likely to put up with his complaining because it's the price that's important and not your relationship with the delivery man. You can put up with his complaining on the rare occasion you see him because you have no necessary strong, long-term relationship with him. Now, if the same guy is your next door neighbor and you regularly have to put up with his negativity, then your CBA might call for a higher need for you to confront him.

The same would hold true for an employee like Todd in IT, known to be a Gloomy Gus who mutters his answers, but is incredibly smart and fixes things fast. Say you only have to deal with Todd on rare occasions and have no intention to have lunch with him on a regular basis. You might decide that confronting Todd about his surliness is not the hill to die on and just leave the situation alone and work around him. On the other hand if Sandra, a star employee who relies on Todd, complains to you that his attitude is impacting her and her ability to get her job done, suddenly *your* relationship with Todd becomes quite important and you'd *better* act or you run the risk of losing Sandra, a 17 percenter.

The CBA is a helpful but risky tool to use. The analysis will help you gather the information you need to take appropriate action. But if you postpone acting, you're now stuck with being responsible for any negative outcomes. Ignorance may be bliss, but that's a luxury the *Unforgettable Boss* has to give up.

You can really become an *Unforgettable Boss* by employing

the CBA tool when counseling or coaching employees. They might be dealing with one or more of the above issues themselves, and guiding them – without *judging or evaluating* their choices – by asking them to think in a CBA manner, is a superb role for you.

If you are in a coaching mode, and trying to help someone work through a CBA, another helpful maxim to keep in mind is that *people are always precisely where they want to be* (unless, of course they are being held prisoner, or in some other way physically restricted). Yes, this goes for you, too. It's helpful to realize this especially if you are dealing with a Victim's Unit member, as they are always thinking that where they are is someone else's doing. In essence, people are always doing a CBA, even unconsciously, and even in staying in what they purport to be an awful situation – personal or job related – because somehow the benefit of staying is outweighing the cost of staying. When I'm coaching clients who may be thinking about changing jobs or careers, the first step we almost always take is to do a CBA on either staying or leaving, and it's always an enlightening – and often sobering – experience for them.

Summary: Here's what I hope you learned in this chapter.

As you learn and practice *The Seven Fundamentals*, keep in mind the concept of *exaggerated learning* where you always try to master the Fundamental at the 100 percent level, knowing that, especially at first, you'll only get halfway there. And don't be too hard on yourself for slipping backward on any of the Fundamentals. I've embraced and written about them for more years than I care to count, and I still mess up way more than I'd like.

To recap, they are:

1. **Always the boss, never the parent.** Of all the bad habits you might have to shake off to become an *Unforgettable Boss*, especially in a smaller enterprise or family business, this may be the most difficult. In my book, it certainly is the most sinister bad habit when it comes to restricting others from growing and becoming more self-reliant and responsible company citizens. When you act like the *parent* (dictating, developing one-way rules and regulations, etc.) your employee quickly and easily becomes the *child* dumbing down, robotically doing what he or she is told, and taking little or no responsibility or initiative. No wonder you're so busy!

2. **Be curious.** All too often, bosses hide from unpredictable or ambiguous situations (quality issues, performance problems, etc.), because they fear not being able to manage the information they might get if they ask about it, or that now *they'll* have to come up with the solution. It's the same problem we have as parents when one of our kids behaves in an unusual manner: Don't ask, don't tell. *Unforgettable Bosses* get past that fear and realize that only by being curious and asking open-ended, non-judgmental questions can real solutions be achieved. What are you afraid of? Information is power.

3. **It's strictly business, nothing personal.** We all get way too involved in the personal lives and motives of the people who work around us – especially in a

smaller enterprise, and even more particularly in a family business. Bosses need to be more at arm's length in their relationships with employees. This is an especially difficult task for bosses who got promoted and now have to lead people who were peers just yesterday. Being at arm's length doesn't at all mean being cold-hearted when an employee is hurting or in trouble. Nor does it mean that you shouldn't show *interest* in their personal or family lives. Just remember that showing interest and getting involved are two different things. Work on taking the emotional factor out of the relationship when guiding an employee. As a boss, you are obliged to listen and observe *non-judgmentally*, then make a fact-based move or decision. Also, erase the word *loyalty* from the lexicon of your enterprise. *Loyalty* is defined as "devoted attachment," and implies an unhealthy connection between people at work, or even ownership of one person over another. Loyalty can sometimes mean turning a blind eye to the facts. Think about the trouble that can occur if you do that in a business setting.

4. **Authorship leads to ownership**. The more that people participate in analyzing a situation, solving a problem, designing a process or planting a shrub, the more they take ownership of the outcome. The opposite is also true, similar to the parent-child relationship. Transferring the ownership means less work for you in the long run. If your style is more of the *high control* type, the transfer will take more effort in terms of letting go. If your style is of the

low control type, the transfer will go faster. For you *low controllers*, though, just be sure you make the goal or desired outcome really clear before turning the employee loose.

5. **Freedom and commitment go hand in hand.** Unless I've been misinformed, slavery in the U.S. ended a long time ago. Employees don't belong to you; they're just there as long as mutual needs are met (I hate when I hear a boss refer to people in the enterprise as "my employees"). Similar to the *authorship-ownership* Fundamental, the more that people have a say in the selection or design of their daily work assignments and their careers in general, the more that they are likely to make choices that appeal to *you*. If they make choices that don't appeal to you, either re-evaluate your position or go look for someone else to do what you want. Don't *ever* force people to do anything they don't want to do. You'll both lose.

6. **The 11 Percent Solution.** In a bell-curved world, roughly 11 percent of the employees in your enterprise don't belong there, and about 17 percent are your superstars. The reasons the 11 percent shouldn't be there usually fall into one or more of four categories: *Fit* (They never did or no longer fit within the current direction or needs of the enterprise.); *Competence* (They are just plain not qualified to do the job, and this includes temperament and attendance issues.); *Prima Donnas* (There is the misperception on your part, and theirs, that the place

would fall apart without their presence.); and *Victims Unit Members* (Perceiving that they have little or no control over the events that occur in their lives.). Keeping the 11 percenters on board is not only a bad idea for the obvious reasons, but continuing to employ them can drive the 17 percenters out the door. As a boss, you are certainly responsible to see to it that all employees are treated with dignity, respect and fairness. You must establish an environment that promotes these company values. Beyond that, you are *not* responsible for anyone else's welfare and happiness. The employee is. The more you get involved in others' personal business, the less able you are to have a healthy relationship of mutual respect.

7. **Life is just one big cost-benefit analysis**. Really good *Unforgettable Bosses* frequently coach employees on how and when to zig or zag. A cost-benefit analysis is a terrific tool for helping them make good decisions. It's your chance to play Yoda to their Luke Skywalker. On a deeper level to you as a boss, the CBA should be employed constantly when analyzing when and how to move people up, sideways or out. Finally, the CBA is a good tool to help you think about your own career.

In for a Penny, In for a Pound. There is an important postscript to this chapter, more rightly a caveat. *The Seven Fundamentals* all sort of fit together into one tightly woven fabric. If you buy into one of them, you need to embrace and carry around with you the entire basket of goodies. I really don't see how you can refute one while practicing the others. As you get into *Part Two: The Manual* of this book, you'll hopefully see this point more clearly and not want to return it, thus helping me with my retirement plans.

3

THE BASIC OBJECTIVES
IN MANAGING OTHERS

For me, the whole field of managing people boils down to understanding and mastering three basic objectives:

1. Being clear about the goal or expectation.
2. Creating an environment where the person's opportunity for successful completion of any task is optimized.
3. Reducing or eliminating all ambiguities about a person's ability or willingness to do a job.

Like going on a diet, though, making this happen is simple to understand but not necessarily easy to accomplish. I mean, it's pretty *simple* to grasp that eating a can of tuna fish with some celery stalks (no mayo, no bread) will help you lose weight. But it's certainly *not easy* to do. Let's examine each of these objectives, or better yet, challenges that *Unforgettable Bosses* face, and let's focus on two specific things: Why they are important and the pitfalls and potholes that make them *not easy* to master.

1) Being Clear About the Goal or Expectation

Of the three main tools for becoming an *Unforgettable Boss*, this one is probably the easiest to master. That's likely because you're flying solo when you are initially determining goals and expectations, not yet requiring input or collaboration from others.

You may argue this point and see yourself as a *Team Leader*, rather than a traditional boss, relying on the team to set goals and expectations from the outset. And this is possibly because you read a book that says you should be fully inclusive in all you do as a boss. But in my view, and don't argue with me on this, the seeds of goals and expectations should always be planted by the boss.

For instance, let's say you feel it's time to review how your organization markets its product or service, or that it's time to examine a better health plan. You may want to use your team to work through these decisions, but you are – or should be – the prime mover in setting the goal or expectation. You are, after all, the person who has, or should have, the widest view of what goals and objectives should be at the forefront of your organization. This doesn't mean you shouldn't use lots of input on the *hows* of goal achievement from others around you. That would certainly be appropriate and wise, and an excellent use of the human resources in your organization.

There was a time when a process called Management By Objectives (MBO) was extremely popular. It essentially preached a bottom-up approach when it came to goal setting. The employee would write up his goals for, let's say, the coming year, and then present them to the boss who would either sign off on them or modify them through a give-and-take dialogue with the employee. In principle, MBO made a lot of sense in that it played on the notion that people should be intimately involved in setting their own goals, because goals personally set by the employee were more likely to be embraced and reached than those set by others. It was all about the idea that if you wrote it you owned it, or what I call the authorship-ownership continuum – the more you author it, the more you own it. The only problem was that in order to work, the MBO process required high levels of trust between employees and management, trust that both sides would approach the process feeling that the other side would play honest and fair. Big mistake.

Don't get me wrong. It's not a big mistake to support the bottom-up concept of MBO. It's just that most often, we didn't take the time and do the required training to improve – or better yet, level off – the relationship between management and subordinates in order for MBO to work. One of the key reasons why MBO lost traction is that we assumed there was a mutually supportive relationship between the two sides. Actually, even the word "sides" connotes winners and losers. As we so often do with any new management idea that comes along, with MBO we completely bypassed the wading pool and threw everyone into the 8-foot end. Joe Employee would be *told* of this new goal-setting process – sometimes by the boss, more often by someone in HR, then sent to a training seminar (probably run by some outside consultant like me) to learn how to do it. The bosses might attend a parallel session – busy schedules permitting – to learn how to play their part.

Do you see where this is going? Pretty much everyone on both "sides" would be grumbling about the nuisance this new process would cause in the flow of work and how unnecessary it all was. Because there is a historic fundamental mistrust between bosses and subordinates, there was a certain fiction to the MBO process. Subordinates, who thought their bosses would automatically doubt the validity of the goals they wrote and jack them up more, would write soft or weak ones. Conversely, bosses, many of whom were taught to think that subordinates were by their nature lazy, went into the goal-tweaking meeting automatically doubting the validity or stretch of the goals written by the subordinate. To be sure, a number of enlightened bosses held very successful tweaking meetings and jointly produced good and meaningful results with staff, but in way too many instances MBO was a struggle at best.

As a result of watching many managers and their staff wrestle with bottom-up concepts like MBO – and while we applaud and support any process that puts the onus of ownership, accountability and responsibility on the subordinate – we've come to believe that goals, objectives and expectations should *initially* be the job of the boss, going top down. The only exception to this rule is where the culture of the organization was *founded* on a bottom-up influence system. W.L. Gore and Associates (the Gore-Tex company) comes to mind.

I recently worked with two partners who ran a successful distribution company. They weren't related, but were the third-generation owners whose respective grandparents had founded the company. The partners – let's call them Noel and Joel – were pretty much forward thinkers and kept up with the latest trends and techniques in operations and management. They had tremendous enthusiasm and were well respected by all who worked there as having a very strong work ethic. Recently, they launched an employee empowerment initiative called "Zap," aimed at giving customers an outrageously positive experience in dealing with the company. Wisely enough, Noel and Joel also considered their employees as key "customers" and of equal importance to the external ones.

Among the first things Noel and Joel did to get things rolling was to form an employee team to generate and implement some out-of-the-box ideas. They named two of their longer-term employees to head the team. In an attempt to model their commitment to empowering the team to not only generate the ideas but to implement them as well, Noel and Joel gave the team leaders a simple assignment:

Take the Zap program and run with it. You needn't come to us for clearance, only if you get stuck.

Talk about bottom-up influence! When I met with them, Noel and Joel were perplexed that the team had come up with little or nothing in the way of exciting ideas over a several-week period, let alone any action initiatives. What they didn't realize – and the point of this story – is that they were trying to superimpose a bottom-up value system on a culture that had been built on protective paternalism; all three generations of ownership considered their employees as being their "extended family." In other words, the committee leaders who had been with the company for a number of years had been *nurtured* to obey and follow, thus, initially at least, being unable to think and act on their own when it came to big issues like changing the course of the organization. Noel and Joel then took charge and provided a clearer vision of what they wanted, along with some needed ground rules, and the team slowly began to get traction and moved more fearlessly, and trustingly, forward.

So this is good counsel for setting larger, broader-reaching goals. But what about smaller, day-to-day goals and objectives? How much direction should the boss be providing, and how much should the employee influence day-to-day goal-setting from a bottom-up perspective?

The way we see it, and unless your organization was built from the ground up on a fully empowered workforce principle, it's your job – as the boss – to set the tone of day-to-day expectations. Certainly, do that until both you and the employee can feel a sense of mutual trust that the job will get done with minimal risk on both sides. You're the one who should be seeing the bigger picture and setting the course of action. You should be seeing when, how and where the employee is succeeding and failing; for instance, that productive interaction with a customer where there were smiles all around, or the time when the employee sent a hostile email to a colleague when he should have visited with the person instead, or the extra mile she went to be sure the job got done on time. You should want to grow each employee to their full potential, and we will show you how to do this in more detail in Chapter 6.

The Three Buckets. In order to simplify the goals and expectations process, think about dividing all tasks and functions into three buckets:; *My Way, Our Way* and *Your Way*. In the *My Way Bucket* are those tasks or functions for which you have a very clear view and methodology of how it should be done and by whom. These are items that you have no interest in getting input from others on, and have no desire to change your mind about. In its simplest form, these would include how you brew your coffee, or mow your lawn, drive to work or plan your day; or at work, whether or not you answer your own phone or greet guests personally. Items in the *My Way Bucket* are most often idiosyncratic; a preferred way of doing things that is comfortable for you and that if someone forced you to change might cause you to start sucking your thumb – again.

One of the neat things about being the boss is that you get to have a *My Way Bucket.* Where a lot of managers I know get into trouble is being fearful or unable to declare that they want certain things done a certain way, then get engaged in trying to *persuade* others to see things his way ("Don't you think this is a good idea?"). It's much better to come out and say: "This is what I want done," or "Here's how I want this done." Even better, add in your reasons why ("I want to meet with you on Wednesdays because it's the middle of the week, so we can examine where we fell short and still have time to fix things."). It's clean, clear and not at all deceptive or negatively manipulative. Another key benefit of telling people the "why" is that it actually increases their self-esteem, giving them a sense of recognition and inclusiveness – more on this below under the second *Basic Objective in Managing Others:* "Creating an Environment..."

Sometimes the items in the *My Way Bucket* don't seem to make a lot of sense, but it doesn't matter, as long as they make sense to you. For years, I insisted on opening all the mail that came into the office, partly out of the habit formed when I was the only one there to do it. It wasn't at all efficient, but it was my little escape hatch from work stress. I could claim some level of productivity while simultaneously avoiding junk I didn't want to deal with at the time. As a boss, you're entitled to a few privileges. Take advantage of them. Your name is on the door, and you always get to park your car in the same space (even though it's not marked). The buck does stop with you. So, go ahead and make a list of what's in the *My Way Bucket*. Just keep two things in mind if you want to become an *Unforgettable Boss*:

- The number of items in the bucket should be few, and

- Everyone who works for you should know what they are, and *why* they are.

This brings us to the *Our Way Bucket*. As you might guess, this bucket contains those tasks and functions you want or need to work with others on in order to get them done. The reasons they are in this bucket vary. They are usually things you might have done yourself in the past or are doing now, but need to be either passed on to or shared with someone else. The *Our Way Bucket* could also be viewed as a transfer station or plateau where you empty out items from the *My Way Bucket* to the *Our* Way *Bucket* and ultimately to the *Your Way Bucket*.

An excellent example of this transition occurred recently with a client who owned a three-store retail company. Ron's family business had grown from one store to three in a rather brief period of time. He ran the company with his wife and two children. We met because he was beginning to pull out what little hair he had left due to feeling overwhelmed with too many responsibilities. He was frustrated by what he perceived to be a lack of initiative on the part of the "kids." "They should be stepping up and taking on more responsibility," he said. He felt more or less alone in dealing with the growing pains of his company. Ron was also courageous as he wanted to hold a family meeting to clarify roles and expectations, facilitated by yours truly. I call it *courageous* because most bosses I've known consider *role clarification* meetings to be right up there with preparing for a colonoscopy. And here was Ron boldly scheduling a *family* meeting for the same purpose. *Courageous?* I'll say. Anyway, here's what we learned as a result of a couple of these meetings:

- Ron's *My Way Bucket* was filled to the point of overflowing.

- The "kids" wanted all along to take on more responsibility, but other than seeing to their original job assignments they had very little clue about what was frustrating Ron, and why.

- Ron had never been specific about what items he wanted to shift from the *My Way* to the *Our Way Buckets*. An example was analyzing the weekly financial reports. Ron had created the report format, and each week looked for certain trends and indicators. He then gave the reports to "the kids" without any guidance on how to read them, but expected them to jump in with both feet.

Here's what we did:

- It was decided that Ron would move the *financial analysis* function from the *My Way Bucket* to the *Our Way Bucket* he began to craft with his daughter.

- This would occur by Ron's sitting with the daughter for a couple of *learning* sessions and explaining how and why he developed the report, what he looked for each week, and why.

- Over time, the daughter would be free to alter the report format and revise the key indicators as she saw fit (thus moving an item from Ron's *My Way Bucket* all the way to his *Your Way Bucket* for his daughter), but only over an extended period of time, so Ron could feel comfortable with the transition plan and process.

- Other responsibilities closely held by Ron were similarly transferred from the *My Way* to the *Our Way Buckets* with both the daughter and the son.

The keys to successful bucket transition are to identify the items to be moved, and then have a clear plan for moving them.

The *Your Way Bucket*, then, would contain roles and responsibilities that you, as the boss, care about only in terms that they get done and by whom, but not necessarily how. As a boss, your ultimate goal should be to have as much as possible in the *Your Way Bucket* by, over time and once mutual trust takes form, continually pouring stuff from the other two into it. We'll look more closely at this process in Chapter 6: *Identifying and Developing Talent.* For now, the important thing to keep in mind in becoming an *Unforgettable Boss* is to be really clear about your expectations of both self and others and not dare others to figure that out by themselves. That's just plain not fair.

Here's one other thing that's "just plain not fair" that comes under the *Your Bucket* heading: I've known some managers who read somewhere that *your job is to get people to think that your ideas were their ideas.* Rubbish! To me, there are few things as deceitful (or plain not fair) as a manager sitting with an employee, asking their thoughts on how to do a job, when the manager has the *right* answer written on a card that's hidden in her lap. Never, I mean *never,* do that! It's stupid tricks like that that get you categorized as *The Unforgettable Boss,* but not in a way you might wish.

2) Creating an Environment Where the Person's Successful Completion of the Task is Optimized

A key question bosses wrestle with is: "When – if ever – can I trust this employee to be more self-managed?" Unfortunately, all too often the employee has to jump through an unnecessary series of hoops or side-step a bunch of land mines to get there. We can call it *Obstacle Course Management.* And, I suppose, if an employee is able to effectively manage this maze, then you've got a real winner on your hands.

Earlier, it was mentioned that most managers never went to management school, but learned and honed their style through a combination of nurture (learning by observing other managers styles) and nature (genetic makeup). As a result, bosses, over time, set up an environment where employees can either thrive or be blunted in terms of their overall effectiveness. In other words, you can shape the behavior of your employees just by the environment you establish. This environment is sometimes called the "organizational culture." The organizational culture usually gets formed over time, and is almost always a direct reflection of the person or persons who set up the company or enterprise. It is a system of values, beliefs and practices of an organization – usually not written – that dictate how things are to be run. As people join the organization, they are usually expected to behave in such a way as to promote, promulgate and support the culture. A healthy culture (environment) provides opportunities for everyone to succeed, employees and bosses, while an unhealthy environment limits people's ability to perform and therefore succeed.

> *A healthy culture (environment) provides opportunities for everyone to succeed, employees and bosses, while an unhealthy environment limits people's ability to perform and therefore succeed.*

Here's a good example of what I mean. A number of years ago when retail powerhouse Nordstrom was about to open a store in a local mall, we were hired by the mall management to do customer service training for all the other stores. As you may know, Nordstrom customer service is legendary; it's the gold standard for retail. Pretty much anyone who has shopped at a Nordstrom store has a terrific story to tell about how superbly they were treated during their shopping experience. In this case, the mall management felt that other stores would benefit (and survive better) if they had an opportunity to enhance their customer service levels. In preparing to do the training, we spent some time in the Nordstrom store, observing employee-customer interactions by acting as sort of mystery shoppers. It was a pretty amazing experience. As a *customer* we were consistently treated as royalty, not in an over-the-top manner, but rather in a soft, nuanced way. We were consulted with, not sold to. Sales staff went out of their way to find us just the item we were looking for, and at no time did we feel pressured to buy anything. If the item wasn't available in this store, they would check inventory in a store as far away as the West Coast and have it shipped directly to us. Free. Wow!

We designed several training modules from what we learned and went on to conduct the training and hold sessions for a number of personnel representing many of the other mall stores. The training was well received, for the most part, but several of the attendees commented along the lines of: "This is good stuff, but our store management wouldn't allow us to bend that much for a customer." Or: "We would give up too much profit if we did that." All in all, attendees got some good tips from the training, yet we couldn't help but notice a certain level of "yeah, right" skepticism among them.

A key insight we had was that the Nordstrom employee had been hired from the very same labor pool as the employees who attended the training, yet there was this distinct difference in attitude and behavior between the two groups. The only thing we could surmise was that it was all about the environment and culture that management at Nordstrom had established – and taught – when it came to customer service expectations.   It seemed to us that Nordstrom had fundamentally different beliefs about the kind of atmosphere a customer should shop in, and the attitude required of store personnel to capture and project that atmosphere.   It was also about how employees or "internal customers" were treated, not just the external ones. Nordstrom seems to believe that in treating employees in a civil manner, they in turn will do the same for their customers.

Obviously, no boss I've ever known actually set out to establish an unhealthy culture or anti-customer environment, but through little, nuanced and maybe even unconscious mechanisms employees can easily become lobotomized, robotized and generally beaten down. Draconian employee policies get written to cover all the bases ["I know Joyce saved Bill's car from burning up by using that fire extinguisher, but she never took the fire prevention training course that's required by anyone using the extinguisher, so we have to write her up!"] True story, by the way.

Big Brother watches, catching people doing things wrong rather than catching them doing things right. We read about a supermarket that docked two employees for taking an unauthorized break because they paused to hold their hands over their hearts as a military funeral procession passed by the store. We also know of a Christian book store in a small Connecticut shoreline strip mall along busy Route 1 with a sign in the window that says: "Don't Even Think of Asking to Use Our Restroom!" What would Jesus think? The sometimes hilarious, but disconcerting examples go on and on.

Just as I suggested in Chapter 1, *Physician, Heal Thyself,* that you need to take a hard look at and work on your personal   strengths   and   weaknesses   to   become   an *Unforgettable Boss,* it's an equally good idea to do a similar assessment of the *culture* you've either created or that gets reinforced by daily practices.

Here's a great way to do this assessment:

The following is a series of questions you could quiz yourself on, or, better yet, put to your management team if you have one; or if it's a family business, one morning over coffee (but not at home over a holiday meal – too high a risk of indigestion). The "survey" items, of course, are based on the *Seven Fundamentals,* which, if embraced and practiced to their fullest, puts you (and your enterprise) in the pantheon of a truly *Unforgettable Boss* running one of the best organizations in the world!

Using a 5-point scale (1 = Not at all; 2 = Somewhat; 3 = Usually; 4 = Most often; 5 = All the time), answer the following:

To what extent does our enterprise…

Always the boss, never the parent
1. Avoid "taking care" of people, preferring to help them become self-reliant and responsible

2. Consider employees to be adults who are capable of making good choices, rather than children who have to be led

Be curious
3. Pursue ambiguous situations, preferring to know the source or cause of a situation rather than avoiding the situation or the people involved

4. Pursue ambiguous situations by asking non-judgmental questions rather than assuming motives, grilling people or putting them on the spot

It's strictly business, nothing personal
5. Value employees more for their performance than their loyalty

6. Avoid getting caught up in the personal lives of employees to the point where this information clouds good judgment

Authorship leads to ownership
7. Get people involved in decisions, especially those that affect their work lives

8. Believe that the more people get involved in workplace decisions, the better they perform

Freedom and commitment go hand-in-hand
9. Actively promote employee development, tuning in more to their needs as they see them, rather than as we think they should be (e.g., the company's paying for courses employees want to take, even though they're not job-related, such as Feng Shui)

10. Support policies like flex-time or work-from-home, trusting that employees will still "git 'er done," and maybe do even better

The 11 Percent Solution

11. Deal head-on with tardiness, absenteeism and general performance issues rather than waiting until performance appraisal time, hoping the person will quit, or best of all, that he or she will get hired by our worst enemy

12. Spend more time thinking about our best employees and how to keep them, than thinking about the 11 percent

Life is just one big cost-benefit analysis

13. Use a guided development tool like a cost-benefit analysis to help employees work through an issue or problem, rather than either directly telling them what to do or leaving them to figure things out on their own

14. Employ a cost-benefit analysis tool when thinking about moving employees up, sideways or out, rather than postponing and hoping these situations will take care of themselves

Assessment surveys like this one are terrific tools for generating a list of improvement actions to energize your enterprise, especially if done as a group exercise. If you can afford it, get a neutral third party to facilitate the meeting. When I'm doing something like this survey for a client, I always suggest that the discussion be more structured than loose, in order to have maximum participation and minimal arguing. The process and ground rules should go something like:

- Everyone privately scores the survey.

- Results are plotted on a whiteboard or newsprint.

- Promote the *Be Curious* Fundamental by having people focus more on questioning the reasoning of other people's scores rather than on presenting their own ideas.

- Everyone's opinion is valid; no arguing or debating (or kicking or biting).

- Try to limit questions to 30 seconds and answers to one minute.

- Depending on whether you want this to be an informal, energizing discussion or a more formal *Cultural Renewal Plan,* you might want to record some action steps for improvement and assign renewal plan "owners."

I've noticed in recent years that many organizations are referring to their employees as "associates," "teammates," and other trendy names. This is an acceptable and perhaps even forward-thinking way of looking at the relationship between bosses and subordinates. However, keep in mind that words like "associate" or "teammate" imply *partnership.* These titles work only if your culture "walks the talk," as they say, of a real partnership. To me, partnership means enlisting, embracing and implementing *The Seven Fundamentals* within your culture, or a similar set of values or principles, and then continually and even brutally evaluating yourself against them.

3) Reducing or Eliminating All Ambiguities About a Person's Ability or Willingness to Do a Job.

As you know from me by now, one of the things that has always driven me crazy is the last line that bosses and HR departments put on job descriptions: *And all other tasks as assigned.* It's essentially a catch-all phrase that some Machiavellian genius thought up years ago so that bosses could *tell* an employee to do a job they had never done before, then point to this line with a "nah-nah-nah-nah-nah" tone if the employee in any way balked at the assignment. What baloney! Right now, before we go any further, if you have such a last line in anyone's job description, I urge you to remove it. Go ahead. I'll wait.

That is a major reason why we have a lot of so-called performance problems. It is also a reason why we have unions. What a great way to start an employer-employee relationship:

"Before you even start to work here, we're assuming we can't trust that we can have an honest, open dialogue with you when it comes to asking you to do new stuff. We assume there's a good chance you won't want to do the new stuff, so having this line in the job description protects us from that happening. Welcome aboard!"

Perhaps linking back to the *Be Curious* Fundamental, we find that a typical shortcoming of many bosses is a basic hesitancy to find out whether a person is not only *able* to do a job, but *willing* as well. It's probably more of the if-I-don't-ask-the-question-I-don't-have-to-deal-with-the-answer disorder. I'm still amazed at the following incredible but true story a colleague shared with me, which so dramatically and perfectly illustrates our sometimes idiocy on this matter of finding out if a person is willing and/or able to do a job.

It seems there was this employee who had for several years been a genuine thorn in the side of management. She habitually used up all her sick time, had a long record of tardiness (regularly claiming she had to tend to a sick mother), and made numerous and costly mistakes on her job. The company, up to this point, had turned its eye away from these issues, partly with the hope that she would eventually leave, and partly because it wanted to avoid coming off as being heartless, with her having a sick mother and all. A third factor was that she was part of a collective bargaining unit and had readily available representation through her shop steward in case she needed it. This isn't to say that unions are either good or bad, it's simply that their presence in a work unit creates a super level of caution, and even fear, within management. In short, this was a situation where management, for a variety of reasons, avoided dealing head-on with an employee performance problem that should have been resolved probably years before.

In deciding to finally take action – after the employee had used up all her possible away-from-work options (vacation, family leave, personal days, etc.), and made no attempt to contact management about her intentions for when she was planning to come back to work, a meeting was held among – ready for this? – two labor lawyers, three members of HR and the company COO for one-and-a-half hours (Do the math for what you think that time cost!). I think a partridge in a pear tree was thrown in along the way, and you'll notice that the employee was not present. The product of this meeting was a letter – a *letter*, mind you – to the employee, outlining the company's position regarding her absenteeism and other problems, and explaining to her the importance of her letting management know when she would return to work. Did I mention this was a *letter* rather than a conversation?

The letter was sent, Certified Mail I'm sure, and at no time did anyone – her boss, the lawyers, the HR staff or the COO – ever actually *speak* to her! The employee never responded; the company sent her a termination letter; and the employee – through her union – then brought action against the company. I'm not making this up.

I wonder what would have happened had someone, somewhere along the line, sat with her in order to eliminate the *ambiguity* of her *ability* or *willingness* to do the job. All it would have taken was speaking the information that was in the letter, then *asking* the employee things like: "Do you understand the gravity of this situation? Is there some reason why you haven't been more responsive or kept us up to date? Do you want to make this situation better? If so, what can you do about it? What would you like us to do?"

I can guess that some of you are cringing just reading some of these questions, having thoughts like, "Why would I want to know that?" Or, "If I were to ask her that, I wouldn't know how to handle her response." Or, "Asking her that would only start an argument."

Stop thinking those thoughts right now! Your fear in pursuing ambiguity is:

- absolutely unfounded,

- used as a weapon against you by the opposition to keep you off balance, and

- the foundation of an entire industry for labor attorneys, union leaders and consultants like myself.

The elimination of ambiguity creates a sort of positive nakedness, or at least transparency, between you and the other person or persons. Supposed secrets get put on the table, and if – as the *Unforgettable Boss* – you establish an atmosphere of trust where whatever the person says gets treated simply as information to help solve a problem and not material for an indictment, you can save lots of time, effort and money. To engage in true efforts of eliminating ambiguity, you simply have to ask yourself, "What's the worst thing that can happen if I ask this question of this person?" Think about it. What's the absolute worst thing that can happen if someone in authority were to sit with this employee and ask her: "What are the reasons why you haven't been keeping us up to date on your absence or plans for return?" Notice, we don't ask poison-dipped, challenging questions like: "Why are you late so often?" The best I can figure about why the *What* style question is superior to the *Why* style one is that the word *What* asks someone to make a list from their conscious mind, which is easier to do than when asked a *Why* question which is more analytical, and creates squirm and discomfort as the person has to struggle with unconscious motivation. Notice the difference in this simple example. Would you personally be more comfortable being asked, "Why did you do that?" or "What made you do that?" The latter, I think.

So, back to our case. What is the worst that could happen if that employee were asked that question and in that way? Her response could fall anywhere along a scale from, "I wasn't aware it was such a major problem and I'll do better," to "Why are you making such a big deal out of nothing?," to "I have so many personal problems that I don't know where to turn," to "I hate your guts and can't stand the thought of having to see you every day." So? There's not a single one of these responses that you can't handle effectively, especially once you read Chapter 4: The Art and Science of Communication.

Admittedly, the story of this employee is an extreme example of avoiding learning about ambiguities that might keep someone from being willing and/or able to do a job, but the point needs to be made that *not* performing this *simple, but not easy* task can get you and the employees in a whole lot of trouble. Remember the story about the supermarket manager asking the clerk about why he wasn't packing out product in the prescribed time allowed? All the manager was doing was *reducing or eliminating all ambiguities about the person's ability or willingness to do a job.* Think about it as *creating a spoken contract* between you and the employee. You have a need to get a certain job done, but the employee might have certain hesitancies, needs or concerns that unless they get negotiated up front could result in a misfire and unhappiness all around. So you find out what the blockages are, if any, to someone wanting or being able to do a new job, reduce or eliminate them, and go from there. This is how adults play in their sandbox. Never, never force people to do something they appear unwilling or unable to do. You will both lose. The question is frequently put to me: "What do I do if this person can't or won't do the job?" The answer: Find someone else. "And, if that person continually shows that same unwillingness?" Do I really have to answer that one?

Summary: Here's what I hope you learned in this chapter.

The *Unforgettable Boss* really has only three roles when it comes to managing people: 1) *Being clear about goals and expectations,* 2) *Creating an environment where the person's opportunity for successful completion of any task is optimized,* and 3) *Reducing or eliminating all ambiguities about a person's ability or willingness to do a job.* Jan Carlzon, legendary CEO of Scandinavian Air Systems (SAS), probably presented this idea best when he said something along the lines of: "[As you grow in the ranks of management] if you are no longer directly serving the customer, you'd better be serving those who are." In graphic terms, this means inverting the hierarchy pyramid, so that instead of you sitting at the top, surrounded by minions who do your bidding, you're at the bottom seeing to the needs of everyone in the enterprise. That's it. Pretty simple.

1. **Being clear about the goal or expectation** is obviously important, because if you and everyone else are rowing in different directions, you go nowhere. But beyond that, sharing goals and expectations is a form of providing people with information. And once individuals have information, they can't help but take responsibility, which by the way, Carlzon also said (Gee, maybe you should be reading his book instead!). Also, sharing goals and expectations is important because they frequently change, especially in smaller enterprises; and while *you* have a pretty good idea where you're going on a day-to-day basis, you'd be amazed at how much your employees are in the dark. And keep it simple. You don't have to have monthly "All-Hands" meetings where you do a PowerPoint presentation with graphs and charts. One-on-one or small, informal group sessions are fine.

2. **Creating an environment where the person's opportunity for successful completion of any task is optimized** involves the learning, embracing and continual practicing of *The Seven Fundamentals* outlined in the previous chapter. And don't be too hard on yourself for slipping backward on any of the Fundamentals. I've embraced and written about them for more years than I care to count, and I still mess up way more than I'd like.

3. **Reducing or eliminating all ambiguities about a person's ability or willingness to do a job** primarily employs the *Be Curious* Fundamental. All too often, bosses assume that just because a person is employed by the company, she or he must do whatever is asked of them. True enough, some bosses will be courteous and ask a person to do a job, but never ask if they are *willing* or *able* to do it. Lots of problems that can occur later on would be forestalled if the boss conducted a brief *interview* with the employee beforehand about not only willingness and ability to do a job, but methodology and expected outcomes as well. Everyone would sleep better.

4

THE ART AND SCIENCE OF COMMUNICATION

Would you buy this piece of meat? Remember Stan Cohen? I mentioned earlier that he was the president of a 26-store supermarket chain where I did some executive coaching early in my career. I also worked with him on other key projects like establishing a training store for future department and store managers, an unheard-of expense at the time. As I said before, Stan, while ahead of his time in many ways, could also come across as intimidating and condescending – partly because of his physical stature, and partly because of how he communicated. By the way, the line, "What we have here is a failure to communicate" is baloney. We are always communicating, even in our silence. Our body gives us away: arms folded, finger pointing, furrowed brow, a grunt, a laugh, a head nod, a head shake, a smiling face, sitting forward, sitting back, folded hands, open hands…they all convey a message.

Anyway, back to Stan. My coaching arrangement with him included accompanying him on store visits, which usually occurred on busy Fridays, the typical day that home-office executives conduct these visits. My assignment during these store visits was to critique Stan on how he came across to the store personnel with whom he would come in contact. Asking me to observe him was pretty courageous on his part, I thought – but typical of Stan. Also, he had gotten feedback from other execs that he was seen as intimidating and overbearing. So, serving as his mirror, I followed Stan into the first store on our Friday visit list.

A store visit in the supermarket industry is very much like a military inspection, with the top brass walking up and down the aisles of canned goods, detergents, cookies and such, serving as the "troops," and the store manager (company commander) walking two steps behind Stan with a clipboard containing an ever-increasing gig-list of problems that need fixing. All in all, it's a somewhat tense situation.

When we arrived at the meat case, Stan picked up a package of top round steak that was a vivid, cherry red, and turning to the store manager, beckoned him over by crooking his index finger, and asked in that trained baritone voice: "So, Harold, would *you* buy this piece of meat?" Without answering, Harold immediately grabbed the steak and strode deliberately into the meat room, where behind the glass wall he berated the meat manager while firing round after round at him with his index finger (It really does all run downhill, doesn't it?). While Harold was going at the meat manager, Stan turned to me and asked: "So, Bob, how am I doing?"

Not quite knowing how to react, I answered: "Well, I really don't know what the problem is, and I'm betting Harold doesn't either." Stan proceeded to explain to me that the cherry red steak was perfectly fine for consuming, but it lacked eye appeal (most steak you buy is more of a brownish red) and should have been ground up into hamburger meat.

Let's go back and think about Stan's question to Harold and the manner in which it was asked. *Would you buy this piece of meat?* It's classed under the heading which I call a *Bag Job Question*; meaning that no matter what answer is given, you're "bagged," as in being snared and thrown in a bag to be cooked for supper. If Harold answered, "Yes," it would imply that he's an idiot, especially by the tone and inflection in Stan's voice. If he answered, "No," then the automatic response of the Stans of the world would be, "Then what's it doing in the case?" I've told this story a hundred times to a hundred audiences, and when I ask them what they think the answer is to the "No" response, almost in unison everyone would say, "Then, what's it doing in the case?" On the face of it, it's hilarious that they know the answer, but it is really sad that they are so familiar with this kind of verbal dance, the Bag Job. In a way, Harold showed a certain kind of self-preserving wisdom by not answering Stan's question at all.

I brought all of this to Stan's attention while Harold was still in the meat room beating up on the meat manager, and he asked me a bit gruffly what he should have done instead. As gently as possible, I said, "If your motive is to teach, then teach. Simply explain what's wrong: 'Harold, this meat is what we call 'cherry meat,' and while it's perfectly fine to eat, it lacks eye appeal. So please remove it from the case and have it ground for hamburger.'" Stan stroked his chin a bit as we left the store, pondering this alternative way of communicating. You could almost see the internal struggle he was having with the subconscious fun of asking a Bag Job question as a way of asserting authority, versus the healthier, but more drab, straight teaching approach.

We arrived at the next store and took our inspection tour, this time with Larry the store manager playing the part of the company commander. The tour was going rather well, with very few items going on Larry's gig-list. We finally came upon a "hypertainer," a large, square wire cage holding a bunch of stuffed bunnies (It was a week before Easter). Stan paused, stared for a moment at the hypertainer, and in his best imitation of himself, boomed to Larry, "So, Larry, would you bring one of these bunnies home to *your* kid?"

Larry started to twitch and stutter with a kind of "Hummina, hummina, hummina...," but before he fainted dead away, Stan interrupted him and said, "Larry, don't answer," and then turned to me and said, "Go ahead, DeLisa. Ask Larry in your way." Befuddled, I took Stan aside and asked him what was wrong, because something obviously was, based on this newest Bag Job question. Before reading on, can you guess what was wrong? Fifty bucks if you get it right.

Stan explained that although merchandising the bunnies in this robust, "buy me" manner is a good way to increase sales, but because the hypertainer is essentially an open box, the bunnies nearest the bottom will get dirty when the porter sweeps the floor. So the hypertainer should be set on a platform a foot or so above the floor. Pretty logical and simple.

I turned to Larry and said, "Larry, the bunnies near the bottom will get dirty when the porter sweeps, so please set the hypertainer higher off the floor." I then threw in, "I do like the idea of merchandising the bunnies this way, though.

I'll bet you'll sell a lot." Larry smiled, and before he could say anything, Stan said, "Okay, Larry. You heard the way I asked you, and then the way DeLisa asked you. Which way would you rather be asked?" Without skipping a beat, Larry said, "Oh, your way, Sir, your way!" Thanks a lot, Larry.

On our way back to the main office, Stan of course acknowledged that Larry's last response was given under duress. He went on to admit that Bag Job questions end up as a lose-lose; no positive learning takes place. At the time, I had been designing a series of supervisory-skills training programs for Stan's company, and I told Stan that the cherry meat and bunnies stories would be excellent examples of poor communication, and that I'd love to be able to use them in the training. He said that by all means I should do so if I felt they would have a positive impact on the training. That's the kind of guy he was, tough and intimidating, but at the same time self-confident and self-effacing enough to let himself be used as an example of how *not* to communicate.

Word War. With a nod of acknowledgement to Stan for what turned out to be an inspiring visit to the two stores, let's delve a little deeper into some don'ts and dos of verbal communication.

Our communication skills were learned at an early age, and a lot of them were learned and honed through interactions at home. Once again, Bag Job questions are ones that can't be responded to without the receiver getting in trouble. Here are some examples of Bag Job questions we probably all heard at home, plus their workplace equivalent:

At Home:
- *"How could you be so ridiculous?"*

- *"Must you always look like a slob?"*

At Work:
- *"What do you think this is, rocket science?"*

- *"Do I have to walk you through every step of this?"*

At Home:
- *"Do you think I'm your servant/I'm your personal bank/I was born yesterday?*

- *"Do you have any idea how lucky you are?"*

At Work:
- *"Why can't you follow directions?"*

- *"How many more of these bad parts are you going to make?"*

At Home (not really questions, but statements to the sky meant to induce guilt):
- *"All I am is the maid around here."*

- *"Something has got to change, and change fast."*

At Work:
- *"If I want anything done right, I'll have to do it myself."*

- *"I suppose it's my fault for not communicating clearly enough."*

Do they look or sound familiar? I remember once testing the limits when my mother asked me how many more times she needed to tell me to clean my room. As if it were yesterday, I can still see and hear myself, arms folded and head slightly cocked to one side: "Twelve, mom. How about twelve more times? Twelve is a good number." What a little twerp I was. Mom walked away in a huff, but I can only imagine what dear, tough old Aunt Jo would have done.

I think one of the underlying causes of Bag Job questions relates back to our inability to practice Fundamental No. 2: *Be Curious*. We too often would rather, what I call, *drop-a-plop*, then run away. We impress no one by our fear of dialogue. Bag Job questions create defensiveness, hurt feelings, anger and frustration in the receiver, and they advance nothing. No problems get solved. No processes improve. No morale gets boosted. Both parties lose. At the least, you have to agree that Bag Job questions are just plain unattractive.

The good news is that since poor communication practices were *learned* and are not genetic, they can be *un-learned*.

Communication is a form of art with an arrangement of items, as in a painting, but in this case, words, which have an effect on the senses, emotions or intellect. For instance, many of us have heard the saying: *Everything before the word "but" doesn't count.* Notice the different emotional responses that might result based on the following *arrangements* of words:

"I like the content of your work, *but* it's sloppy."
"Your work is sloppy, *but* I like the content."

The first *arrangement* leaves the listener with a sense of failure or non-acceptance, while the second creates a sense of success and acceptance to the listener. In essence, the enduring message is the one that comes after the word, *but.*

Communication is also defined as a science, because we've learned through the work of behavioral science researchers like B.F. Skinner, Abraham Maslow and Douglas McGregor that the way we treat others – with our words, behavior and manipulation of people's environments – can result in predictable behaviors in those people, and these outcomes will repeat themselves over time. A good example is the *Crazy Eights* game I described in Chapter 1, where through my words and actions I was able to manipulate others in order to get predictable emotional and behavioral outcomes in and from the people in the small groups.

Within the art and science of communication we are either *presenting* ourselves to others or *listening* to others. "Black Belt" communicators do both equally well, and seamlessly.

Communication Skill 1: How to Present Yourself. Take a look at these next few sentences:

"You're stupid."
"I think you're stupid."
"I think what you did was stupid."

While none of these is pleasant, let's say you *had* to hear one of these three sentences spoken to you by someone else. Which one would you pick? I hope you chose the third one. In analyzing why you'd likely choose the third, we would recognize the first one as being a value judgment, putting an unpleasant label on the person. The second is a little less distasteful, because the speaker is at least taking *ownership* of the comment [using the word : "I"], thus making it more of an opinion, not a fact. Here, at least there's wiggle room enough for a discussion. In the third sentence, not only is there ownership for the comment on the speaker's part, but in addition, the allegation isn't about the person, just the behavior. Remember that old line from Child Rearing 101? *Assault the behavior, not the child.*

The first lesson to learn then, when *presenting* yourself, is to use what we call "I" statements, where the word "I" is the subject of the sentence, not "you." Beginning your sentences with the word "you" usually violates Fundamental No. 1: *Always the Boss, Never the Parent.* In addition to the "You're stupid" example, consider these:

- "You have to…"
- "You'd better not…"
- "You should…"
- "You need to…"
- "You're wrong."

Even the sentence "You're right." makes this *don'ts* list because it appears you are stating an *objective* fact, but it is actually your *subjective* opinion.

All of the above can be found in The Book of Bad Parenting. In brief, sentences beginning with the word "you" convey judgment and non-acceptance to others, resulting in the receiver becoming resistant, defensive and silent. When people are resistant, defensive or silent, problems stay problems, and once again, no one wins. Remember, too, one of the Cornerstones of Trust (under Fundamental No. 3: *It's*

Strictly Business, Nothing Personal) states: *Never judge or evaluate <u>anything</u> a person says, thinks or feels.*

Look what happens when the subject of each of those same sentences is "I":

- "I think you have to..."
- "I feel it would be best if you didn't..."
- "I want you to..."
- "What I think you need to do is..."
- "I think you're wrong."

"I" messages place responsibility where it belongs, with the sender, and they reduce the receiver's defensiveness and resistance to further communication. "I" messages require some courage, because as the sender you're putting yourself and your opinion out there on the tightrope without a net, and someone's forceful disagreement could easily throw you off balance.

A lot of why we select certain words in "presenting" ourselves has to do with motive: What are we trying to achieve? What's the end result we're looking for? If the motive is to achieve the desired results outlined in Chapter 3: The Basic Objectives in Managing Others...

- Being clear about the goal or expectation,

- Creating an environment where the person's opportunity for successful completion of any task is optimized, and

- Reducing or eliminating all ambiguities about a person's ability or willingness to do a job

...then follow an adult interaction model (see *Fundamental*

No. 1: Always the Boss, Never the Parent) by showing your hand early and presenting yourself with "I" statements.

On the other hand, if you have a Win-Lose motive to preach, cajole, gain the upper hand, push others to your way of thinking, or get revenge; then by all means go back to the "you" statements. They work beautifully!

Speaking of "Win-Lose," let's clarify how the various pairings actually work. There are four possible pairings; consider yourself to be the word to the left in each pair: Win-Win, Win-Lose, Lose-Win, and Lose-Lose. "Win-Win" means I want us both to win and will work to establish an environment or an interaction to help "us" get there, such as in everything this book is about. In a "Win-Lose" pairing, I'm more interested in coming out ahead, and either don't care about your position or want to defeat your position. Debating teams or Congress come to mind, where a motive is to find the flaw in the other guy's argument and attack it. The third pairing, "Lose-Win," is interpreted to mean you've given yourself over to the other person or their argument and let yourself lose, because the Cost-Benefit Analysis (Fundamental No. 7) tells you, for instance, that' it's best to lose the battle and try to win the war. An example here is giving up on where to hold the Christmas Party and storing up your ammunition for fighting the increase in the number of sick days HR wants to pitch to you. "Lose-Win can also occur when you feel weaker than or intimidated by the other person and you surrender to them. "Lose-Lose" is pretty much what it seems: Both parties lose, probably because both sides were so invested in their own position the thought of giving in (e.g. listening) was too scary to contemplate. In my view, what actually happens in any pairing other than "Win-Win" is "Lose-Lose." When one party suffers an initial loss, there is almost always a payback, so any gain by either side is short-lived. Consider the situation where the boss ridicules a suggestion made by an employee, especially in front of others. The boss "wins" the round, but with a now demoralized, or at the least embarrassed, employee, the boss ends up with a loss all around. Turning the other cheek is certainly a laudable act, but I suspect the slapee is actually making a nasty face at the perpetrator when looking away.

"Describe and Ask": The Bridge Between Presenting and Listening. Many people tell me that when they're reading a "how-to" book, they are very happy to find one really good thing, one gold nugget they can take away and use. "Describe and Ask" may be that nugget in this book.

"Describe and Ask" is simply an invitation to a dialogue, an examination of the *space* between you and another person. You have a thought, idea, feeling, perception or reason for an action. So does the other person. The objective of "Describe and Ask" is to get all that information out there, so that work gets done well (Remember, it's all about productivity.).

Here's how it works.

Always begin the dialogue with a statement that *Describes...*

- Your view...of a situation as you see or infer from it, without the benefit of any dialogue.

- Your need...for more information before taking a next step or reaching a conclusion.

• Your interpretation...of a situation or information based on what you heard from someone else.

Then *Ask* an appropriate question (<u>not</u> of the Bag Job class). Some examples:

Describe your view: "From the way you seem to drift off, it looks to me like you don't want to be here."

Ask: "Is that true?"
"Were you aware you were coming across that way?"

Describe your need: "Before I can respond to these complaints, I need to find out more about what's happening."

Ask: "What's your analysis of what's going on, and why?"
"What have you tried in order to resolve things?"

Describe your Interpretation: "From what you've told me, you seem to be having difficulty in buying into the team's mission because the goals are unclear."

Ask: "Do I have that right?"
"What needs to be clarified?"

Other versions of *Describe* type of statements are what I call the "I noticed" variety, as in the following:

"I noticed...
...you became silent when the subject of new customers came up."
...you take the opposite view of nearly everything Joan has suggested."

...you haven't said much today."

...you work hard at getting everyone's opinions, and that helps the whole department."

...you got very enthusiastic over the possibility of our changing software."

Complete the bridge to listening by *Ask*-ing questions like:

"Are you aware of that? If so, what's behind it?"
"What's on your mind?"
"Is it normal, or unusual, for you to react that way?"

The last example of the bridge to listening is what I call the *Reporter's Directive*: "Tell me..." *Tell me* gets its own category, because it's not quite a question, but invites information just the same, maybe in an even softer way than some of the sample questions above. The next time you're watching a news program like *Meet The Press*, *60 Minutes*, or *Face The Nation* (OK, OK, even *Access Hollywood*), notice how many times the interviewer uses the term: "Tell me..." as in

"Tell me...
...about your stand on socialized medicine."
...about how scared you were."
...what you think the reasons are behind why we're in this mess."
...what drove you to divorce after only three months of marriage."

"Tell me" (or more recently heard: "Talk about") are probably the first words learned in journalism school, and psychiatry school, too ("Tell me what made you feel that way about your mother."). I think the other words psychiatrists learned at Shrink School are: "I'm sorry, but our time is up." "Tell me" are two words that absolutely unlock the door to dialogue. They are so sincere that people can't help but open up. Is that being manipulative? You bet. But as stated much earlier in this book, if we're always manipulating anyway, why not do it constructively?

Now that we've built this bridge between *presenting ourselves* and *listening*, what do we do to manage the possible bombardment of information we'll be getting, a lot of which we were avoiding in the first place?

Communication Skill 2: How to Be a World Class Listener.

Listening conditions usually occur within one of three situations:

1. You are seeking information, such as in the *Describe and Ask* examples above, or...

2. Someone comes to you with a simple question, clearly seeking a straight, simple answer from you, such as: "What do you think is the fastest way to get downtown during rush hour?," or...

3. Someone comes to you with a desire to be heard along a 10-point emotional scale from the very subtle to virtual howitzer rounds of need. Examples of "subtle" messages expressing someone's need to be listened to might be a sigh of mild frustration or a "statement to the sky" (e.g., "All I am is the maid around here"). A "howitzer round" example would be one where the person is totally exasperated and needs your attention right away.

A memorable example of this last situation occurred for me with my daughter, Lauren, a number of years ago when she was in her first year of junior high. For me, it was the end of a long day of training for a group of nursing supervisors at a nearby hospital. Coincidentally and ironically, the subject matter that day was "Effective Listening Skills."

I was really looking forward to that cold beer waiting for me when, as I walked up the stairs to the kitchen, there was Lauren blocking my way with a serious case of the "hiffers." You all know what "hiffers" is. It's that sound one makes while crying and trying to talk and breathe at the same time. It went sort of like:

"Da – hiff, hiff – ad. I'm real – hiff, hiff – ly upset to – hiff, hiff – day."

Then my turn. This from the "listening expert" who just dazzled a group of trainees with his deft skills: "What is it now, Lauren?" You should of course easily recognize this as a Bag Job question; one for which there was no real desire for an answer. However, I was dealing with Lauren, whom the family knows as a heat-seeking missile when she wants to be heard.

"Every – hiff, hiff – body hates – hiff, hiff – me. My friends – hiff, hiff – hate me. Hiff, hiff – My teach – hiff, hiff – er hates me. My..."

At this point, I hold my hand up as a stop sign, signaling I've had enough and I'm ready to fix things with my sound advice. After all, I silently reason, there are a bunch of clients out there who pay me good money for the advice I'm about to give Lauren. I proceed: "Now, look Lauren, here's what you do. First, make an appointment with your teacher. Then..." Right around here Lauren switches from hiffers to full-sob mode. My very next line goes: "What is it NOW Lauren?" Keep remembering I'm the very guy who just did six hours on effective *listening* skills. Unbelievable!

Lauren blurts out. "I don't need you to tell me what to do, dad. I already know what to do. Right now, I just need you to *listen*." I bet you saw that coming. Embarrassed and a bit ashamed, now *I* come down with a case of the hiffers. Once both Lauren and I calmed down, I was able to complete the assignment I was given in the first place – listen!

In addition to illustrating how easy it is to fall off the listening skills wagon, this story is important because it shows how difficult it is – especially as a boss, or even as a parent – to avoid the Mr. Fix-it role. Avoiding the Mr. Fix-it role is even tougher when the emotional content from the *problem-presenter* is highly charged. But, as we will see, maintaining an emotional distance and not getting caught up in fixing the problem are essential to mastering listening skills.

A Quick Listening Test. As you are reading the following quoted lines, and assuming you are this person's boss think about the words you might use in responding to what's being said:

"I came in this morning to a pile of work twice the size of any-one else's and at least four rush emails or "Why isn't this ready?" voicemails. I've got people coming at me from every direction. I have vacation time coming, but I'm not even going to use it – what's the point? I'd have my mind on work anyway!'

Now, before reading on, and to respond in a more spontaneous than planned way, quickly write down on a piece of paper the response you would normally give to this kind of presentation. Be honest with yourself. No one's looking. It'll be fun.

(Cue *Jeopardy* theme here.)

This "test" assumes there are six likely categories of response when in the listening role:

- Chiding,
- Recommending,
- Sympathizing,
- Hijacking,
- Seeking, and
- Paraphrasing.

I've provided definitions and examples of all six. Identify which one comes closest to the one you wrote down.

Chiding. Registering a form of judgment or criticism about what the person has said or feels (see the Lauren story above). That's a violation of *Fundamental No. 3: It's Strictly Business, Nothing Personal,* and maybe No. 2, *Be Curious.* You may think you're being helpful by pointing out a flaw in the person's position or thought process, but the time for such lesson-giving is not now!

Example of a *Chiding* response:

"You know, it's really not that bad. You should be happy you're not stuck in Steve's department."

Recommending. Offering advice, even though it isn't being sought (see the Lauren story above). This is a violation of *Fundamental No. 1: Always the Boss, Never the Parent,* and *No. 4 Authorship Leads to Ownership.* "Recommending" is the most common trap listeners fall into, especially bosses and parents. You think it's your job to slip into your Mighty Mouse outfit and save the day by doling out your matchless wisdom. If they don't ask, don't tell. Do you see a question mark at the end of the person's *speech*?

Example of a *Recommending* response:

"Why don't you put a 'Do Not Disturb' sign on your door for a couple of hours until you get caught up? At the least, you should prioritize what you need to get done."

Sympathizing. Feeling sorry for; comes across as patronizing or condescending. Here's a violation of Fundamental No. 2 *Be Curious* and maybe No. 1 *Always the Boss, Never the Parent*. Instead of pursuing causes and options with the speaker, you put a Band-Aid on the problem. You might just as well go ahead and pat the person on the head. "Sympathizing" is often confused with "empathizing (see below)," but they are very different responses.

Example of a *Sympathizing* response.:

"That's too bad. I'm sorry for you."

Hijacking. Turning the spotlight on yourself, either because you are uncomfortable with where the conversation is going and worried about how to respond, or you truly see yourself as the center of the universe. Now you have a violation of *Fundamental #2: Be Curious*. I know you want to be helpful, and probably think you're doing so by sharing a story about a similar situation that happened to you or (worse yet) your Aunt Mary, who this person probably doesn't even know and couldn't care less about. Trust me. Hijacking is not helpful at all. This is the speaker's time. Yours will come later. The only time hijacking is acceptable is to *very briefly* illustrate you are tuned in, as in: "Boy, I remember being in a similar situation, but tell me more about what happened to you." Notice the deft and appropriate use of the "tell me" door key.

Example of a *Hijacking* response.:

"Yeah, I know. I'm having the same kind of morning. Maybe worse, because I've got a deadline to meet."

Seeking. Asking for more information, ideally in order to help speakers resolve their own issues. This is an excellent application of *Fundamentals* No. 2: *Be Curious;* No. 4: *Authorship Leads to Ownership;* and even No. 5: *Freedom and Commitment Go Hand in Hand.* Now we're getting into *Unforgettable Boss* territory. This is *Guided Problem Solving,* where the boss promotes a dialogue journey. Unfortunately, the *Seeking* option is not utilized often enough, probably because it takes more time than the busy boss just jumping to a "Recommending" response, which is *clean* and *simple,* but clearly not adult.

Example of a *Seeking* response:

"Is this typical of what's been going on for you? What options do you have to get out of the situation?" (Feel good if what you wrote is similar to this one.)

Paraphrasing (aka empathizing). Using words and phrases that show you truly identify with or understand another person's feelings, emotions or difficulties, without – and this is very important – taking them onto yourself. Paraphrasing is a terrific example of *Fundamentals* No. 1, *Always* *the Boss, Never the Parent* and *No. 3: It's Strictly Business, Nothing Personal* with a subtle touch of *No. 5: Freedom and Commitment Go Hand in Hand.* According to research I've read and even conducted, of all the possible response pattern choices used by listeners, especially in the boss or parent role, *Paraphrasing* comes in dead last. And yet it might be the most potent and valuable. I think one of the reasons for this is that on the face of it, *Paraphrasing* at first seems to be so baby cereal; all mushy, colorless and tasteless.

Example of a *Paraphrasing* response:

"Boy, you seem to be having a grueling day and it's hardly started. It's got to be frustrating to have to deal with this stuff just before vacation."

When promoting the paraphrasing response in a training seminar I'm often met with participant comments like: "It doesn't advance anything. These comments appear to be simply parroting back to people what they just said. They lack intelligence and seem patronizing, and are generally a waste of time." I understand that people usually have that as an initial reaction to this listening skill. To illustrate the value of paraphrasing, what I'll sometimes do in real time is begin using it to respond to these very comments by saying something like: "So, paraphrasing looks to you like the conversation just stalls. It seems to you that all you'd be doing is awkwardly repeating the exact words back to the person and it would almost be embarrassing to do that. Furthermore, you'd feel stupid and not very helpful if you used paraphrasing." Invariably, they get themselves caught in the warm bath feeling of actually being listened to and understood to boot. That's what paraphrasing does. Its proper use lets speakers know they've been heard. And if a person feels heard, they feel valued. And if they feel valued, they get positively motivated. And if they get positively motivated, they perform better! What's so hard to understand about that? Now, when you couple *Paraphrasing* with *Seeking*, you're in world-class, grand-slam listening territory as an *Unforgettable Boss*.

Look at this superb combination:

"Boy, you seem to be having a grueling day and it's hardly started. It's got to be frustrating to have to deal with this stuff just before vacation.

Pause here for a moment and notice the look and sounds of relief and gratitude you'll get. Then continue.

"Is this typical of what's been going on for you?

Wait for the response. Then, depending on how the person responds to the previous question, continue with something like:

"What options do you have to get out of the situation?"

As I said earlier, *Describe and Ask* may be the one really good thing you take away from reading this book. In subsequent chapters, you'll see just how often you can rely on it as a terrific technique for developing a dialogue and moving forward on just about any situation where talking is involved. *Describe and Ask* is built on the notion of putting all your cards on the table and leaving your weapons at the door. Your objective in using this tool is to explore the nature of problems and arrive at solutions that are beneficial to all involved. There is no intent to trap someone or even to teach a lesson. The lessons are jointly learned through the process.

Describe and Ask might feel a bit awkward or foreign as a way to communicate, but I think that issue only holds true if you find yourself in a situation where there seems to be little or no trust, or there's a Win-Lose orientation between parties. Think politics, courtrooms, any negotiations between management and labor, and debating teams. Unfortunately, too many bosses have been raised on notions like, *"Get them before they get you."* If, as a boss, you have not been raised on that Win-Lose view of work life, but frequently find yourself in those kinds of situations or relationships, then get out of the situation or the relationship. Don't fight fire with fire, fight it with water.

The only other kinds of bosses who might find it difficult to master the skill of *Describe and Ask* are those who see themselves as Miss or Mister Fix-it and can't fight the urge to just jump in and resolve the situation. They often see using *Describe and Ask* as too time consuming ("It's easier to just git 'er done"), even though they know intellectually it's the wrong thing to do.

With some practice and rehearsing, you'll love what *Describe and Ask* can do to help you and everyone around you to grow.

Other Advice on The Art and Science of Communication

Who goes first? There is a long-standing debate among bosses as to who should present first when trying to brainstorm new ideas or resolve an issue – the boss or the employee? On the one side are those who feel the employee should present her ideas first, so the employee opinions are more pure and less clouded by those of the boss. The flip side, of course, is the notion that it's better for the boss to go first, so the employee doesn't waste any advance energy trying to figure out what the boss is looking for before she answers. In my experience, it seems the latter approach works best. The boss should go first with the following conditions:

- The idea or solution the boss presents should only be *an* idea or solution, <u>not</u> *the* idea or solution, and

- Every boss should also be aware of her own style (along the scale of *Autocratic* [highly directive] to *Laissez-faire* [highly non-directive]) and present accordingly. This means if you are more *highly directive* you'll need to emphasize your desire for inputs from others after you present – and then you should clam up and wait.

What if after all is said and done, I really do want to give my advice, and it's not being sought? *Describe and Ask* is built on the foundation of most of the Fundamentals, especially No. 4; *Authorship Leads to Ownership*, No. 5; *Freedom and Commitment Go Hand in Hand*, and most certainly No. 6; *Life is Just One Big Cost-Benefit Analysis*. On your way to becoming an *Unforgettable Boss*, you're using *Describe and Ask* as a self-discovery tool, guiding employees to their own Promised Lands. Achieving this level of success on behalf of all the people you might touch in your career as a boss is a wonderful thing.

On the other hand, there are those times when as a boss *Describe and Ask* is simply too frustrating a tool to pull out of the box. I'm thinking here of those times when – from what you see as a perspective built on your years of experience and substantial knowledge – you have the answer to what people should do sitting right in the palm of your hand. And all they have to do to avail themselves of this vast wisdom is ask you for it. But they don't! In these situations you'd probably figure the last thing you want to do is go with *Describe and Ask*.

So, what to do?

My son, Bob, upon graduating from Babson College with a degree in Entrepreneurial Studies, began a rather lengthy search looking for himself. For the first month or so, the search was conducted in his bedroom, and then soon moved to the family room where he searched for himself on the couch, under the couch, and sometimes behind the couch – while occasionally reading that year's edition of *What Color is Your Parachute?* (I should have guessed the search would take some time, as one of the elective courses he took that year was titled: *On Being Young* (no lie)).

Each day I would come home, again longing for that cold beer, and observe Bob as he carried on the search-for-self. I was trying really hard to keep a safe distance from the search area, but I also had some brilliant ideas about where he should look next (one being Australia). After several weeks of keeping my distance, I began casually offering small pieces of advice that usually began with words like: "How about....?" "Have you tried...?" "Maybe you should..." "What if you..." Each of these forays into the no man's land of Bob's search mission was gently rebuffed by him with "thanks-but-no-thanks-Dad" verbiage.

It was right around this time that I was putting the finishing touches on the *Describe and Ask* approach and thought about how to apply it to this situation – which was now spilling over into total exasperation for me. So I wrote my script (something I always do when I'm pushing my communication comfort zone envelope) and rehearsed it several times, fully expecting success when I ran it by Bob. I arrived home on D-Day and found Bob continuing his search for himself, but now the area had been expanded to the kitchen, and specifically the refrigerator.

This was the speech:

[Describe] "Bob, I've been getting really anxious and frustrated with the amount of time you seem to be taking to get your career going, and I would assume you're getting a bit frustrated as well, at least with me. I feel I've got some good insights as to how you can move forward and would like to share them with you"

[Ask] "Are you interested in my advice?"

(Pretty good, huh?)

But, you know what he said? He said, "No, Dad, not really."

I was frankly stunned by his response, partly because it was so immediate and, of course, partly because it was totally unexpected. After all, I'm a consultant and people hire me for this very purpose; to get my advice. What was wrong with this kid? Once getting over the initial shock, I realized that my son was simply giving me an honest answer, and wisely remembering not to *judge or evaluate anything a person says, thinks or feels*, I simply thanked him for being straight up with me and went on with the rest of my evening, albeit with a slight flesh wound.

To be sure, things remained a bit rocky between Bob and me for a while as he continued his search (now on his own and without my advice), but that episode was one of the most freeing moments of my life. I no longer invested any time or energy in trying to direct his career. And even though it was sometimes painful to watch him go through his struggle, and as much as I was tempted to make a sarcastic remark or two about parachute colors, I pretty much kept it all to myself.

The postscript to this story is that Bob went on to set up his own very successful company in the world of Information Technology, where he currently employs about 20 people. He and I spend lots of time together playing golf and taking father-son getaway trips every year and hardly ever talk business, except for those occasional times when he'll say, "Dad, I need your advice." What a rush!

Here's the point. When you want to give your advice and it's not being directly sought during a communication interaction, you have to ask for permission to give it, according to *The Fundamentals* rules. What will happen – at least based on my own experience in asking family, friends and clients if they want my advice – is that about 75 percent of the time they'll say yes, and the rest of the time, no. In those 75 out of 100 situations you have license to kill, so go ahead and load up the other person with your collected wisdom. The other times? Put a sock in it and move on. As you should know by now, people are better off finding their own way. Your journey is tough enough without taking on someone else's. The very quotable Bern Williams, who appeared regularly in

Reader's Digest's "Quotable Quotes" (though few other traces of him seem to exist) once said, "Unsolicited advice is the junk mail of life," and I think he was so right.

What about the value of body language? Tons of books have been written about the fascinating language of the body; what we say to others without actually speaking. These books often give guidance on how we should effectively "speak" with our bodies. For instance, we are told to...

- Maintain eye contact with the person as a way of showing we are listening

- Keep our hands folded so we won't distract the other person

- Offer an occasional head-nod to make the other person feel comfortable in continuing

- Utter an occasional "uh-huh," again, to show we are listening

- Avoid finger-pointing, as this is interpreted as a hostile act (the finger representing a gun!)

- Lean forward in our conversations with others to appear interested

- Avoid folding the arms when in conversation, as this conveys we dislike or feel uncomfortable about something being said and are closing ourselves off from further dialogue or trying to suppress anger

- Avoid touching our nose during conversation as this sends a signal we are getting ready to fight (similar to a boxer thumbing at his nose)

I happen to believe a lot in these *body language* actions as a doorway to what's really going on in a person's mind when they are speaking. As a consultant and executive coach, I try to maintain constant awareness of what the person's body is saying while we're engaged in conversation. When I see some of the so-called "non-verbal" cues mentioned above, I'm better able to guide the conversation in a more appropriate direction, sometimes actually *describing* to the person I'm listening to what I observe their body doing, then *asking* the right follow-up question (man, that *Describe and Ask* tool is unbelievable).

The problem with trying to control our bodies to give off the right signals is that we really can't consistently control our physical responses to the conversational conditions we are experiencing. If, for instance, we are truly uninterested in someone's message, it's very difficult to maintain eye contact, throw off the old head-nod, or say "uh-huh" with any real degree of sincerity. Or, if someone is saying something to us that really grates or creates discomfort in us, it's very hard not to fold our arms as an act of self-protection. Besides, trying too hard to control our body language will likely result in our looking stilted and wooden. In essence, over time, our bodies give us away no matter how hard we try to control the signals.

My suggestion is to find and read a well-rated book on body language and use what you learn as another communication tool, especially when interviewing job candidates or during performance reviews. Just hope the people with whom you are engaged in conversation didn't read the same book, because they'll be reading you like crazy at the same time. Now that I think of it, that's kind of an hilarious picture – two people in conversation occasionally excusing themselves from each other so they can consult their body language book ("Hold that thought").

Email. A tool or a weapon? I know of at least one company that has declared *No-Email Fridays*. The policy permitted employees to send emails to anyone outside the building, but not to another employee within the building. The deal was that if you wanted to communicate with someone in the building – at least on Fridays as a start – you should either get on the phone, or preferably, go directly to see that person. What a novel idea! What apparently drove this policy was the growing use of email throughout the company as a method of either avoiding or enhancing conflict; aka Win-Lose postures. You know the drill: writing in all-caps, copying the person's boss and the rest of the world, etc. Exasperated clients have frequently shown me copies of emails of jaw-dropping length between two or more employees, filled with vitriolic accusations and counter-accusations and no resolution.

The company that adopted the *No Email Fridays* evidently did the math and calculated that the time it took to think about, then compose these often lengthy and back-and-forth terrifying tracts was way more than the time it would take to talk by phone or meet in person.

Email is supposed to be a valuable tool for communicating information in as rapid a manner as possible. Instead, in too many cases, it has become the weapon of choice for people who lack the courage or skill to deal directly with people. It's too easy to hide within email. A form of The Golden Rule has to apply here. If the email you are about to send is one you wouldn't want to receive, don't send it! End of story.

Summary: Here's what I hope you learned in this chapter.

- We are always communicating with others, sending or receiving messages. Sometimes the messages we send are received by others in ways we never intended. Sometimes we interpret the messages we receive in a way the sender didn't mean. To communicate most effectively, then, we need to ensure that the messages going out, as well as those we receive, are clear. This chapter offers us tools with which to do this.

- Think about using "I" language over "You" language when presenting yourself to others. The word "I" as the subject of a sentence conveys ownership and self-responsibility, while the word "You" as the subject tends to send a message of judgment, accusation or non-acceptance.

- To be a truly *Unforgettable Boss*, in any dialogue with employees you need to always be thinking in terms of Win-Win (both parties gaining). Because so many of us have learned Win-Lose communication habits ("Would you buy this piece of meat?"), it helps to actually write a script of what you intend to say and rehearse it with a "study-buddy," colleague or coach.

- *Describe and Ask* is an amazing tool to use as a framework for sending clear messages and then learning about the receiver's understanding of the message, and willingness to comply if a request is involved.

- Being a world-class listener doesn't come easy, especially for bosses who are often cast in the role of doer, director or problem solver. Effective listening requires a bias toward *guiding* versus *directing*, and this is best done by avoiding listening blunders like *chiding, recommending (unsought advice is the worst kind), sympathy (feel for, not sorry for),* and *hijacking (sometimes it isn't about you).* Instead, work hard on *paraphrasing (or empathizing)* and *seeking* types of responses where the effort is toward helping employees resolve issues and formulate plans on their own. *Paraphrasing* and *Seeking* are the underpinnings of *Describe and Ask.*

- Learning about and reading body language rounds out the communication skills tool kit. People may try to mask their true feelings with the words they choose to use, but their body movements give them away. Take care not to misread a person's body language by not learning about the subject in enough depth. That would be unfair. After all, as an Italian-American, I have a tendency to flail around a lot with my hands when I'm talking, but that doesn't mean I intend to hit anyone. I think.

- Emails can be a tool for good or evil. All too often, employees use email as a device for blaming or vengeance. The half-life of a scathing email is quite long, and the wounds take a while to heal. Have an all-hands meeting or one with key people to talk about the use and abuse of email, and do it now. Email wars cause a lot of emotional damage, and they are getting worse every day, not to mention the productivity lost by the effort expended to write these ridiculous, lengthy documents.

PART TWO:
THE MANUAL

5

FINDING, INTERVIEWING, SELECTING AND ORIENTING GOOD PEOPLE.

The beginning is half of the whole, so a bad start does as much harm as all the later mistakes put together.

- Aristotle

A Tale of Two Cultures

The ABC Plastic Box Company was privately owned by a wonderful guy who had invented a durable plastic clasp mechanism, and then began to design and manufacture various plastic boxes to put them on. If you have any small power tools in your garage or basement, they might well be housed in one of the company's blow-molded plastic boxes. Spencer had a nice little operation going for him. When I got involved, his son-in-law Warren was taking over the day-to-day operations, while his daughter Jill was taking over the administrative duties: accounting, HR, etc.

Spencer wanted me to help groom Warren in his managerial skills as well as work with the family on a management transition plan that would allow Spencer to retire in the next couple of years, leaving Jill and Warren to own and run the entire enterprise. With an employee population of about 20 people, the company enjoyed solid annual sales that provided a more than adequate living for the family. It turned out Jill and Warren were terrific people, too.

As an aside to the core of this story, to illustrate the kinds of business views and values Spencer held, one day a few years before I became engaged to work with ABC Plastic Box, the company's sales manager excitedly ran in to see Spencer with the announcement that he had a commitment from Chrysler Corporation for ABC to make all the plastic windshield washer bottles for several of their models. The sales manager could hardly contain himself, likely thinking of the size of the bonus he would get as a result of this kind of sale (the company had no sales commission structure, and people worked on a company performance bonus system).

Spencer brought Warren into the conversation, and neither one of them had to think very long about a response to what looked like an incredible opportunity for the company. Their answer was "No." Sound wacky? Not really. You see, the company had a very clear vision and accompanying strategic plan that included among other tenets:

- Slow and steady wins the race, and

- No more than 20 percent of our business with any one customer.

Of course, the Chrysler deal would violate both these strongly held beliefs in a big way. ABC would be forced to at least triple their manufacturing capacity almost overnight (a chaotic situation), and they would run the risk of being at the mercy of one huge customer representing way more than 20 percent of the business.

Still sound like a wacky decision? You can be your own judge, but the decision represents the kind of stable, predictable and secure culture Spencer had established, espoused and manifested every day. I'm sure the sales manager went bonkers for a while, but I was told that the rest of the enterprise exhaled a sigh of relief.

Back to the original purpose of this story and what it has to do with adopting a good hiring process. The production machines and processes were fairly simple and straightforward, therefore not requiring high skill levels to operate. The factory was in a fairly wealthy suburban community, but most production employees were from the city of New Haven about 10 miles away.

And here was the fascinating thing. When anyone walked into The ABC Plastic Box Company to apply for a job, they were offered coffee and doughnuts if it was morning, and cookies and soft drinks in the afternoon. Also, they were immediately, and I mean "immediately," brought into a small conference room where they met someone from the office, usually Jill, and walked through the employment application process. Not only was this applicant-friendly assistance of great value to the job seeker – all of us at one point or another in our work lives have had to fill out one of those stupid, impersonal job applications that ask for stuff that isn't even pertinent to the position [*Do you have a Class C driver's license?*] – but the process also provided the company representative with an opportunity to get a good impression of the applicant via this mini-interview.

Furthermore, all applicants were contacted within 24 hours and told whether or not they had the job; that is assuming there was a position available. Finally, if the applicant was hired and lacked private transportation to and from work, the company's shuttle van would pick them up in New Haven.

So, think about it. A small company. A semi-skilled, largely minority workforce. Coffee and doughnuts/cookies, soda. No waiting. Private interview with assistance in completing the job application form. You'd think they were hiring their next COO. Well, the way Spencer, Jill and Warren looked at it, they might be. It was part of their culture. Stature or station in life didn't matter. I have to say, working with this family was one of the most pleasant and gratifying experiences I've ever had in this management consulting business.

In sharp contrast to that story, around the same time that I was working with ABC, a few towns away I was conducting a series of seminars on supervisory skills at the headquarters of a regional bank that had 12 branches. Remember regional banks? Early on in any training project, I would have one or two planning meetings with the head of HR or the training director to get a feel for the client's specific training goals, as most everything we do is customized.

On that particular day, a planning meeting was scheduled, and as I was sitting in the lobby/reception area waiting to be met by my client, I noticed a young lady sitting nearby, filling out a job application. She was kind of scrunched up trying to get the lap board she was writing on into a comfortable position on her knees, while at the same time covering up what she was writing with her opposite arm. Every so often she would gaze up at the ceiling, looking for an answer to a particularly thorny question on the form. As she struggled, another young lady walked in and went up to the reception desk, and gave her name and said she had a job interview scheduled for 2:00 (it was then about 1:45). It was a fairly small lobby/reception area, and I could easily hear the conversation. This second woman was waved to a chair by the receptionist who was busy at her keyboard and barely glanced up. A few minutes later, the first woman finished filling out the form and brought it up to the receptionist who said someone would get in touch with her in the next two or three weeks *if* there was an interest. Then she was dismissed without even a "have a nice day."

Visions of The ABC Plastic Box Company began to dance in my head, and I began to think about how de-humanizing – and quite common – this whole job application process is. Here were two people who anyone who walked into the lobby/reception area would know are either out of work or unhappy in their current job, neither reason being anyone's business. Clearly, Spencer and his family were in the minority when it came to welcoming strangers into their enterprise. I further got to wondering at what point on the job classification scale management offers an applicant coffee and doughnuts, or at what point a free lunch kicks in, and at what point in this class system the applicant gets taken out to dinner at La Maison Ritz.

To complete the story, I went with my client to the planning meeting, which ran about an hour, and on my way out I saw that the second woman, the one with the appointment, was still sitting there waiting to be interviewed. I guess the interviewer was having a busy day. It was their culture.

This is not a very difficult lesson for *Unforgettable Bosses* to learn and apply. Simply step back and look at every job applicant – from the maintenance worker to the CFO aspirant and everyone in between – as a guest in your home. As you treat one, you should treat all. The applicant is hoping to make a good first impression. You should as well. Why wouldn't you want to?

This chapter is going to help you look at every facet of the hiring process, to not only make you an *Unforgettable Boss*, but to make your enterprise equally unforgettable. Remember, one of the three Basic Objectives in Managing Others as outlined in Chapter 3 is about *creating an environment where people can be fully successful.* Whether the current economy is robust or in the tank, you need to create a consistently positive experience for all people who apply for employment at your enterprise.

As part of an assessment of the kind of first impressions the possible *next president* of your enterprise might get, look around and examine things like:

- Is there assigned executive parking? A possible sign of elitism or a caste system.

- What's the entryway/lobby like – cold or welcoming?

- How are people greeted? Is there even anyone there to do so? I once arrived for an appointment with a potential new client, and I noticed that the three best parking spaces reserved for the owner, his wife and his son. The lobby was a stark white with one folding chair and a buzzer next to a windowless steel door bearing a sign: "Push for Service." I did so, and a husky female voice came out of a ceiling speaker, asking what I wanted. After explaining that I had an appointment with the company owner, the voice said, "Wait a minute," and then came back to say, "He's busy right now and can see you in about a half hour." I thought to myself, *He's the one who called me for this appointment!* I walked (actually, I think I ran) the 50 steps to my car and left. Good thing I was having a good month.

- What are the restrooms like? Do you let guests use them?

- What signage or kinds of artwork is in the entryway/lobby? I remember going into a retail store that had a sign taped to the doorway, which read "No Solicitors," then one at the cash register, which read, "All bounced checks will carry a $25 recovery fee." By the time I got to talk to the clerk, I was petrified.

You get the idea.

Now, let's turn to some very helpful tips for finding, interviewing, selecting, and orienting your next company president.

Kelly McDaniel, whose name joins mine on the cover of this book, is a terrific recruiter and interviewer. Kelly joined our enterprise a number of years ago and – in addition to being an outstanding management consultant in her own right – she took what was then the fledgling recruiting services unit of our business and honed it into a significant asset to us and a valued resource to our clients. Kelly is way more talented and knowledgeable than me when it comes to the current nuances and tools of the recruiting function in an enterprise, so she'll be taking charge of the rest of this chapter to impart that wisdom to you.

And now, heeeere's Kelly!

If Only There Were More of Me to Go Around.

Recruiting is really a relatively simple process that gets mucked up by human nature. Things like subjective decision-making, desperation, lack of skill, interest, and/or time to do things right cause us to hire the wrong people, for the wrong reasons, and often at the wrong time. For the small enterprise leader, this time element is really the killer, since a smaller organization doesn't usually have a full blown HR department with specialists trained in recruiting to help the leader get back to the business of being an *Unforgettable Boss*.

We're often asked how long it should take to fill a position. The answer depends on the particular job. Is it one with an abundant, primed labor force ready to start for you tomorrow, like a customer service representative, or is it a hard-to-fill niche job that's custom-designed for your company ("We need an engineer who's good with the customers and can design cogs as well as our marketing materials.")? Time required to fill a job also depends on the *pickiness* level of the hiring manager and hiring team. People hire like they shop, and there are two categories: "Grab this one, I'll try it on later," or "I must visit every store in town to ensure that I have the very best quality for the very best price."

These factors considered, when it comes to recruiting, *Unforgettable Bosses* bear one key distinction from their peers: They *plan* their hires. And I don't mean planning in the sense that they create a job description before hiring someone (a must, by the way), but rather they look at what's happening with their business – how they're spending their time, how their key people are spending theirs, where they want things to go, and what's happening outside the business: competitors, the labor market, the economy. Then they decide what kind of hiring needs to be done.

We have a client who is getting particularly good at this plan-for-hire thing. It's a technical firm consisting of about 100 engineers of varying levels of experience across different engineering disciplines. Steven, the president, and his HR manager, Georgia make a refreshingly progressive team when it comes to managing their human resources. They're inclusive, they understand just how much good morale leads to productivity, and they're well organized without being rigid. Steven heads up his leadership team in strategic planning every year; and for the last few years, the plan has been growth oriented, which in a service business, means adding head count.

As they got to discussing hiring needs this past go-round, Steven, Georgia, and the leadership team began to notice a few things about their business. First, even though employee survey results and exit interview notes indicated very high morale, they seemed to be losing 5-7 percent of their work force every year, either through voluntary exits or forced terminations. They also realized that the time it takes to identify, interview and hire new people took so long that they had to turn down work or at times overburden the existing work force due to understaffing, and sometimes there were no qualified candidates available at the time they wanted to hire. Steven and Georgia came to see that by the time they realized they needed to find a replacement for an exiting employee, they were a day late and a dollar short. They became aware that they needed to begin to hire proactively, and working with us began the practice of *filling the pipeline* – continuously sourcing, interviewing and sometimes hiring candidates whether they [knew they] needed people or not.

Sounds risky? Sure, but this data-driven method was actually more coordinated than the unpredictable way they had approached recruiting in the past. Plus, a new phenomenon emerged: Managers and the marketing team, who, with the new system, now had extra employees to keep busy, were actually working harder to ensure the work kept coming in. Proactive hiring actually increased sales! "Necessity [really] is the Mother of Invention," as Plato said, or was that Frank Zappa?

Some managers didn't buy into the concept and maintained the status quo of hiring only when there was a hole, despite Steven's reinforced encouragement in quarterly leadership meetings. Over time though, it caught on. Engaging in this practice, they sometimes found candidates they loved but had no spot for. Luckily for this company, they had the funds available to hire anyway, considering this a good problem to have. And though they did occasionally find themselves understaffed or unable to fill a tough slot, they also found they made better hiring decisions on the whole because they were no longer desperate.

While it makes sense in theory, this proactive hiring idea is a scary philosophical leap of faith to take for a small enterprise leader, especially when operating on a thin margin, and adding even one more person simply busts the budget. For those not yet won over, we'll take one more stab at convincing you to consider going this route and say that *under-hiring greatly reduces your potential for growth*. The client examples are too numerous to regale you with, so I'll relate my own:

Different from a headhunter's model, at DeLisaGroup, I charge an hourly rate for my recruiting services instead of a flat fee at the conclusion of a search – which, by the way, is a much better deal for our clients. Call me.

The recruiting part of our business ebbs and flows, and, as is the curse of any small business person, there are times when I have more projects to do than time to do them. During these high times, I'm known to throw myself into the work, putting in late nights and weekend mornings to meet the needs of the clients. I always get the work done, and done to a good quality standard. I'm a cheapskate by most measures and take pride in the fact that I am able to save our company money by not hiring an assistant. Plus, I'm of the firm belief that no assistant could do things the way I do them (see the section on *BOSS 2000* in the next chapter), and that I couldn't put anyone else in front of the client because they don't have the rapport I have. Sound familiar? How about: "It would take too long to train someone, and it's easier for me to just do it myself." OK, now it sounds familiar.

If recruiting were the only thing I had to do, this could work well and for a long time. It's not my only job function though – I also have to do other consulting projects, along with marketing the business, networking with colleagues, paying the taxes, finding out why my computer is sluggish, managing vendors, ordering pens…you get the idea. Thank goodness I don't have to manage people.

You see, something has to give, and in my case, until I wrestled this issue to the ground and actually hired and assistant, it was always the business development work that got shelved because it was in the non-urgent pile. I can't be a face to the outside if I'm buried in buying pens, which is just as much of a lesson in delegation as it is in proactive hiring. But we'll get to more on the subject of delegation in the next chapter. What finally got me going was the realization that if we were properly staffed, I'd be better able to fill my future role as business owner, which is just as much (usually more) about growing and developing the business as it is about making things work. Clearly, this one is easy to preach but hard to live.

Our proactive hiring concept based on turnover analysis tells us when to hire and how many people to hire, but for us practical types, we still need the "how," or method. For this, we turn again to Steven, Georgia, and their 100 engineers who recently faced a very difficult recruiting challenge: A much-liked department manager, who led a group of 20 or so engineers, abruptly left the company because of a very serious family issue. His departure opened a gaping hole in an important profit center of the enterprise.

Steven saw this departure as an opportunity to experiment with improving the existing hiring process. Not that it was necessarily flawed in any major way, but because he generally operates under the notion: *If it ain't broke, fix it.* Remember, he's an engineer. So, he brought Bob and me in to help him and Georgia take an evaluative look at their hiring methodology.

During our first meeting, Steven made it clear that he was intent on promoting from within, if possible. *Promoting in-*

ternally is always the first and most-preferred approach, especially in a small business that isn't often able to offer people vertical growth and many chances at promotion.

By the time we came on board, a few internal candidates had already visited Steven and made their ambitions known. The company had a formal posting procedure in its policies, but it was randomly practiced. What both Steven and Georgia were looking for was a good, fair process they could apply consistently. What we developed that day with Steven and Georgia was a mixture of processes, procedures and system designs that we had created for other clients, either as stand-alone elements or as two or three strung together. However, this particular strategy was extremely comprehensive and we offer it to you as an excellent recipe for establishing a world-class recruiting process for the smaller enterprise.

Step 1: Update (or create) the job description, highlighting the five to seven key duties this person will perform, and the requisite skills and experiences necessary to carry out those functions. If your company doesn't use job descriptions, now is the time to start. Answering a few key questions through a technique called *Job Analysis* gives you simple insights you may not have uncovered and is a great feeder for a job description:

- What does the employee do? (Five to seven key things he/she will be responsible for)

- What is the end product or objective of the job? (What's his/her purpose?)

- What standards are used to evaluate performance? (How will he/she be measured?)

- What skills/experience does the person need to turn in a good performance? (What do you want to see on the resume?)

- What qualities characterize the supervisor and the employees in the work unit? (Who will best fit into or round out our culture?)

The last item here is really a key one that's often over-looked. Studies show that not only is the supervisor the most important person in the employee's life (no brainer), but also that *a bad manager/supervisor is the No. 1 reason why employees leave an enterprise.* Got that? Not pay. The boss! Understanding what kind of supervisory style you and your managers have and finding employees to *match* that style, not fight it, is a great way to ensure better hires. Likewise, finding people to fit into the culture of a work group is essential, since employees have interesting ways of *purging* those who don't fit, regardless of how competent they are. A lot of leaders in enterprises we know, and books written on the subject of *style diversity* in the workplace, will preach, and attractively so, that the hiring manager should always be seeking to enrich the team by bringing on people with varying styles or personality profiles. That idea works well on paper, but creates a havoc of conflict when put into operation. If you've been able to attract and keep a diverse personality group, good for you, but you're in the minority, and I'm sure that keeping them all singing from the same hymnal is a little like herding cats. When we use team personality tests to measure member styles, the group almost always clusters around the same *acceptable* norms. Opposites may attract in marriage, but not so much at work. To reinforce our belief that *fit* is at least as important as *ability*, we encourage the more and more commonly practiced technique of including departmental employees as part of a hiring team unit. More on this *hiring team* idea in a bit.

Once you've completed the Job Analysis, you're ready to cruise on to formulating the job description, which for many managers or their HR people often becomes more involved than it needs to be, as forms become loaded with legalese. Bob and I strongly agree with each other on omitting what has been the obligatory "and all other duties as required" statement, and opt for a simple, clean, unencumbered format such as:

Job Description XYZ Company

1. Job Title:	Customer Service Representative
2. Department:	Sales
3. Reports to (*job title*):	Sales Manager
4. Main Responsibilities/authority:	To respond to customer needs and resolve customer problems.
5. Main Tasks:	1. Answer incoming calls, faxes, emails from customers. 2. Follow up on customer complaints. 3. Check in quarterly with customers to ensure satisfaction. 4. Notify customers of promotions and sales. 5. Maintain customer database. 6. Provide backup support to receptionist.

6. Job Requirements:	
a) Education and experience	2-5 Years customer service experience in an office setting; familiarity with email, internet and MS Word; familiarity with database software
b) Personal skills/attributes	Friendly and outgoing; detail oriented; organized

Note that the items in *6. Job Requirements* should match up with *5. Main Tasks*. In other words, you don't need someone with good interpersonal skills if they work alone in a lab all day.

Step 2: Get the hiring team together. Identify the best people able to contribute to making this decision. In the case with Steven, we had him as the hiring manager along with the human resources manager, the technical chief of the firm, and two outside consultants who could provide an unbiased view. The only constituency not represented up to that point was the department staff. So, with Steven's blessing, we took the extraordinary step of holding an election in the department to choose an employee representative to sit on the hiring team. Pretty daring, but cool, idea. And, no, this isn't the same elect-your-boss occurrence mentioned in our book's introduction; that was another daring and *Unforgettable Boss*.

Step 3: Set Up an Interview Form like the one seen here, to provide objectivity to your recruiting process. This form is especially important because you're using a hiring team, and it will prompt you to discuss requirements until all can become of one mind.

DELISAGROUP
Candidate Evaluation Form

Candidate Name:		Client Company:	
Interviewed by:		Client Contact:	
Date Interviewed:		Position:	

Weighting Factors:

3 = *Critical* to Successful Job Performance
2 = *Important* to Successful Job Performance
1 = *Helpful* to Successful Job Performance

Rating Scale:
3 = Expert/Excellent Match
2 = High/Good Match
1 = Satisfactory/Acceptable
0 = Unacceptable

Selection Criteria	Weighted Factor	x	Interviewer Rating	=	Total Rating
Job Specific					
Technical Expertise	3				
Supervisory Experience	3				
Ability to Develop & Maintain Customer Relationships	2				
Design Engineering Background	1				
General Traits					
Mentoring Style	3				
Assertiveness	2				
Organized	2				
Able to Execute	1				
		Actual Total Rating			
		Possible Total			51
		% of Possible Total			

Notice that this form asks you to assign weight factors to different traits or experiences. Since no one candidate will possess *everything* on your list, these weight factors provide a way for you to differentiate your *must have* from your *nice to have* traits. This form will later be filled out by every interviewer at the conclusion of each interview, and the numbers will be calculated. You can't get much more balanced or fair than this!

Step 4: Identify the Ideal Personality Type by using an assessment tool like the Hogan Personality Inventory mentioned in Chapter 1. This will help you get a handle on all those *intangible* things (e.g. Is she self-reliant? Will he rub people the wrong way?) that are sometimes difficult to find out about in an interview.

Step 5: Create an Internal Job Posting that describes the duties and requirements of the position, and incorporates elements of the personality profile developed. Committing yourself to doing internal job postings can be a bit risky, especially when you're worried that Marty Maudlin or Vicky Victim might apply. Consider, though, that not only can you provide a rare-to-come-by vertical growth opportunity, but you might have a real diamond-in-the-rough that you may not have noticed just waiting to sparkle. This is one of those cost-benefit analyses (Fundamental No. 7) where the potential cost of internal posting is far outweighed by the potential benefit. Be fearless!

When advertising outside, be sure to *talk up* the enterprise, focusing on what sets it apart from other companies in an effort to attract the very best candidates. If you haven't figured out compensation by this point, get that issue resolved by doing a little market research. In your ad, ask candidates to respond with their salary expectations, so you can check your assumptions about what the job is paying in the outside world.

Step 6: Source Candidates by advertising your job, searching resume databases, and networking, networking, networking. Let everyone know who you're looking for – the best source is a referral from someone you trust. When hiring externally, be sure to put the ad in places where your target market is likely to see it. Get creative here – if you're hiring a junior person, use free portals like social media. If you're after a highly technical type, turn to industry-related websites or schools as a way to identify talent.

Step 7: Screen Each Candidate by reviewing the resume and conducting a brief phone interview if the candidate isn't familiar to you. Some tips for reading the resume:

- **Reliable Stereotype No. 1:** The person who has spent 10 or more years with his current or most recent employer usually has a tough time adjusting to the next job or two. You usually don't want to be the first date after the divorce.

- **Reliable Stereotype No. 2:** The person who wants to move from a large organization to a smaller enterprise or vice versa often suffers culture shock and doesn't adapt well. ("You mean you don't have an IT department? How will I get this fixed?")

- **Job hoppers. Toss or Take a Second Look?** The traditional view of two-way loyalty and cradle-to-grave employment has changed dramatically as the younger work force is pretty much expected to make three or four job changes by the time they're 30. If you're a traditionalist, you might have to get over it. Also, you're very likely the parent of a kid who fits this profile. Sorry.

- **Check for Reliability of Education Credentials.** More and more people are getting *creative* regarding their degrees. It's a fairly easy thing to check by calling the college. I know, I know, it's an added burden in your otherwise already busy day, but either pay now or possibly pay later. Remember what Aristotle said about the "Beginning" being half of the whole.

- **Be Prepared to Question "Accomplishment" Statements** (e.g. "Saved the company $2.5M through inventory reduction). You'll want to know how they did this.

- **Look for Gaps in the Work History and/or Mock "Consulting" Work.** There's nothing essentially wrong with people trying to make themselves look better by glossing up these things. You just need to gently find out more details.

- **Look for Instances Where the Candidate Took Demotions When Switching Jobs.** Check to see if he or she stayed in the same position for a long time without a promotion. Again, there's nothing wrong with either of these situations, but you'll want to know more about their work-motivation drives.

- **Look for Multiple Career Changes.** This could indicate the person really doesn't know what they want to do in life, regardless of age or generation.

- **Look at Overall Appearance.** Neatness, spelling, grammar, and articulately written cover letter.

- **What Good is a Resume Without a Cover Letter?** Not much. Taking the time to write a cover letter shows something about the person's whole attitude toward work.

Step 8: Interview Your Top Picks. This step is going to require a little preparation time in the form of making a list of questions in advance, which relate to both the items on your candidate evaluation form, as well as what you determined was your ideal personality "fit" type.

Now, many bosses have no problem finding out what kind of technical, job-related experience a candidate has ("Tell me, Mary, about your expertise with launching rockets.") because they are usually experts in the field. It's that fuzzy personality stuff that trips up a lot of them. They have a hard time forming questions around the intangibles like the ones mentioned above in the *General Traits* on the Candidate Evaluation Form, and without a skill in this area, the tendency is to lob a softball at the candidate as a way of partially covering a topic. Say one of the items on the evaluation form is *self-reliant; takes initiative*. Here's how that line of questioning usually goes.

Interviewer: "Mary, are you self-reliant?"
Say it with her now:
Mary: "Yes, very." [Smiles]

Let's make the line of questions just a bit more penetrating for her, and see if we can learn a little something more about Mary. We're going to use a technique called *Behavioral Based Interviewing*, a topic worthy of having many books written about it, yet so simple we're going to cover it here in a paragraph or two. The idea behind Behavioral Based Interviewing is that the best predictor of a person's future behavior is their past behavior in certain situations. With that in mind, the typical behaviorally based interview question has two parts. It starts with the phrase that makes the candidate recollect past behavior, something like: "Tell me about a time when you..." and ends with a request for an example related to the personality trait or characteristic you're looking to find out more about: "...showed initiative or had to become self-reliant." With her answer, we're getting a whole lot of good information from Mary. Not only do we find out more about whether or not she possesses this trait, but we get to judge her example as well – we get a little insight into what she defines as taking initiative. When she says, "Getting out of bed every day to come to work," does it match our expectations? Falls short? Exceeds? (Yes, *Falls short* should be the correct answer here.)

The beginning of this chapter encourages employers to follow one of the Basic Objectives in Managing Others: *Creating an environment where people can be successful.* The interview situation is no different in those terms. I often hear poorly skilled interviewers brag about what a tough interview they conduct, and how they challenge potential recruits to sell them a pen or demonstrate some other such unrelated skill in an overly intimidating setting that has nothing to do with the real-life environment of the job. They don't understand that by putting the person at ease they'll tell you way more than you'd ever expect them to. With that comes our basic rule of thumb when it comes to interviewing: *In all cases, notice and learn that the candidate should be treated respectfully and brought to a point of trust with you, so that she will feel comfortable in disclosing the information you need to make the right choice.*

If you get that much, and combine it with your commitment to *Be Curious*, you're already a much better interviewer than when you first thumbed to this chapter. If you're feeling really ambitious and you want to achieve *elite* interviewer status, follow these tips as well:

- **Prepare for the Interview** by studying the resume and being on time.

- **Establish the Right Environment**, like a private office with desk/table between you; no interruptions or other distractions. There was a time when sandal-and-tofu types preached that a table between you and the candidate created a barrier to interview intimacy, and that it was better to just have two chairs facing each other. It wasn't long before bosses came to realize that the awkwardness of this configuration actually created way too much discomfort for both parties, so everyone retreated behind their desks again. A few chose to use a round table for interviews, a modified barrier, and those are fine. Regardless, everyone knows which one of you is the boss.

- **Put the Applicant at Ease.** Offer refreshment, and begin with some small talk ("How was your ride/trip?").

- **The World's Best Opening Statement and Question.** *"I have two goals for this interview. One is to learn all I can about you, and the other is to answer all your questions about this job and our company. It doesn't matter to me where we start as long as we cover both. What's your preference?"* An interesting note: Even though the candidate probably should choose to *interview you* first and ask questions about the job and company in order to get important insights for questions he or she will be answering later, they almost always choose to have the boss ask them questions first. Our best guess as to why this phenomenon exists is that either the candidate expects to answer questions first, or they're just desperate to talk about themselves. In just making this opening statement and asking the question though – and applying the principles of *Fundamental No. 5: Freedom and Commitment Go Hand-in-Hand* and *Fundamental No. 2: Be Curious* – you're setting a tone of openness, curiosity, and ease. Goal accomplished!

- **Explain the Process.** Tell the candidate up front that you're going to be asking them for specific examples and details of how they've handled time deadlines, pressures, unexpected situations, and adversity in the past. In other words, prepare them for your behaviorally-based questions. It's only fair to do this, and why wouldn't you?

- **Follow the 70/30 Communication Rule** wherein the applicant talks 70 percent of the time. It's usually the other way around, but logic says, if you're doing most of the talking, you're not finding out anything about the other person. I'm often in a situation where a client and I are separately interviewing the same candidate, and I'll be doing the second interview. I'll usually begin my interview by asking the candidate how the interview with the boss went. It's extraordinary the number of times the candidate will answer, "I'm not sure. He did all the talking."

- **Start by Going from Back to Front.** "Let's take a walk through your life. What made you decide to go to XYZ University? What made you choose your first job?" By talking about the person's history, you'll get key insights into her motivations, especially why the candidate left past jobs.

- **Share Some of Your Experiences** in order to get them to open up and feel comfortable revealing weaknesses. "On my last job, the boss' son who took over the business didn't have a clue about how to manage people. This sounds similar to your situation. Is it? How so?" Remember the "70/30 Communication Rule" though and don't get carried away with your war stories.

- **Pursue Ambiguity.** If something's not clear or sounds like a potential red flag, don't let it go. Follow up with specific questions until you're sure you understand the candidate's response or feel comfortable with whether or not you have identified a potential issue. "I'm really not clear on why you responded that way. Tell me more."

Step 9: Hash It Out with the hiring team, if you're using one, to determine your top two or three candidates. Refer back to the candidate evaluation form *scores* and interview notes to decide who will move on to second interviews.

Step 10: Do the Due Diligence by conducting second interviews, personality testing your final candidates, and conducting reference checks.

I have several clients who opt not to do reference checks, citing they don't get any good information from them or that people refuse to talk. As someone who makes these calls, I rarely find this to be the case, but when I do run into a stone wall, I simply put the task of finding someone who *will* open up back on the candidate. If they can't find three people they've worked with in the past who will talk about them, then you've got to do some thinking about whether or not you have the right person in front of you. As a more preferred alternative, think about who you might be able to network with who knows the candidate and is willing to give you the real scoop. Once you do get the references on the phone, and you've dug around the edges of the candidate's reputation to find out what they *most need to learn to be better at*, expect glorious things to be said. Anything short of very positive reviews should be a red flag to you. After all, these people are references, defined as people who "recommend" or "pay tribute."

Step 11: Onboard Them with Purpose by keeping with the tone we've set for demonstrating respect and courtesy for new hires/promotes. If the new person is coming in from the outside, welcome them warmly, and pay them the proper attention. This is first impression territory, so make it count. Plan for the new hire's first week, and build flexibility into the plan, so he or she isn't sitting idle.

For a new employee to connect with the company, he needs to bond with his manager and peers and get a proper indoctrination. Here are some ways to ensure this will happen:

- **Let People Know What's Going On** by announcing the new hire before he arrives, and letting people in the work area and the company know what he'll be doing.

- **Cover the Logistics** by having her fill out her paperwork in advance, and by having phone and computer access, an email account and an ID badge, if necessary, ready to go.

- **Be There and Involved** to schedule the start date for a time when you can not only welcome the new person, but also be available to spend real time with him. Use that time to bond, to go over the job description and expectations, and to introduce him to his coworkers and other managers around the company. Don't just shuffle him off to *shadow* a peer for the week. Check in regularly, and provide training yourself whenever possible. The section on *BOSS 2000* in the next chapter will provide you with lots of tips on how to do this really well.

- **Use the Buddy System,** because starting a new job is socially daunting. The new recruit may be hesitant to ask you "stupid" questions, or may feel intimidated, not knowing anyone. Assign a buddy who you think will mesh well with the new person, to help her learn the ropes and the important things, like where the best place is for lunch.

Summary: Here's what I hope you learned in this chapter.

- **Develop a Healthy Culture Around Hiring** that treats each candidate, external or internal, as if he or she were the next president of the company. Demonstrate respect, courtesy, and openness, so the person will not only show you her cards, but if she joins you, will stay with you for the long haul.

- **Plan and Control Your Hiring** by experimenting with and hopefully embracing a proactive versus reactive approach. Reduce panic and desperate de-cision-making by filling the talent pipeline and con-tinuously looking to hire whether you need people or not. Remember *Fundamental No 6: The 11 Percent Solution.* Roughly 11 percent of the people in your enterprise really shouldn't be there. Being on a con-tinual lookout for new talent can help reduce the *agita* of continuing to put up with sub-par perfor-mance.

- **Develop and Refine a Recruiting Process** that in-volves getting the right people in the room and working together as objectively as possible to hire not only for the technical aspects of a position, but the interpersonal traits and qualities you're looking for as well. We think you'll be amazed at the quality results you get when using a team approach, espe-cially if you *elect* an employee from that department to be part of this team.

- **Rely on Curiosity, Not Intimidation** when inter-viewing people, and prepare behaviorally-based questions that get to the nooks and crannies of can-didate personalities to determine how they will fit with the *personality* of the enterprise, as well as the job.

- **Orient and Indoctrinate** people with an eye on building relationships, not just filling them in on the technical aspects of the job. It's sad how few enter-prises have a formal "Welcome Aboard" process in place or in use. *Unforgettable Bosses* wouldn't even think about *not* having one.

6

IDENTIFYING AND
DEVELOPING TALENT

*Feeling gratitude and not expressing it is like wrapping a present
and not giving it.* -William Arthur Ward

K elly and I are often fans of John Rosemond, renowned family psychologist whose books and
articles I believe should be required reading for
all managers or manager wannabes. Rosemond's repeated
teachings on it being a parent's job to build personal responsibility and accountability in their children dovetail perfectly
with so many of the messages in this book.

In a recent Rosemond article, he responds to the question
of whether or not he agrees with "the currently popular parenting adage that 'rules without relationship lead to rebel-
lion.'" He resoundingly answers, "No, I do not." His fascinating but absolutely logical reasoning includes this: "When
the thin line between having a relationship and being in a
relationship is crossed by a person in a leadership position –
and parenting is a leadership role – authority is sacri-
ficed...When someone who has established a close relation-

ship with someone else then tries to exercise authority over that person, resentment is the inevitable outcome." (Rosemond, 2011)

Rosemond explains that the "ethical" leader wants a relationship [with an employee] but won't rush it. "His aim is to bring out so much 'best' in the people he is leading that they are eventually qualified for a relationship with him. So, the private advances through the ranks and becomes an officer, the salesperson is eventually promoted to sales manager, and the child eventually becomes a truly grown-up responsible adult who is in a peer-to-peer relationship with his parents." Whether it's effective parenting or effective managing, the message is the same, it's just the ages that are different.

There's a subtle implication in what John Rosemond says: Led properly, employees will eventually become "officer[s]" or "manager[s]." But let's not kid ourselves; not everyone who works with or for you is destined to become the next *Unforgettable Boss.* However – and according to the point I hope we drove home in the previous chapter – everyone who comes under your care in the hiring process should be looked upon as a potentially very big deal indeed, from the minute they walk in the door to setting up shop in their work area.

Mentor, guru, guide or advisor, somewhere along the line in your career, you likely had one or more of these people in your life who actively – through direct guidance or simply modeling admirable behavior – had a positive impact on your life choices. The person could have been a parent, teacher, neighbor, relative (think Aunt Jo), or most desirably, a boss. Think about who they might be, and as the names and faces of these people pop up on the screen of your mental search engine, I'm going to bet you're smiling, at least a little, over the fond recollection. That's good.

This chapter is going to beef up the mentoring skills in you so that one day when one of your mentees (sorry, but it's really a recognized term in organization-speak) is reading this section of this book, they'll be thinking of you, and smiling.

BOSS 2000.

Back in the late 1970s, Paul Hersey and Ken Blanchard (many of you may recall Ken Blanchard as the author of the incredibly successful and abundantly readable book, *The One Minute Manager*) developed a model called *Situational Leadership* that essentially says the leadership style one should employ depends on the situation, and to some extent the person being supervised (Blanchard, Hersey, 1977). They staged the model in four segments: *Telling, Selling, Negotiating* and *Delegating*.

I was intrigued by their concept, but had always felt – and still do – that it's not so easy for bosses to just pull out of their pocket the style that applies to a given situation. In Chapter 1: Physician, Heal Thyself, I spent a healthy chunk of your reading time making a case for learning about your own style and its impact on others, and the difficulties involved in trying to be a chameleon about it. The point was made in Chapter 1 that we probably can't change the default setting on our management styles very much, at least not without an enormous amount of work, but we can practice new behaviors and/or adjust our environments a bit in order to either soften or strengthen an aspect of style.

What I did get from and liked about the Hersey-Blanchard model was that it showed the boss as being more (and appropriately) highly directive in the initial *Telling* segment, or quadrant as they illustrate it, than in the other three. So the way I saw it, the so-called style one would use was not so much *situational* as it was a continuum toward a constant goal of moving each employee from a position of dependency to one of total independency. For me, a key aspect of the job of managers is to actually work themselves out of the job by serving as a sort of booster rocket for people whom they manage, getting them to a point where they can fly on their own as fully independent and accountable performers. *Unforgettable Bosses* do this in a series of carefully planned and measured steps that can occur over a brief or lengthy period of time, depending on the job function (responsibility) being taught.

I was working with Kelly and our colleague team, within our own enterprise, doing all this theorizing and mental maneuvering on this subject in the late 1990s, and with the millennium approaching we cleverly decided to call our model *BOSS 2000*. What we wanted was to create a conceptual framework built on the foundational principles of *The Basic Objectives in Managing Others* as explained in Chapter 3, namely...

- Being clear about goals and expectations

- Creating an environment where people can be fully successful

- Finding out about a person's willingness or ability to do a job

Built into this framework, we needed a map of sorts to serve as a step-by-step guide for achieving these *basic objectives,* and – to show we knew what we were talking about – we needed to have each of the steps coincide with what would become the *Seven Fundamentals.* In short, we wanted to keep our ongoing pledge to ourselves and our clients that it isn't enough to just point out what has to be done, but to show *how* to do it, relying on a few rules consistently applied. Without the *how,* the *what* is just a sieve.

So, with a bow to Hersey-Blanchard and a whole bunch of other insightful and provocative management and leadership theorists of the past 60+ years, here's how *BOSS 2000* works.

BOSS 2000©

Leading Others to INDEPENDENCE...One Function at a Time

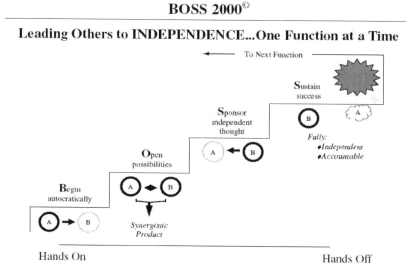

The underpinnings of *BOSS 2000* are every one of the *Seven Fundamentals,* and connections will be made to the applicable ones as we walk through each step of the *BOSS 2000* model.

If you agree with the previously mentioned notion that a key aspect of the job of managers is to actually work themselves out of the job, then you will immediately see that the only way to achieve that lofty goal is to work toward making everyone fully independent; otherwise you can never just disappear and go sit on the beach. Now, you may be thinking – and rightly so – that not everyone can or wants to be the boss. Or you may be thinking about those few (the 11 percent) whom you feel shouldn't even be on the planet. Stay with me on this; it will all work out.

As a practical matter, getting everyone who works for you to this lofty state of total *Independence* is an almost impossible feat. This is partly because there are usually one or more *newbies* coming on board at regular intervals, so unless you freeze your enterprise in time, the road to total *Independence* for all will never end. Plus, we're talking *one function at a time* here, which means that while Jane Marie might have mastered to a point of independence the function of grant writing, there's still a whole basketful of other functions she has to master, such as purchasing, customer relations, and supervising her first new hire. But, and especially keeping the notion of *exaggerated learning* in mind, you should always have your eye on the prize of *Independence* for everyone, unless or until the signs show you otherwise, as we shall see.

In the broadest sense, the conceptual framework for leading others to *Independence* is within the practice of and relates directly to: *Fundamental No. 4: Authorship Leads to Ownership,* and *Fundamental No. 5: Freedom and Commitment Go Hand in Hand.*

Under *Fundamental No. 4: Authorship Leads to Ownership,* you want to be thinking that your tactics within *BOSS 2000* should be to eventually involve the person in any re-design of the work function you want him or her to *own*. With *Fundamental No. 5: Freedom and Commitment Go Hand in Hand*, you're thinking that as the person is being guided through the various phases of *BOSS 2000*, the wider the avenue of freedom he or she has to make choices, the more likely you'll have developed a long-term, *committed* player, an investment of your time and effort that will pay off in spades down what you should expect to be a very long road. Remember, whatever carrots of money or promotion you may not be able to give as a way of ensuring a long-term stay from your top people, you can easily make up for – and get the same result – by providing them the most enjoyable work experience possible.

You'll notice there are four stages or steps to the *BOSS 2000* model, ending in the starburst, which is meant to indicate the point at which both you and the person being groomed for *Independence* have arrived! You'll also notice just after the starburst, there is a return line marked "To Next Function." This refers to the point made above that *BOSS 2000* considers a person's journey to *Independence* to be function-specific. Let's begin at the beginning and you'll see better what I mean and how all this works.

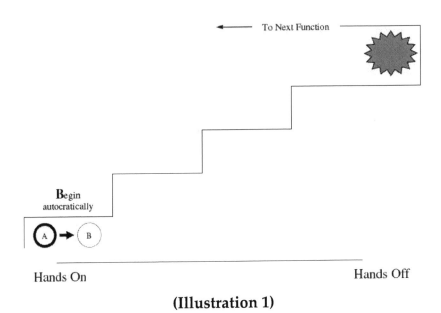

To Next Function

Begin
autocratically

A → B

Hands On   Hands Off

(Illustration 1)

I must confess that when we first conceptualized the *BOSS 2000* model, we first came up with the acronym "BOSS," which we liked a lot, and then backed into coming up with suitable words to fit it. Hopefully, you'll agree that we did a nice job in the way we dressed up the acronym.

The first letter in *BOSS 2000* stands for "Begin," as in:

Begin Autocratically

When introducing a new task or function to anyone within the enterprise, whether a new hire or someone who's been on board for a length of time, you should want to call on whatever directive traits you have and autocratically request the job be done in exactly the way it's been prescribed up to now. For those of us who are dyed-in-the-wool autocrats, this part of *BOSS 2000* will come easy. For those of you who are toward or at the other end of the scale and more democratic, this part will be more difficult. "Why autocratic?" you might ask. In my experience, it seems that most people in a subordinate situation prefer more direction than less direction, and would rather be over-explained to than second-guessed after the fact. Also, most bosses, if being completely honest, will admit they have a preferred way of doing things (think slicing tomatoes), and will wince at least a little if someone does the task another way without prior consent. So, in designing this first phase of *BOSS 2000*, we figured it would be better to be safe than sorry.

If you want to create *an environment where people can be fully successful,* by being highly directive in the manner of an autocrat at this early stage you eliminate most of the ambiguity about job expectations. The resulting sense of safety the employee feels becomes a big part of that environment for success. See how nicely all that fits together and how this *Directive* action is faithful to The Basic Objectives of Managing Others? I call this a low-risk/high-success option for both the employee and the boss. Neither of you is running a high risk when the directions are so clear and the control so rigid. Therefore, the likelihood of success is very high. When training clients on this portion of the model, we urge them to explain to the employee how the whole process will go and why you are taking each step. So, for instance, we want clients to explain to the subordinate that they are deliberately acting in an autocratic manner as part of a longer range goal of the employee becoming totally independent.

Perhaps this process would be a lot easier to understand if I use an example. When Kelly McDaniel first joined our company, part of her job responsibility was the *function* of writing proposals. Now, whether or not Kelly had any previous experience writing proposals didn't matter. In following the *BOSS 2000* view of life the conversation went something like this... (NOTE: I represent the bold-circled letter "A" in Illustration1, with Kelly being the letter "B." The **A** → B interaction is intended to illustrate the boss appropriately taking the lead in the dialogue, since at this point bosses are holding most of the cards, and to appear to be less in charge would be at best patronizing and at worst deceitful.)

- I gave Kelly copies of several randomly selected proposals we had written in the past, and started our conversation by expressing a wish that I hoped would become a realized goal of her completely taking over the proposal writing function.

- Because this was her introduction to the *BOSS 2000* model, I spent a few minutes explaining the concept of the autocratic, high-control initial phase of the process and how it should help ensure a *low-risk/high-success* experience for the two of us. I then made Kelly aware that after the *autocratic* start, I would be letting out the string of autonomy over a designated period of time until she could become fully independent and therefore fully accountable for the proposal writing *function.* It should also be noted that at each touch point of our conversation, I checked with Kelly to find out what her thoughts, understandings, reactions or questions might be *(Fundamental No. 2: Be Curious).* Some may argue that because this phase is so top-down/one-way, it violates the principles of *Fundamental No. 1: Always the Boss, Never the Parent.* After all, isn't it the parent in us that tells people they have no choice in any-thing: "My way or the highway?" I would argue back that the open-ended quality of our conversation, plus fully explaining my motives for the rigidity of this phase, actually illustrated an adult-to-adult conversation. Can you buy that?

- With the above foundation in place, I then went over each of several sample proposals with Kelly, reviewing the rationale and nuances of each part. As we reviewed each one – and this is an extremely important part of the *Begin Autocratically* step – I expressed to her that I was fully aware there were parts of our proposal format and process that could be improved, but at this point she was only to make note of those parts she felt could be improved without actually making any changes in the process or format. However, I made it clear that at the next step of *BOSS 2000,* we would have a back-and-forth dialogue on what to change and what to keep.

- Before sending Kelly off to write her first proposal – coloring within the prescribed lines, but along the way making notes for improvement – I presented her with the last but again extremely important piece of the *Begin Autocratically* step, and that was to select a specific date on which we would formally meet to go over the changes she wanted to suggest.

Here's why this setting a date is so important. Way back in Chapter 1, the point was made that once identified, we really can't change our management styles very much; that without a lot of practice or getting a frontal lobotomy, we will usually default to either autocratic or laissez-faire behaviors. As said above, Step 1 in *BOSS 2000* should be quite easy to accomplish for the autocrat, because it plays to a strength: high control. At the same time, the laissez-faires among us would have difficulty with Step 1, as giving what feels and looks like heavy-handed orders is anathema to this kind of manager. The remedy offered by the *BOSS 2000* model to offset this dilemma is to select what I call a *Moving Day*. *Moving Day* is a specific calendar date the boss selects to build the bridge from Step 1 to Step 2. This involves meeting with the person being trained in the selected function to review the trainee's suggestions for improvements and their state of readiness to *move* to and through Step 2. Why the "specific" date? It seemed to us when conceptualizing *BOSS 2000* that without a specific *Moving Day* set in cement, the autocrat might never let go of the control, or certainly take way too much time to do so. Conversely, the laissez-faire manager, in an unconscious effort to avoid a commitment or possible conflict, might similarly avoid or postpone holding the meeting. So, the specific calendar date forces both management style types to act. The date for *Moving Day* should be one that suits the function being worked on. For instance, in Kelly's case, where she was learning to master the proposal process, I determined that she should write at least five proposals before we would best be able to sit down and talk about changes in the process or format and/or determine if she was ready to fly more on her own in this function. I also determined, based on past records, that we typically wrote three proposals a month. Therefore, it seemed that we should set a date for two months out. The initial meeting ran about an hour-and-a-half, and we parted company with the understanding that we would meet formally in exactly two months (logging the date on our calendars), but that I would be available as much as possible to answer questions or provide guidance. I was also at peace, because I knew it would be at least two months before I would have to hear any assaults on *my* perfectly suitable and workable proposal writing process.

As an asterisk to the *Begin Autocratically* step, it should be pointed out that as the boss you might not be the best candidate for guiding the employee to become fully proficient in a particular function. In these situations, you would logically enlist the assistance of the resident expert in that function. But that person should also follow the procedures and spirit of the *BOSS 2000* steps. For instance, with Kelly, part of her job was to maintain appropriate records for billing and other purposes. If you knew me at all, you'd clearly understand why, when it comes to record keeping, I would seek a third party to help in teaching Kelly this responsibility. Alice, the bookkeeper, had a similar *Begin Autocratically* meeting with Kelly to explain the existing process for record keeping, to *color within the lines* of that process, and to make a list of improvement suggestions for the *Moving Day* meeting. Kelly and Alice then went on to follow the subsequent *BOSS 2000* steps, just as Kelly and I had done with proposal writing.

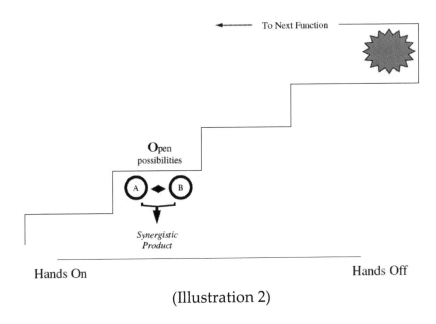

(Illustration 2)

The second letter in *BOSS 2000* stands for "Open" as in:

Open Possibilities

This second step in *BOSS 2000* is probably the most complex but rewarding phase, partly because it combines elements of both autocratic and laissez-faire styles and partly because it's where synergistic creativity gets spawned. Creativity is sometimes defined as: *That place where no one has ever been.* Synergy, a wildly popular notion during the heyday of Total Quality Management (TQM), can be defined as two or more people working together to produce a result not available by each person working separately. Say your queen-size bed has to be made and you're doing it alone. You know what a drag it is to have to go from one side, stretching here, then to the other side, pulling there, then back to the first side, tucking here, then back to the other side, adjusting there. In a separate bedroom is your spouse making another queen-size bed, going through the same rigmarole as you. The theory behind synergy says that if you and your spouse worked together making both beds, you would finish in much less than half the time it takes to do them separately. In other words, the two of you, working together, could probably make three or four beds in the time it would take for you to make one bed apiece! Also, consider what a nice spousal bonding experience this can be.

You'll notice in Illustration 2 that "A" and "B" are in bold circles, implying a balanced interaction between the *Unforgettable Boss* and employee. And so it was with Kelly and me. During the two-month bridge period between Step 1 and Step 2, and along with other more simple jobs she was doing and new *functions* she was learning, she completed several proposals, following the format and process as originally defined. All in all, she did a very nice job. But that led us to *Moving Day*, and it was time for her to offer her suggestions. In short, we breezed through that meeting, going back and forth with ideas, points and counterpoints, all aimed at improving our proposal format and process. It was a little like an old Judy Garland and Mickey Rooney movie where they took over the barn to put on a play. No egos, no defensiveness, and no bad ideas, all because Kelly and I did what we did in Step 1, coloring within the lines before breaking loose. The proposal process was substantially changed and we knew for sure that the new version could have only been produced by this *creative synergy* we experienced together; that neither of us on our own could have matched the quality of the new product. We decided to let out more string, and Kelly went off to try out some of the new ideas we had agreed upon, with her checking in with me when needed to make appropriate corrections.

I can't say enough about this synergy business and how incredibly valuable it is, not only in growing people, but in the new *products* that come from the exercise. By applying the principles of *Fundamental No. 2: Be Curious; Fundamental No. 4: Authorship Leads to Ownership;* and *Fundamental No. 5: Freedom and Commitment Go Hand in Hand,* you reduce defensiveness; and when you reduce defensiveness, ideas flow; and when ideas flow, you have creativity. OK, maybe now I've said enough.

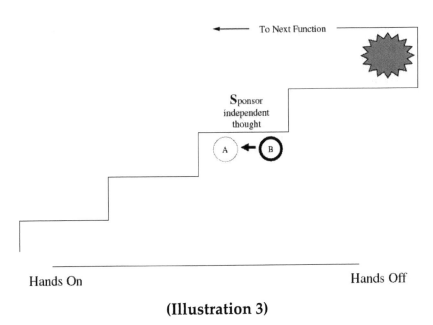

(Illustration 3)

The hard part is over. We now turn to the first "S" in *BOSS 2000,* which stands for...

<u>S</u>ponsor Independent Thought.

Here's where you as the *Unforgettable Boss* first get to thinking about grabbing those golf clubs or that fishing rod from the garage in preparation for vacating the premises.

You are now becoming a *Mentor*. Who'da thunk that way back when you bought your first piece of equipment at the formative stages of your enterprise you'd one day get to wear the mantle of a *Mentor*. Your job now is to be more in the responsive role than the directive one, as in Illustration 3 with the bold outlined "B," or as in my example, Kelly. As she continued to develop in the proposal writing function, Kelly became more and more the driver, and thusly the owner, of DeLisaGroup proposals. In my *responsive* role, I became more the cheerleader, providing less and less frequent feedback and coaching, while also becoming the clearer-of-blockages guy, helping her (and us as an enterprise) become successful in the function. The continued synergy between us got us to producing a clearer, more consistent proposal document, a better set of guidelines for pricing projects, and more definitive client-consultant responsibilities during a project – all the while allowing me time to buy a new golf bag and hit the driving range.

Kelly and I were now ready for the final step, the second "S" in *BOSS2000* which stands for:

Sustain Success

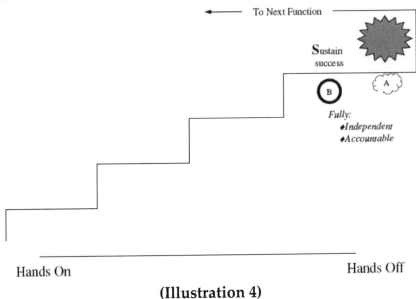

(Illustration 4)

You'll notice this step is pretty much about "B" (Kelly). I, as the "A," am just a wispy figure off to the side, floating within a cloud. The above graphic implies that as the boss I'm certainly available for sage guidance whenever needed, but my role that at one time was chief proposal writer had now diminished substantially. As a real fact in our enterprise – and between Kelly, who is now the proposal chief, and me – I rarely, if at all look at proposals. To be sure, I am fully aware of and involved in the discussion regarding the scope of all potential client projects and engagements, but the format, content and flow of all DeLisaGroup proposals are in her capable hands. So far, so good. Kelly had risen to the occasion and became, as stated in the graphic above, "fully independent" and "accountable" for this important function. As you can see, *BOSS 2000* is a fairly easy management model to understand and navigate. If you were paying attention in Chapter 3: The Basic Objectives of Managing Others, and especially the section on *The Three Buckets*, *BOSS 2000* is a formal way of moving things from the *My Way Bucket* to the *Our Way Bucket*, and finally to the *Your Way Bucket*. Because each step of the way is designed to have a low-risk/high-success experience for both the boss and subordinate, the process itself is rather enjoyable; uplifting even. In fact, if managed as designed and with full use of the *Seven Fundamentals*, you very likely could avoid developing any kind of formal performance appraisal system, or blow up the one you've got. Now, wouldn't that be terrific! More on this point later.

Right now at least some of you have to be thinking, what if the Kellys of the world can't master a function? What then, smart guy?

Funny you should ask, because that's precisely what happened to me when developing the *BOSS 2000* model. And it happened with Kelly, the seeming superstar. While working with Kelly on developing her skills as a proposal writer, we began a conversation about her doing some marketing of our company's services. Up to that point, DeLisa-Group's approach to expanding our client base was to rely mostly on referrals. The only active marketing we did was to maintain steady contact with existing clients through occasional newsletters and meeting with them over coffee, lunch, or dinner. It was entirely casual, but very effective. Being with our clients in this way gave us insights to their current issues, problems and successes. Most often, these get-togethers did not result in immediate business for us, but this face time with them helped fortify the relationship. And relationships are what our business was and is all about.

All of this philosophy was explained to Kelly as we initiated Step 1 of *BOSS 2000*, with me *autocratically* telling her that I wanted her to make at least three informal appointments with clients, and I provided her with the steps we followed as a company in setting up these appointments and conversation points we cover during the meetings. Under the *Fundamental No. 2: Be Curious* banner, I asked Kelly what her thoughts were about the assignment, what additional help or information she might need, and if she felt she could do it. She expressed some mild anxiety about calling on what to her were "strangers," but felt she could give it a good go, especially if I would provide her with a list of clients who would "go easy" on her. I gladly provided her with several names. *Moving Day* was set for three days out from that meeting.

On the eve of *Moving Day*, Kelly stopped by my office and (in a bit of a sheepish tone) asked if we could postpone the meeting until the following week as she was pretty much on overload with other tasks. I certainly obliged and should make a point here. Although emphasized earlier that *Moving Day* should be considered a sacred event, and not readily cancelled or postponed – especially by the *Unforgettable Boss* – in realistic terms, though, stuff happens, and there should be some degree of flexibility in keeping to the committed day. As in all *exaggerated learning* efforts, try to *never* violate the date, and then you will only about half the time. It was unlike Kelly to ask for a postponement, so I was a little surprised, but it was no big deal.

On *Moving Day* redux, Kelly, who never beat around the bush, came right out and confessed having a hard time getting herself to make the phone calls. In the couple of calls that she actually did make, she found herself hoping for voicemail (who hasn't wished for that before?), and got tongue-tied in requesting the get-together; feeling a bit like she was selling life insurance (no intention of alienating any of the life insurance salespeople who read this book). In short, our *marketing* process was daunting for Kelly, to say the least. And for her to press on with it was certainly not going to meet our *BOSS 2000* criteria of low-risk/high-success experience. So it was time to apply the lessons of *Fundamental No. 7: Life is Just One Big Cost-Benefit Analysis* (CBA) to this situation. The basic concept of *BOSS 2000* is to keep moving people up the steps toward *Independence,* function by function. That's the goal. However, the model also recognizes that not everyone will master all the functions, or in some cases not even get past *Moving Day.* The CBA question for me in this instance was: Does the benefit of taking Kelly off the hook of mastering the *marketing* function worth the cost of taking her off the hook? This one was easy. Kelly was knocking the cover off the ball on at least three other functions she had been assigned to become proficient at: proposal writing, stand-up presentation skills, and seminar design. It was a no-brainer for me to tell her to dump the marketing efforts to possibly re-visit another day, another month, or even another year. As far as I was concerned, DeLisaGroup was way ahead of the game just having Kelly in the house.

As I said, this CBA was easy. But in other situations with other employees, the CBA didn't work out so well – for either them or me. Let's say Kelly's job as a consultant within our enterprise was to perform the four functions mentioned: proposal writing, marketing, stand-up presentations [training], and seminar design. In terms of importance, the seminar design work had a weight factor of 30 percent; the stand-up presentations 40 percent, and the proposal writing 20 percent; leaving a weight factor of 10 percent for marketing. As you can see, if Kelly's issues were with either of the first two functions, the CBA might have come out differently. This *weight factor* idea is a good one to employ when doing a CBA, but it isn't always reliable. Sometimes you have to go with *feel* or intuition, as in the case of a bookkeeper (not Alice, by the way) we once had working with us. She was the most accurate and well-organized person we had ever had in that position, but she was a she-bear with clients: harsh, uncooperative, alienating, and just plain mean spirited. One client reported to me that dealing with her was like being kept after school and getting your knuckles rapped with a ruler. If you were to ask me before the fact what the weight factor for *Pleasantness* should be for a bookkeeper, I would have said 10 to15 %, with the other 85 % being distributed equally between *Accuracy* and *Well Organized*. But in her case, we threw the percentages out the window and showed her the door.

The postscript to the story of Kelly and her marketing skills is that today she generates well over 50 percent of our new business through marketing efforts that were *synergistically* revised between us and others over time. Much of the reason why she is so successful in this function today is that she had the freedom to choose *not* to be measured on that function at the beginning of her employment with DeLisa-Group. Given that she could then have a more or less guilt-free period where she could hone her other skills, she then could comfortably choose the time to become more engaged in marketing efforts. Throughout this period of re-evaluation on her part, I'd like to think Kelly never felt unfairly judged or evaluated (a la The Cornerstones of Trust) by me or anyone else in the enterprise. I guess you'd have to ask her, though.

BOSS 2000 can be an all-encompassing tool for you in homing in on and developing the talent of the people who work in your enterprise. However, it does take time and a real commitment for it to work well. One of the time and effort payback benefits of using this model is the possibility, as mentioned above, of dismantling (or avoiding instituting) a formal performance appraisal system, because in its own way and like any good performance appraisal system, *BOSS 2000* is a continuous measurement tool that allows the *Unforgettable Boss* to stay on top of a person's performance, positively reinforcing the good stuff, tweaking progress plans, or counseling weak performance.

The Pain and Payoffs of Performance Appraisal Systems.

If you have a formal performance appraisal system in place, I don't have to tell you what a dreaded activity it is. If you don't have a performance appraisal system, it's probably because you heard from a colleague what a dreaded activity it is. I could write a whole other book just on this subject, and many have already been written. In fact, I've recently read a couple that make a case for eliminating a formal performance appraisal process altogether (although I haven't read about any really good suggestions for what to do instead). Let's at least devote some space to tips on making performance appraisal less *dreadful*; then *you* decide if you either want to fix yours, never institute one, or use *BOSS*

2000 or a modified version of it instead.

In all the years that I've been a management consultant, I can still count on the fingers of one hand those enterprise owners/managers who actually look forward to conducting performance appraisal meetings, not to mention a similar dread the employee feels in having to sit through what is often a grueling session. For both parties, it's a little like going through a tooth extraction without Novocain.

This anxiety is one of the reasons a lot of smaller enterprises don't have a formal performance appraisal system. Leaders or owners of these organizations will often promise themselves they'll get to implementing one when the enterprise gets bigger. "Right now, because we're such a small shop, everyone here pretty much knows where they stand when it comes to doing their job well." Sure they do. Our management feedback survey results show that across industries, the *No. 1 complaint* employees have about their bosses is: "No one ever tells me how I'm doing unless I screw up. Then I hear about it big time!"

Even from our own company's perspective, at DeLisa-Group we're not really big fans of performance appraisal systems, especially as they are designed and used in most enterprises today. And yet, most everyone agrees there is a need to regularly provide some sort of feedback to employees if we want high performance and high morale. It's also true that having a formal performance appraisal system in place, and actually *in use*, provides the company with written documentation in the event it's needed for warnings or terminations (We don't like suspensions [with or without pay] by the way, but that's a subject for the next chapter). However, the *need for written documentation* motive is far down our list of reasons why you should do performance appraisals at all.

As I see it, among the reasons for the discomfort and dread, on the part of both management and employees, regarding performance appraisal systems and their use are the following:

- **Lack of Clear, Measurable Performance Goals and/or Plans for Getting There.** Without clearly stated goals within job functions (e.g. proposal writing), it's difficult to know where to start the discussion about performance. Remember: "A goal without a plan is just a wish."

- **Lack of Regular Communication Between Boss and Subordinate Regarding Glitches, Speed Bumps or Potholes in the Work Relationship, or Lack of Progress Toward Goal Achievement.** The tendency is to store up the negatives and dump them out at performance appraisal time. Coupled with this is an inability or hesitancy on the boss's part to give praise because the person might get a big head and start goofing off, or worse, want more money. Can't we get past that frayed belief?

- **The Boss's Tendency to do Most of the Talking and Very Little Listening.** I see the avoidance of listening as a fear of dealing with the unknown. After all, if you're doing all the talking, you never have to deal with what's on the mind of the employee; essentially, you're controlling the outcome and never getting at the root cause of problems or even successes. By now you should automatically be thinking of *Fundamental No. 2: Be Curious.*

- **Worrying About How to Argue About the Difference Between a *Good* and *Outstanding* rating.** And certainly, no boss I've ever known looks forward to labeling someone *Average,* or goodness forbid, *Below Average.*

- **Having to Talk About Money and Performance in the Same Meeting.** Most managers don't want to have this discussion, so they go for the safe middle on both the ratings and pay increases. As a result, if the person is really not performing up to standard, there's no documentation of it on file. My colleagues who are human resource professionals will tell you it happens all the time.

Here are a few tips for off-setting these fears and missteps in managing the performance appraisal system. First off, we like to get our clients to use the term *Performance Planning* when defining and designing their process, because we see it more as looking *forward* than looking *backward*:

- **Beginning on the Date-of-Hire, Introduce the New Employee to the Performance *Planning* System.** It often happens that new employees never even see the performance "appraisal" form until the actual formal review meeting is held. The form or system should really be a re-stating of the job description for the position. Review each of the line items on the job description (that now becomes a performance planning sheet), and try to be as specific as possible about what you expect on each one in terms of performance. See how much this is like the *Begin Autocratically* step in BOSS 2000? If you can tie the expectation to a number (e.g., produce 37 to 40 parts/hr), that's even better. If you are just setting up a performance planning system, have this same conversation with existing employees at least three months before the formal meeting in order to reduce the number of surprises.

- **Regular Verbal Communication About Performance During the Year Helps Reduce Anxiety on Both Sides.** This means getting out and wandering around more; checking in with employees to see how they are doing, briefly discussing goals, offering helpful tips, and directly confronting performance issues *as they happen* (and with as much privacy as possible). Also, don't overlook opportunities to catch them doing something *right!* This way, when formal performance planning/review time comes around, there are fewer surprises. Again, this suggestion is pretty much a duplication of the BOSS 2000, especially the middle steps. Leave it to us consultants to find three or four different ways to say the same thing. Job security, I guess.

- **Follow the 70/30 Communication Rule During the Actual Review/Planning Meeting.** Similar to what Kelly preached in the previous chapter on candidate interviewing, you should do 30 percent of the talking while the employee does 70 percent. The more the employee talks, the more ownership he or she takes for the results. For this to happen, you have to really work on learning and applying the skills taught in *Fundamental No. 2: Be Curious; Fundamental No. 4: Authorship Leads to Ownership;* and *Fundamental No. 5: Freedom and Commitment Go Hand in Hand.* It can't hurt to repeat some earlier messages by stating that applying these *Fundamentals* in this situation means you're showing a genuine, sincere and non-judgmental interest in the other person's views, thoughts, ideas and explanations. This further means an over-emphasis on your part on *open-ended* questions such as: *"What are the obstacles keeping you from getting higher quality output?"; "Are you ready to move on to more complicated work?"; "If so, what kinds of jobs would you like to try?"; "What are you doing about trying to be more consistent in getting jobs done on time?"; "I notice you seem to be struggling with that new software. What's that all about?"* Try looking at the meeting as an opportunity for two people to have a dialogue that includes both good and bad news. And don't fret in anticipation of the answers you might get to your *Be Curious* questions. As I asked before, what's the worst thing that can happen? Besides, you're still the boss, no matter what. You might want to actually electronically record a performance planning meeting and do a word count to see if you're keeping to the *70/30 Communication Rule* as one of my engineering clients once did (not to stereotype anyone).

- **Avoid the Use of a Grading System and Try a "Pass-Fail" One Instead.** Whether it's a letter grade system (A, B, C, D, F) or a word grade system (Walks on Water, Above Average, Average, Below Average, Should Disappear), none of them works well, because people (boss and employee) get hung up on the letter/word score. Nobody wants to be *average*, or even *above average*, as long as there's a score above that one. A *pass-fail"* system is two columns headed by *Meets Expectations* over one column and *Needs Improvement* over the other. Leave room on the form for written comments that support the rating, plus additional room for writing up a brief *Action Plan* for where there's a *Needs Improvement* issue. You might ask: "What about the really exceptional job a person did on a project?" Easy. Make note of that in the written comments section. Or, you might ask: "What about the person who needs the lowest possible score in order to get the message?" Easy again. First, do you really think giving a person a "failing" grade will actually serve to improve his performance, or is he likely to become [more] embittered? Second, a person who gets the very bottom score in any category on the performance planning form should either have been counseled months before or be in someone else's company. But we'll deal with this more in the next chapter.

- **Unbundle the Compensation Discussion from the Discussion on Performance.** This one is a bit tricky, and there are several ways to approach it. Generally speaking, discussing both these important topics, money and performance, at the same time, results in Linda Lou wanting only to look at the number at the bottom of page 2 that shows her increase, and she's probably not listening a whole lot to the performance stuff. We try to get our clients to find a way to give pay increases at the end of the fiscal year and do reviews on the employee's date-of-hire anniversary. We get a lot of push back on this, largely because clients would prefer to "get it all over with" at once, and we don't blame them. But thinking about it, if you follow the tips I've outlined above, the whole process becomes less dreaded, plus our belief has always been that compensation increases should be based, among other things, on the company's performance, which is information you have at hand at fiscal year-end. In brief, if you can find a way to unbundle these two events, the performance planning meeting becomes that much richer and worthwhile.

One final thought and one that might be the most valuable in terms of reducing the dread of the event: "Dialogue before draft." Before committing anything at all to writing, meet with the employee first to ensure both of you are familiar with the components of the process, then to have an informal discussion about general performance; maybe even each of you doing a rough draft that you'll bring to the formal meeting. Any of these tactics is way better than you showing up with a performance review document, in "ink," with a compensation amount written in on the bottom of page 2 that's already logged in to the payroll system – no wiggle room, and just another of the many reasons why performance appraisal is such a burdensome and taxing experience for everyone. Another potential and positive payoff to this informal meeting is that you might well learn about activities and efforts the employee has engaged in that are to her credit and you don't even know about. No matter how much of an *Unforgettable Boss* you think you are, you can't know everything!

Summary: Here's what I hope you learned in this chapter.

• **The *BOSS 2000* model** is designed to show a simple but highly effective procedure for growing people, especially the ones you never want to lose. A subtlety of the model plays off *Fundamental No. 5: Freedom and Commitment Go Hand in Hand.* It usually works out that an employee who knows she can choose to take on a task or choose not to, for whatever reason, is way more likely to stay and grow in an environment that projects this value. *BOSS 2000* also plays heavily to *Fundamental No. 2: Be Curious*, because the information the employee shares with you throughout the process not only enriches that person's experience and ability to perform, but also the job function itself, through synergistically produced improvements. The most obvious of the *Seven Fundamentals* that applies to *BOSS 2000* is *No. 4: Authorship Leads to Ownership* because the whole idea behind this model is to transfer accountability (aka *ownership*) from you to that person. Here are the key points of each step...

- **Begin Autocratically**

1. The new assignment (new function) needs to be delivered in a highly directive fashion in order to increase the guarantee of high success resulting from low risk on the part of both parties.

2. Give clear messages. "I'd like you to do things in this order, and for you to have typed notes available every Friday morning so we can be sure you're on the right track."

3. Prepare the employee for *Moving Day* in phase two by having her make notes on any changes she would suggest that might improve the task or function.

4. Set a specific date for going from phase one to phase two. Without such specificity, you might let go of your authority too soon or hold on to it forever.

5. Always check for the employee's understanding. "What's still unclear to you? What questions can I answer? How about repeating back to me your understanding of the assignment so we'll know we're on the same page."

- **Open Possibilities**

1. This step, *Moving Day*, is the time at which you begin to *move* ownership of the function from the incumbent to the employee.

2. Be sure to use this time to synergistically find ways to improve the way the function can be

performed in the future. "Let's go over what you've been doing, and any ideas you might have to make the job more efficient." For synergy to blossom consider that it's OK to *attack* the ideas, but always support the person.

3. At this point, you'll also be getting clues regarding whether or not the person can really handle the function at the desired optimum level of performance. If the signs (postponements, complaints, unreasonable excuses, etc.) point to a real performance blockage, do a Cost Benefit Analysis (*Fundamental No. 7*) to help you decide to push a little harder, back away or find someone else who is better able to do it.

• **Sponsor Independent Thought**

1. The employee should at this point be trying out some of the agreed-upon changes and meeting with you along the way to do progress checks.

2. The *ownership* of the job should now be in full shift mode as the employee does more and more of the authoring, with you functioning now as the mentor, *guiding, encouraging, praising* and *correcting* as needed. Just be sure you're doing all four things in balance. The *Unforgettable Boss*, as mentor, also leads the way in securing resources the employee needs or removing blockages.

3. You can also now book a hotel and get theatre tickets for the trip you've wanted to take.

- **Sustain Success**

    1. This is where you want to be. Valhalla! Heaven! Nirvana! At the beginning of this chapter, I quoted a message from John Rosemond when he talked about not rushing to have a *relationship* with an employee; that your efforts should be to bring out the *best* in the people you are leading so that they *qualify* for that relationship with you. This is where that happens in the *BOSS 2000* world. The employee is *fully independent and accountable*, allowing you to be colleagues with each other when it comes to the particular function being mastered.

    2. As the functions get mastered one by one, the collegial relationship advances to a point where it is more therapeutic than anything else. You offer the relationship occasional pieces of wisdom and gentle challenges, and the employee brings you issues he or she can't share with anyone else, and perhaps vice versa. You are now more *partners* than anything else. As the Beach Boys sang, "Wouldn't it be nice!"

- **Performance Appraisals are a Painful Event** for both employee and boss for a lot of reasons, not the least of which is that most performance appraisal systems are designed to create a win-lose interaction – having forms and new pay levels filled in before the meeting, the employee being unaware of what's being evaluated until the meeting is held, the boss being lousy at *interviewing* the employee to find out why he is doing so poorly, or even a general awkwardness in delivering bad or good news. Perhaps most prominently, traditional performance appraisals are ineffective because in meeting with the employee once or even twice a year you are usually dealing with stale information about events that happened in the then-and-there versus the here-and-now, thereby opening the door to arguing over the validity of recalled rather than current information and feedback. The *BOSS 2000* model, if used properly, can take the place of a formal performance appraisal, and because it's an ongoing process all the pertinent data are fresh. Adding the flavor of *BOSS* 2000 to the proceedings helps the process be more about performance *planning* instead of *appraisal,* focusing on setting and monitoring future goals rather than looking backward. If you are committed to using a formal procedure, then in addition to following the performance appraisal dos and don'ts offered in this chapter, remember to use the meeting to get feedback from the employee on how *you* are doing as a boss. You do want to be *Unforgettable,* don't you?

7

THE TOUGHEST PART OF THE JOB – COUNSELING AND TERMINATING

"A relationship, I think, is like a shark...it has to constantly move forward or it dies...What we got on our hands is a dead shark."
                              - Woody Allen as Alvy Singer in Annie Hall

If you can't change the people, change the people.
                              -Attributed to more consultants than one could count

Personnel Policy Manuals: Cure or Curse?

The subject of personnel policy manuals has been raised several times in this book, and I think my feelings have been made known about bosses relying too heavily on them, often at the surrender of good common sense. For those of you who are founders of your enterprise, or joined it at its earliest stages, I'm sure you remember those blissful days when it was just you and the few others there running things. You all understood the goal, worked hard, generally liked each other, and probably socialized or even vacationed together. You overlooked what you saw as each other's shortcomings because you had a common interest in growing and nurturing the enterprise. No work rules or policies had to be written because each of you understood the expectations of the others and the job you had to do. Knowing it or not, you were forming an inner circle the textbooks call *The Dominant Coalition.* Those who fall into this category can now refer to themselves as *The Dominant Coalition,* which is a much cooler and more regal title than *The Over The Hill Gang.*

But how things do change as the enterprise grows. As you add rings of new people around this inner circle, you add the need for more clarification and separation of duties and responsibilities, a crucial activity most business builders don't do all that well. Conflicts begin to arise, and some people appear to *misbehave,* especially in terms of doing things differently than the norm. To clarify: *Norms* are a set of expected behaviors within the enterprise that are *not* written down anywhere, but exist in the minds and hearts of the good old *Dominant Coalition.*

At home, the parents are considered to be the *Dominant Coalition,* because they established the enterprise and therefore set the norms of acceptable behavior. (Lately, though, the more I see of the *Self-Esteem Movement,* where the kids have been made the center of the universe, the more I wonder who actually is holding the winning hand at norm-setting. But that's a subject for a whole 'nother book.) Examples of *norms* in our home lives are: trash removal, when and who; leftovers night; who gets the chair with the hassock for TV viewing; or even when the TV gets turned on and off.

Norms in the workplace take the shape of things such as:

assumed parking spaces, who sits where in the conference room during meetings and who talks first or last; clothing preferences (e.g., casual or dressy); bringing lunch to work or ordering out; or even political leanings. Now here's the curious thing about *norms:* If, by definition, *norms* are accepted forms of behavior and are not written down anywhere, then the only way a person usually learns about a norm is to *violate* it. In other words, normative behavior evolves over time, and no one within the enterprise, be it a family household or workplace organization, thinks to remind newcomers about them. So, for instance, the first time Laurie Ann has her boyfriend over for a family dinner, and he chooses to sit in the chair by the window, he finds out by the shocked looks on the family faces that he's in Big Bart's chair. Obviously, families don't have a dining table seating chart posted on the refrigerator, so it should be understandable that the boyfriend would make this *mistake.* Nor would it be expected that after such an event the family would now create such a chart (read as: *new policy*). That would be ridiculous.

Similarly, if a new hire violates a norm by not wearing a tie on the first day at work, would we now write a policy about wearing ties to work? Wouldn't that be just as ridiculous? Or would it? Think here about how often we jump to creating policy when a good old fashioned chat would serve just as well – most likely, even better.

So much for *norms.* They're interesting and even fun to think about (*engineers use pocket protectors*), but this section of this chapter is really about how norms become policy. At some point in the evolution of any smaller enterprise, and especially as those rings of new employees come on board, there is a compelling need to formalize *how we do things around here,* which spawns written policies, known by various titles such as *Personnel Policies and Procedures* and *Employee Handbook.* I've already made the case that all too often it's only about 11 percent of the people in the enterprise for whom we write personnel policy manuals. They're often referred to as the *Rest Room Lawyers,* spending all their spare time (and some of the enterprise's time, too!) looking for the loophole in the policy; the one thing you've overlooked so they can drive their *Gotcha* truck right through it. As Netflix says on their website describing their culture, "Rules annoy us." They should annoy you, too. It should annoy you that you get forced into a chess match with just those few people in your enterprise who will never be happy with anything you do or don't do. It should annoy you that about 90 percent of the people who make good to excellent contributions to the enterprise have to suffer being treated like children by having another limiting and finger-wagging policy written. Finally, it should annoy you that whoever heads up HR in your enterprise is spending way more time writing and rewriting policy when that person could and should be spending that time seeking new ways to attract and keep good people.

Mark Soycher is an attorney and human resources counsel at the Connecticut Business and Industry Association (CBIA). He is CBIA's point person to answer questions for and to guide the hundreds of member companies and organizations in their human resources issues, especially in the area of compliance. Many of these organizations have fewer than 50 employees, and therefore no HR professional on staff.

Mark has been a valued colleague and friend for years, and shares my concern that we can get policy-happy, writing and sticking one in every new hole in the dike. Mark espouses common sense over policy whenever possible. Remember Spencer who owned The ABC Plastic Box Company, where doughnuts awaited the job applicants? His Personnel Policy Manual was one line: *Treat others as you would like to be treated* (The Golden Rule). Really. Mark Soycher echoes that same sensibility when he advises CBIA members that a policy that says, *We try to treat our employees fairly and expect them to do the same with each other and the company,* is a great start, and the rest of whatever gets written should be in the form of referential guidelines for carrying out that spirit, rather than hard and fast rules. A *guideline,* as opposed to a *rule,* offers ideas and suggestions, but in work-related terms, leaves it up to the manager to *do the right thing.* To the question that Mark and I often hear, *"What about those people who need more hard and fast definitions of the limits?",* we both say maybe you've got the wrong people. Mark recently told me of a workshop he led with a bunch of HR folks in attendance, and they were challenged to write policies in 25 words or less. He reports it was a difficult exercise, but a valuable learning event for almost everyone there. For those of you who have a policy manual, you might want to check out your word counts, plus see if you may be trying to cover too much territory.

Of course, because of certain federal and state requirements, there are some rules that must be in writing. But, as much as you are able, rule with your head and even your heart, not a book. And don't even mention the concern about one department allowing latitudes another doesn't, like what time people show up for work or the time they leave. *Be Curious.* Ask questions and get a dialogue going about why different departments or work units do things differently and how you can form what are popularly called *best practices.* Yes, it is riskier than having a written policy to rely on or to hide behind, but you'll work it out. Oh, and be sure to check the rest rooms from time to time to see whether anyone is in there grousing.

The Case Against Progressive Discipline...Which Isn't Very Progressive at All

Before we finally get to discussing the dos and don'ts of counseling and termination, here's another beauty of an idea that needs to be put out to pasture. The term *Progressive Discipline* derives from there being a step-by-step process or *progression* when disciplining an employee. And it usually is set up in this manner:

- **Step One: Verbal Warning,** where the employee is told she'd better stop or start doing something different than what she's been doing or she could get into trouble. Excessive tardiness is a common example of a situation where *Progressive Discipline* gets initiated. Sometimes a *policy* has been written stating what precisely constitutes "excessive tardiness" – six times in a calendar quarter, for instance. Admittedly, having specific numbers involved occurs mostly in union shops, but there are some obsessive-compulsive enterprises that have an over-the-line number for everything.

- **Step Two: Verbal and Written Warning.** If the tardiness continues, a similar verbal warning is given, along with a written one that gets placed in the employee's file. The written warning usually states that the employee's *job is in jeopardy.*

- **Step Three: Suspension Without Pay.** Probably many tedious weeks after the initial verbal warning was issued, the employee gets sent home for several days without pay. Now here's where this setup really loses me. With a suspension-without-pay move, the assumption on the part of management is that the employee will suddenly have a blinding flash of insight and realize just how wrong he has been, and spend the three or four days doing penance and lighting candles to the company management. Can't you just see the scene when he walks in the door: "Hi, hon...I'm home. Guess what? I just got suspended for three days without pay, and boy did I ever deserve it!" C'mon. Are you kidding me? A line like that can only occur in a really bad movie. What really happens is the employee becomes irate, bitter and self-righteous, eventually marching up to Step Four.

- **Step Four: Termination.** Both sides finally part company. Unfortunately, and in my experience with watching clients and the terminated employees go through this joint agony, the time between Step One and Step Four can take months! It's a little like Purgatory, where both souls are suspended somewhere between Heaven and Hell, and for a very long time.

I *do* believe there needs to be a formal process for counseling an employee, one that might eventually lead to termination. But the traditional *Progressive Discipline* course of action is built around negativity and is clearly antithetical to what has been preached under *Fundamental No. 1: Always the Boss, Never the Parent. Progressive?* I think not. *Regressive* is more like it. What we need, then, is a methodology that has the best possibility for a positive outcome, while still conveying to the employee that what he or she is doing or not doing is unacceptable. This methodology should also contain an element in which the employee can have a voice in determining what constitutes acceptable work behavior (similar to the *synergy* opportunities reviewed back in *BOSS 2000*). Such an element in the process promotes the practice of *Fundamental No. 4: Authorship Leads to Ownership.*

A good place to begin the search for an alternative to traditional *Progressive Discipline* is to briefly examine what initially appears to be an odd contradiction in terms; a principle called *Non-Punitive Discipline,* or discipline without punishment. The term has its roots in child psychology and gained traction in the '90s, largely at the efforts of Alfie Kohn, a widely recognized – and seen by some as controversial – author and lecturer on child-rearing and education (Kohn, 2005). One of Kohn's gems is: *"'Give 'em an inch and they'll take a mile' mostly describes the behavior of people who have hitherto been given only inches."* The way *Non-Punitive Discipline* works in an at-work setting is as follows:

- The employee, let's say, Mildred, has been advised numerous times about her excessive tardiness and absenteeism, a whole calendar of X's. She has been written up a few times, but there has been very little improvement.

- Mildred meets with her boss, Martina, for the umpteenth time and is told she's being suspended for one day, but *with pay* (yes, you read that right, *with pay*). Her one day suspension is called her Decision-Making Day, during which she has to reflect on whether or not she wants to stay and play by the rules, or if she really can't live up to the expectations and therefore will *choose* (notice *Fundamental No. 5: Freedom and Commitment Go Hand in Hand*) to leave. In other words, it's her call.

- Mildred is home the next day, having been disciplined but not punished, because she still gets paid. It is hoped that she ponders her decision.

- Mildred comes in the next day and gives her answer, which historically in most cases is: "Yes, I want to stay and abide by the rules." Mildred leaves the meeting with the understanding that if the tardiness and absenteeism continue, it will be interpreted as her breaking the deal struck with Martina; thus, she will have essentially decided (*chosen*) to leave. How simple. How adult.

Now, whenever I've explained the *Non-Punitive Discipline* process in a seminar of bosses, there are always a few who scoff at this notion and offer comments like: "I'll bet there's a whole bunch of people who would line up to get a paid day off like that." Or: "Why would I pay someone who's broken the rules?" Or: "DeLisa, you don't live in the real world."

I'd guess the number of people who express these arguments in my seminars equates to roughly 11 percent of the group. Hmmm.

Hitting People in Their Pocketbook

One more point before diving into a better model for counseling employees: I'm not a compensation specialist, nor do I play one on TV. That said, I'd like to briefly address another anachronism that no longer belongs in workplace practices: the habit of trying to improve performance by withholding rewards. I'll get right to the point. Giving an employee a 1 percent increase at review time (when the average increase is 3 percent) as a way to send a message that he must improve his performance makes as much sense to me as suspending him without pay for two days. Yet another episode of: "Honey, I know I'm home early, but guess what? I not only got suspended for two days without pay, I also only got a 1 percent increase because of my poor work output. I just can't wait to get back there on Monday to show them how much better I can do! Let's go out and celebrate my new insights."

In my experience, the *1 percent increase philosophy* has never worked the way it was intended. Like the two-day suspension without pay, instead of an energized, pumped up employee parading around dressed in company colors, all you get as the boss is bitterness, *Victim Unit* behavior, and another member of the *Restroom Lawyers' Association*.

Two points to consider here that will help fix this situation:

1. Any and all performance problems (which include time and attendance as well as quality and behav-

ioral issues) should be managed as they occur, not stored up to be dumped out at compensation review time.

2. Everyone in the enterprise should be given the same base increase (bonuses for outstanding performance is a fine idea, but a matter for a separate discussion). If you feel the person doesn't deserve the same base increase as others, and you counseled him, as suggested in the first point above, then the person shouldn't be in the enterprise. Hitting him in the pocketbook is a cop-out, and you haven't done your job. And if you have the secret hope that getting only the 1 percent increase will motivate him to leave the enterprise, then we both know you're kidding yourself.

As full disclosure: This second point on compensation is clearly a minority view in the world of consulting and has always been a difficult one for my clients to embrace and put into practice. Except for a small handful, most of them still maintain a three-tier compensation system, usually 1 percent for poor performers, 3 percent for average performers, and 4 to 5 percent for top dogs. They just can't seem to get their heads around paying a malingerer the 3 percent.

Every couple of years we have the same discussion about it, and at least most of them have worked on implementing the first point of dealing with performance issues in the present, so the needle is moving in the right direction. I'm just not a big fan of any multi-grading system, whether it's in performance appraisal or compensation. Please don't misunderstand me on this point. It's not that I feel, as *Self-*

Esteem Movement advocates do, that everyone should get a trophy just for showing up. Not at all. It's more that unless you're on jury duty, I have a tough time with the notion of anyone sitting in judgment of anyone else, ever. I know we all fall victim to being judgmental, some of us more often than others. But we should always strive to find alternative behaviors in those situations, which actually is what the *Seven Fundamentals* is mostly about.

All the multi-grading systems I know of just don't play out well. There are too many bruises caused when we use grading systems based on some sort of a bell curve. And even though most enterprise leaders talk the talk of bell curve distribution, whenever we look in the personnel files of employees – and HR professionals usually will nod in agreement with me on this – there is no real curve. Everyone pretty much gets the same performance appraisal grades and/or compensation; somewhere right down the middle. But, again, this is a subject for another whole conversation, so give me a call if you want to kick it around. Maybe we'll come up with something really clever together.

Toward a Healthy Model for Counseling

Way back in Chapter 1, *Physician, Heal Thyself,* I made a case for self-examination, a portion of which is to consider the part you, as a boss, play in the health of relationships you have with your employees. When there is positive electricity and energy between you and them, there's a part you play, and you should take credit for it. Likewise, when there is heat and conflict, you also play a part and need to take *credit* for that as well. Here's a good illustration:

Aaron is a client who works as hard as anyone I know in trying to do the right thing as a boss in managing the people in his modest-sized enterprise (a 50-person service firm). One day, while he was doing a performance review for Lucille, one of the office staff, he very gently (at least according to his recollection) mentioned a few areas where she needed to improve. Almost immediately, she broke down in tears, bolted from the room, got her coat, jumped in her car and went home! And this was in the middle of the afternoon. Aaron was "flabbergasted," to use his word. He couldn't imagine what could have possibly triggered Lucille's response to the feedback he was giving to her. She did have a reputation for being a bit thorny and defensive (performance factors he was addressing during the review), but he hardly thought she would react in such an extreme way.

When Lucille came in to work the next day, Aaron could have done several different things. He could have channeled Tom Hanks as the baseball manager in *A League of Their Own (1992)*, and confronted Lucille with: "Crying? There's no crying in office work!" Or he could have done what I know a lot of bosses would do – hide out for a few days, avoiding Lucille at all costs until things blew over, probably promising himself to never again meet with her without someone else in the room. What Aaron actually did was, I thought, quite courageous. His first act of courage was to spend some time mulling over what he might have done to lead to Lucille's meltdown, recalling that earlier in the day he and a couple of other folks in the office were making ominous, exaggerated comments about the *looming* performance review meetings everyone had to go through. Behind these comments, which Aaron was now realizing were juvenile, was Lucille's anxiety with the performance review process, which she had expressed several times earlier in the week. Aaron figured the joking around, while not maliciously intended, might have contributed to Lucille's emotional eruption. So his second act of courage was to meet with Lucille as soon as she showed up for work the next day and check out his hunch. Of course he was also clearly playing the *Fundamental No. 2: Be Curious* card. Very nice move, Aaron!

The short of the story is that Aaron was dead on in his hunch that the jokes pushed Lucille over the edge. He sincerely apologized to her, which was followed by Lucille's apology for overreacting, which was followed by Aaron commending Lucille for her willingness to own her part in the clash between them, which was followed by Lucille suddenly becoming a much happier camper and more productive to boot. I can attest first-hand to this last part of the story, because on my next several visits to the company subsequent to this episode, Lucille was absolutely more upbeat, friendly and cooperative than I had ever seen her before. Do you think Aaron's no-excuse apology, coupled with the fact that he was willing to talk about the situation with Lucille in non-judgmental and *Be Curious* tones was instrumental in her softening? I do. Very, *very* nice move, Aaron!

In preparing ourselves for a counseling session, then, the first step is to think deeply about the part we might be playing in the need for such counseling. Ask yourself whether you have all the facts, whether this is a pattern or a single instance, whether this is the only person who does this, and maybe most importantly, whether this is an oil-and-water mix with you and this person only, and not between her and others.

I don't know about you, but in my history as a boss, there have been a few people in the various enterprises I owned or ran who pushed me to the edge, but with whom others had no problem. Ralph Waldo Emerson wrote, "We boil at different degrees," which I take to mean that our lack of, or patience with, other people varies. A most simple example would be movie actors who some of us come close to worshipping, while others of us wouldn't even enter the multiplex cinemas where their film is showing (If I have to hear Julia Roberts' cackle one more time, I think I'll get sick!). You perhaps remember my mentioning earlier in the book the situation where one manager replaced another in a regional office. Both were equally good at managing people, but one employee who thrived under the first manager clashed with the second. Neither the new boss nor the subordinate was right or wrong in any specific way; they just saw work life through different lenses.

One reason for the above phenomenon of boiling at different degrees might be in the notion that while opposites may attract in marriage, they don't as much at work. For instance, as a boss, you might be a sequential thinker, preferring to follow one subject to its logical conclusion without distractions. And the person you're considering counseling may function more like a spontaneous-combustion engine, firing on all cylinders at once. You can see where that kind of relationship could be a hotbed of conflict and irritation. This is not an easy fix, because objectively speaking, a strong case could be made for the importance of having both types in the enterprise. You might never fully embrace, or even accept, this person's work style, and at times it will take a mighty struggle on your part to co-exist with it. In some instances where it's been clear that the employee is a real asset to the enterprise, and his behavior is not aberrant as much as it is just annoying to the boss, we have coached bosses to step aside and let this person report to someone else with whom the chemistry is better. Sometimes, it's whatever works. Now, if your situation is such that there really is no one else who this person can report to, then I suggest you take another look at whose name is over your door and act accordingly. Hint: You're still the boss.

As an added thought, if you have, or are trying to develop, a management team, consider this: during our consulting work on building and fixing work teams, we have consistently found that in spite of team leaders (bosses) trying to build a unit of diverse styles, the most harmonious teams are the ones where members are more alike than different. Further, while it's logical to believe that diverse teams are usually more creative and dynamic, they require a lot more conflict management skills to survive, again for the same reason that opposites don't really attract as much as you'd like to think.

I've now devoted several pages to the idea of extensive self-examination one should engage in prior to entering the counseling arena. That self-examination includes giving thought to:

1. What part do I play, or might I be playing, in the problem I'm having with this person?

2. What *opposite* behavior is this person demonstrating that is turning me off? And is there a redeeming quality to this behavior that I'm not seeing that is really beneficial to me or the enterprise?

This self-reflective exercise gains in importance the more you avoid painting yourself into a corner with a lot of written policies. It's a given that the more written personnel policies you have, the more arms-length objectivity you have in determining when a transgression has occurred, the extent of the transgression, and the consequence of the transgression (e.g., six events of tardiness in three consecutive months results in a written warning). Conversely, the fewer written policies you have for the enterprise, the more you need to rely on subjective judgment. Now, I admit that if those two statements don't look like a compelling case for *having* written employee policies, I don't know what does. I still maintain, though, you'll be a better and more content boss using the *Seven Fundamentals* as the underpinnings of good, common-sense counseling and termination decisions, and not being hampered by the constrictions of a thick, onerous volume of written personnel policies. And I'll even go so far as to guarantee the contentment – if you follow the counseling and termination models that follow.

As one last swing of the bat at the danger of trying to write your way out of trouble, I place in evidence the following policy on bereavement leave taken from an actual employee personnel policy manual:

...Eligible employees may take bereavement time for immediate family, defined as spouse, parent, child, sister, brother, grandparent, father-in-law, mother-in-law, and same-sex domestic partner...The length of the leave depends upon the circumstances, but up to three working days are granted if needed. On other occasions, permission to attend services for deceased colleagues and other close relatives or friends can be made at the supervisor's dis-

cretion. In these cases, employees may be paid up to three hours to attend local services without deductions from personal or vacation time.

(Getting a headache yet? Wait, there's more.)

If an employee is on vacation, and an immediate family member dies, bereavement leave will be provided in place of vacation. An employee on an unpaid leave of absence is not eligible for bereavement leave pay. Please see the following policies for additional information...

(OK, now I'm done, and you should be too. I can just hear the buzz going on in this company's restroom.)

Level One Counseling: Preparation

The preparation steps for a counseling session can be worked out by yourself, but the ideal is to have a colleague *study buddy* or professional coach to guide you. In any case, here are the key points to consider. I suggest you actually write down your answers to these bulleted items. (NOTE: For the purposes of this exercise, we'll assume you've already spent the required time in analyzing "the part I play," and "the behavior that's turning me off"):

- *What's the Violation?* Was a written policy or procedure involved, or was it more in the realm of norms? Is the *violation* a subjective call on your part (therefore possibly one of which the *violator* is not aware, such as what hours salaried people are really expected to work), or is it an objective breach of which the person should have been aware, such as missing deadlines?

- *What Are My Goals, and Are They Realistic?* What outcomes do I expect, so that I can convey them to this person during our meeting? Can this person actually change enough to achieve them? For instance, counseling someone to be more leader-like is probably unfair if she is an extreme introvert.

- *Be on the Lookout for Conciliatory Gestures,* which is a sign from the employee that he wants to improve, cooperate, or take ownership of the problem. A good example is what happened between Aaron and Lucille when she offered a return apology. Conciliatory gestures are crucial to a win-win outcome, and they usually occur about midway through the session. Always positively support them and never abuse them. Aaron showed positive support when he thanked Lucille for acknowledging her overreaction rather than abusing her gesture by saying something stupid like: "Well, see to it that it never happens again."

- *Manage Meeting Logistics*
  - o Find a private place, and be sure it's not just used for such meetings (*"Uh-oh, the boss is meeting Jerome in the boiler room...Jerome's in big trouble"*).

  - o Should anyone else be present? Try to meet one-on-one, especially if it's the first time on this issue. Witnesses or corroborating testimony comes later.

  - o Ensure you won't be interrupted. I can't think of anything more rude, except for taking two parking spaces at the mall.

○ The meeting should be held as close to the in-fraction event as possible, or at least once you've done a cost-benefit analysis. The script should always be, "Could you please come with me to [name of room]?" Telling someone you'd like to meet with them on Monday or even two hours from now is the act of a terrorist.

Level One Counseling: The Meeting

Now that you've done all this advance preparation, the rest of the process, while still anxiety laden, should be a bit easier to navigate. Back in Chapter 4, on communication skills, I introduced you to the *Describe and Ask* tool, calling it "the bridge between presenting and listening." Let's pull that handy gadget right back out of the tool box and use it again, because this meeting is about a dialogue, not a speech. In other words, whether, as in *BOSS 2000*, you're helping someone develop or hone a skill set, delegating a new task or responsibility to them, or you're in a less comfortable counseling session, you still must have a two-way interaction, primarily to ensure there is an effective transfer of ownership (*Fundamental No. 4*). And *Describe and Ask* is the vehicle to get you there. Are you ready? Here we go:

• **Describe** the behavior or incident being addressed, and explain how it violates a policy (written or un-written), procedure, norm or expectation. Examples (Notice I use the people's names when addressing them; makes it a less formal, more personal situation):

○ "Joe, you've been late five days in the past month,

and even though we don't have a written policy for tardiness, I think this is excessive."

o "Mary, you often appear to huff and roll your eyes when I'm giving directions on something I want done. Not only is it annoying, but it makes me think there's something going on with you that you're not telling me about."

o "Ronnie, I find that I have to check your work for mistakes more often than I should, and the mistakes I find are threatening our quality rating with our customers."

Notice that each of these *Describe* scripts are just that, *descriptive.* There's no threat, sense of finger wagging, or pejorative tone. When a statement is descriptive such as these are, there's an implication that a dialogue is coming, one that's open to an alternative opinion. And that's precisely what you want at this stage.

- **Ask** the employee if he understands or is aware of the violation. Remember that oftentimes there is a really poor orientation to the job, or the *violation* could be against one of those speed-bump norms we keep dropping under the employee's feet. So, it behooves us to determine if simple ignorance of an expected behavior is involved. Secondly, you want to *Ask* the employee to explain the cause of, or reason behind, the "violation."

o [Joe] "Are you aware of the number of late days, and do you agree that it's excessive? (Wait for the answer)...What's the reason for it?"

o [Mary] "Are you aware that you're giving off these signals? (Wait for the answer)...Is my interpretation correct, or is there another reason for your reactions?"

o [Ronnie] "Are you aware you've been making numerous mistakes? (Wait for the answer)...What's causing them to happen?"

This *Ask* step is probably the most important, yet most overlooked part of the counseling process. When first describing *Fundamental No. 2: Be Curious* back in Chapter 3, it was mentioned that in the role of parents and bosses, we fear information, especially the kind we think will burden us with an unwanted task in the end, or a problem for which we don't have an answer. Let me emphatically state that the problems (*violations*) you're dealing with in these counseling sessions are *not* yours to solve! Elements of the first four of the *Seven Fundamentals* are in play here, and you should rely on them to help you get your arms around this *toughest part of the job*.

Start by realizing that counseling is nothing more than guiding people to their own solution, one that, if you're the boss, you should be able to agree with (but not design). Then use the following *Fundamentals* as the poles you can lean on as you walk someone through the process:

- *Fundamental No. 1: Always the Boss, Never the Parent.* Avoid dictating the remedy, because when you do, you become responsible for the success or failure of the outcome, and the game goes on with the *child* doing better only to either please you or to keep you off his back. Neither of these motives is good for the growth of the employee or the resolution of the problem.

- *Fundamental No. 2: Be Curious.* Without your being curious about the cause of the problem and its potential solutions, it just sits there buried under a mulch heap. It will never get better on its own, and you certainly can't expect the employee to *Be Curious* on her own and open the communication door by coming to you and asking how *you* think *she's* doing!

- *Fundamental No. 3: It's Strictly Business, Nothing Personal.* Counseling sessions should always be an arms-length deal, and have little or no emotional content to them. I, of course, acknowledge that in a situation like the Aaron-Lucille interaction, there can be an emotional element involved, but it should never be initiated by the boss, especially an *Unforgettable* one. If emotions come into play, whether tears or temper, do your very best not to engage or get put off by them. What I do under these conditions is channel Aunt Jo and wait it out until the emotions die down, always keeping the goal in mind of getting this thing solved one way or the other. Another thing to remember about this *Fundamental* is that this person, even if a family member, does not *belong* to you. Their life is their life, and this enterprise where you both work offers (or should offer) the mutually beneficial opportunity to earn dollars to help you both live your personal lives in the way you want.

- *Fundamental No. 4: Authorship Leads to Ownership.* This one's easy. The more the employee participates in the solution, the more the employee will live by it, because he *authored* it. The reverse is true as well; no authorship, no ownership.

Managing the Responses

Supported by the *Fundamentals'* reinforcements, let's go back and first examine some possibilities for the answers that Joe, Mary, and Ronnie might have given to our *Asks*, and then figure out how we might now deal with that information while not violating any of the *Fundamentals*.

- "Joe, you've been late five days in the past month and even though we don't have a written policy for tardiness, I think this is excessive. Are you aware of the number of late days, and do you agree that it's excessive?"

Joe Might Say	You Might Respond
"I knew I'd been late, but didn't think it was that often. Is it such a big deal?"	"Yes, it is a big deal. I need to count on people to be here on time, because of the way our work flows. What's the reason for the tardiness?"
Then Joe Might Say	Then You Might Respond
"I've been having some problems with my car. I never know when it's going to act up on me in the morning."	"I know cars can be unreliable. What can you do to take care of it, so you can get here on time?"

Or Joe Might Say	Then You Might Respond
"One of my kids has been getting into trouble, comes home late, and we've been having arguments at 3:00 a.m., so I'm not getting much sleep."	"I'm sorry to hear that. I know kids can be difficult to handle at times. What steps are you taking to resolve the situation?"

- "Mary, you often appear to huff and roll your eyes when I'm giving directions on something I want done. Not only is it annoying, but it makes me think there's something going on with you that you're not telling me about. Are you aware that you're giving off these signals? Is my interpretation correct, or is there another reason for your reactions?"

Mary Might Say	You Might Respond
"No, I'm not aware of doing anything like that."	"Well, you do. Next time it happens, I'll point it out to you. But in the meantime, is my interpretation correct? Is there something going on?"
Or Mary Might Say	Then You Might Respond
"Now that you ask, I feel like you give *me* all the tough assignments, and it's not fair."	"Wow. I wasn't aware of that. What would you like to see done about it?"

- "Ronnie, I find that I have to check your work for mistakes more often than I should, and the mistakes I find are threatening our quality rating with our customers. Were you aware you've been making numerous mistakes? What's causing them to happen?"

Ronnie Might Say "Look, if there is a quality problem, I'm not aware of it."	You Might Respond "Well, there is and has been. Do you know what's causing them to happen?"
Then Ronnie Might Say "If mistakes are being made, it's not my fault. It's that way when the work gets to my desk."	Then You Might Respond "Have you ever taken any steps to find out what's happening?"
Or Ronnie Might Say "I really haven't. I thought my work has generally been OK."	Then You Might Respond "I'm afraid 'OK' isn't good enough. I need you to dig deeper to determine the cause and the fixes. Are you willing to do that?"

It's impossible to cover all the various scenarios of the interactions between you and Joe, Mary, or Ronnie, but I hope these examples provide you with enough realism to get a good idea of how this part of the model works. You'll notice throughout the examples, the boss (you) avoids getting emotionally entangled in any back-and-forth debating, and through the script, you maintain a focused attitude of wanting to get to the bottom of the issue, so a solution can be discovered and applied. You should also note that the boss is practicing the *Cornerstones of Trust* by not judging or evaluating responses given by any of these employees (Joe's attribution of his tardiness to the problem he's having with his kid is assumed to be his honest answer, and even though it might not be the way you'd react in his situation, this is Joe's way, not yours). Finally, notice that the boss (again, you) avoids giving unsought advice or solutions. At this juncture, there is a strong temptation to offer a fix, and in the end you may actually participate in designing a solution. However, in the spirit of *exaggerated learning,* and keeping *Fundamental No. 4.*in the forefront, rein in the advice-giving even more than you normally would (*When you exaggerate the effort, you'll only get halfway there, so go for 100 percent and settle for 50 percent*).

One of my summer jobs while in college was selling pots and pans – or as we were trained to more elegantly describe to the potential buyer, *stainless steel cookware* – door-to-door. Our target market was non-college bound, 18+ year-old girls who had a job (Please don't judge me too harshly; it was the customer profile, and it was the '60s, and I needed a job). This was cold-call selling, and anyone who has ever done it will tell you it's a grueling way to make a buck. Before we went live and on the road we had two days of classroom training on how to pitch, er, *demonstrate* the cookware to "Suzie," which was the euphemistic name for the girl on the other side of the door. The trainer was very good at his craft of cold-call selling, and he was also very animated in his delivery. In addition to showing us how to demonstrate cooking an entire meal on one burner by stacking several pots on top of each other (you might wonder why anyone would want to do that, and so did I), among the key lessons he taught us was how to close the sale, using the *closing question*: "So, Suzie, would you prefer to pay cash or go on our easy time-payment program?" (Two choices, either of which was acceptable) Then the trainer practically screamed at us – no, he actually did scream at us: "Now, you SHUT UP, you SHUT UP, [a third time] you SHUT UP!" His point was, by keeping your mouth shut after asking the closing question, the burden of resolution is on "Suzie," not you; she would become the *owner* of the solution. As I now realize, this is probably when I first learned of the Authorship-Ownership connection, or *Fundamental No. 4*. Who'da thunk such an insight would come from a class on selling cookware?

On second glance, this whole exercise with "Suzie" may look to you to be highly manipulative, and therefore somewhat distasteful, but as pointed out back in Chapter 1, consciously or unconsciously we are manipulating each other all the time. We can argue whether or not getting "Suzie" to buy the cookware was good for her, and therefore a positive manipulation (In fact, the set was of high quality, and I even bought one when I got married.). But I don't think anyone would argue against using the same *closing question followed by shutting up* technique with the Joe/Mary/Ronnie character as a way for transferring problem and solution ownership. The *shutting up* part is quite difficult to pull off, and certainly hard to master. And to be sure, there is some initial uncomfortable squirming on both the boss' and employee's part when the few initial moments of what feels like an interminable silence kick in; but if you're successful with it, you'll be pleasantly surprised at the usefulness of the technique.

Forming a Plan of Action

What usually happens after you've posed the *closing question* and suffered through the inevitable moments of silence, is that Joe/Mary/Ronnie will respond in some way with a soft to moderate, to perhaps even a definitive, commitment to improve, such as was the case with Aaron and Lucille. So much depends on the issue you have, the person's ability to accept responsibility, and your delivery. In any and all situations, however, you *must* have some plan of action before you adjourn the meeting. Otherwise, all you had was a conversation without closure. Remember, *a goal without a plan is just a wish.*

To illustrate how a simple plan – a commitment for improvement – might be formulated, let's go back and finish our discussions with Joe, Mary, and Ronnie:

- In the case of Joe, the *closing question* put to him was, "What steps are you taking to resolve the situation [tardiness based on issues he is having with one of his kids]?" Let's assume he says that he and his wife plan to get some family counseling assistance. Or, he might say that he's grounding the kid for a couple of weeks. Either way, your job is to express support and confidence without getting personally involved in the situation. In other words, you should be telling Joe that you hope it all works out for him; that he's been a good employee and you don't want a poor attendance record to hurt him. Do not offer to speak to the kid yourself, names of good therapists you know, or any advice on how

Joe should be raising his kid (*Fundamental No. 3: It's Strictly Business, Nothing Personal*).

- In the case of Mary, the *closing question* put to her was, "What would you like to see done about it [her feeling you've been giving her all the tough jobs]?" Let's assume she says she's not sure what she wants; that she has mixed feelings about it because she doesn't want to come across as being a shirker, but at the same time can't keep up the pace. Here you are actually free to offer advice, but only if she gives you permission. So, you say, "Mary, would you be interested in an idea I have?" Of course, Mary says yes (What else can she say?). Then you say, "How about we sit down and go over the stuff you're currently working on and see whether we can either re-order your priorities, or off-load some of the work to someone else?" Once again, you're utilizing the Cornerstones of Trust principle of not judging or evaluating Mary's rationale for the problem, plus you're even getting appropriately involved in the solution. How *Unforgettable* are you, huh? Even if you feel strongly about the lack of legitimacy of either Joe or Mary's reasoning, let it go for now. You'll get a chance to right the ship later if, for some unfortunate reason, this initial plan doesn't work.

- In the case of Ronnie, the *closing question* put to him was, "Are you willing to do that [dig deeper to determine the cause and fix of the excessive errors]?" Just by the testy and defensive tone of Ronnie's responses so far, I think it's safe to say that this situation might be a bit more problematic to resolve. So, in this situation, let's assume Ronnie says that he's willing to give some thought to the cause and fix, *but* he doesn't really see value in the effort. Given that *everything before the word "but" doesn't count*, you are justifiably concerned whether Ronnie's investigation will be fruitful. At this point, you could make a strong case for telling Ronnie you don't really trust that he's going to work at this, because of the negativity with which he seems to be dealing with this problem, and I would agree with and support your effort to git 'er done right now by pressing Ronnie on this observation. However, and for the purposes of this lesson, let's accept the rules I've established thus far, and accept and support Ronnie's statements and attitude by telling him you're glad to have had this conversation and you hope he's successful in his efforts. At the least, you're being truthful about hoping he's successful, even though you're hearing and feeling the grinding of your teeth.

So far, so good. If you've colored within the lines of *Level One Counseling*, I'm going to bet you a nickel and lunch that at least two out of these three situations will resolve themselves without further need for sit-downs. Similar to Aaron's and Lucille's interchange, and all the way back to the supermarket example where Walter the store manager worked with Adam the clerk to help him improve his packout rate, just holding the (*Be Curious*) counseling meeting, showing an interest and non-judgmentally accepting and supporting the employee's response, results in a performance surge. It almost always does. As an added measure, you need to recognize and positively reinforce any and all improvements demonstrated on the part of the counseled employee. Let Joe know you appreciate his showing up on time, assuming he does. You might even ask him how things are going with his kid, but be careful here to stay at arms length and not get immersed in Joe's private life. If Mary is doing less huffing and eye rolling, be sure to let her know you notice it. You should also ask how the adjusted workload is going for her. Remember, behavior that gets reinforced will likely be repeated.

Level Two Counseling: The Meeting

OK, let's look at the Ronnie situation. Unfortunately, as we secretly feared, a few weeks go by and not only do the mistakes continue, but Ronnie has never gotten back to you with the results of his research into the cause or fix of the problem. In Level Two Counseling, you will be turning up the heat a little bit, slightly scaling back on *Fundamental No. 5: Freedom and Commitment Go Hand-in-Hand* and relying a bit more on *Fundamental No. 3; It's Strictly Business, Nothing Personal.*

The meeting format utilizes a modified version of the *Describe and Ask* technique, and works like this:

- **Remind** Ronnie of the deal *he* made in which he had agreed to work on the cause and solution to the work quality problem: "Ronnie, I thought we had a deal; you said you would find out why you're having the quality problems and how to fix them. The quality problems are continuing, and I was expecting to get an answer from you, or at least an update on your progress, by now."

- **Ask** Ronnie a couple of appropriate questions like: "What's the reason I haven't heard back from you?" Or: "What progress have you made?" Regardless of Ronnie's responses to these questions, avoid debate and stay focused on resolution. Finding causes was important in Level One Counseling, but going back too far and rehashing will only bog the two of you down in a thrust-and-parry, parry-and-thrust engagement. Right now, you want to look more toward the future, or what happens next. He says: "I didn't know I was supposed to report back at a certain time." You say: "Perhaps I should have been clearer, *but* I thought you knew I was pretty serious about this situation." He says: "There's no real progress, because I still don't really think it's my problem." You say: "It is your problem and until you begin to accept your role in it, we'll be dealing with a bigger one."

- **Designate** a specific time when you expect to receive a plan or resolution. Ronnie is showing signs of not being able to play in an adult sandbox, so instead of relying on him to function as a full grown-up, start to plan for what might be an inevitable termination. The first step is to be more directive by your *designating* a date for resolution, clearly stating your expectations and a possible consequence. It might sound something like: "I really don't like taking this next step, *but* (yes, I remember what I said earlier about the word "but") by next Friday, I expect you to come to me with an answer to the cause of the quality problem and measurable steps to fix it. You can come to me along the way with questions, and I must also tell you that if this problem continues, you're putting your job in jeopardy. That's a conversation I really don't want to have with you, so I hope you don't put me in that position."

You should go on to ask Ronnie if he's clear on what you expect or if he has any questions; but beyond that, if he continues to argue, you might want to employ the non-punitive discipline day-off-with-pay option illustrated earlier. If you do take this step, remember the script Barney and his staff used when they were trying to weed out the 11 percent *(see Fundamental No. 6)*: *"You can come back after the day off and tell me you want to stay and comply with what's being asked of you. Or, you can come back and tell me you can't play by these rules, so you've chosen to leave. But the one thing you can't do is decide to stay and continue to complain about the realities of this job while collecting a paycheck. That would be unethical."* Ronnie would have to get that same speech. Remember also, if you decide to keep Ronnie on board, you need to live by a variation of the same rule and script. If Ronnie continues not to meet job expectations, you can let him go or keep him. But you can't keep him and continue to complain to yourself or others about his weak performance. That would be equally unethical, or at the least unfair.

Fundamental No. 1: Always the Boss, Never the Parent calls for the *Unforgettable Boss* to avoid managing by dictating rules, regulations and behaviors, and generally acting re-strictively toward employees, because that's what parents do. Instead, you are urged to promote self-reliance and per-sonal accountability. Situations like the one developing with Ronnie push you toward the *Parent* function and away from the *Adult* one, and you don't want that to happen. At most, you should settle on a willingness to visit the *Parent-Child* sandbox, but stay only as long as it takes to resolve this is-sue. This is where I see too many bosses (especially new ones) develop a crusty, pessimistic attitude toward employ-ees in general ("Get them before they get you"). Some of them not only visit the child sandbox, but build skyscrapers there! By now, it should be abundantly clear that the *Ronnie* part of your population equals only about one in 10 people. And maybe this *Ronnie* isn't one of them. The Level Two counseling session may serve to scare him straight. Let's hope so. In fact, in my experience – both first-hand as a boss, and in coaching clients on counseling and terminating – the actual need to have a termination meeting (see Level Three Counseling below) is reduced significantly if the Level One and Level Two meetings are managed properly. I recall Mark Soycher, the CBIA attorney and human resources counsel referred to in Chapter 7, telling me that an intriguing question he often challenges managers with is: *If you could never fire someone, what would you do differently?* Level One and Level Two Counseling might offer some good answers.

- **Document** the meeting by utilizing a form such as the Employee Counseling Record shown below. Whether or not the *Ronnie* character signs it is less important than him knowing that's it's going to be put in his file. By the way, almost every human resources professional I know who gets called on by management to help fire someone has the same complaint – lack of documentation. Finally, notice that this form matches up well with the idea of *Describe and Ask* (i.e.., the "Employee's Response").

Bob DeLisa

EMPLOYEE COUNSELING RECORD

Employee's Name _____

Date of
Counseling _____

Nature of need for Counseling:

- ○ Substandard Work
- ○ Carelessness
- ○ Safety Violations
- ○ Insubordination

- ○ Excessive Tardiness
- ○ Excessive Absenteeism
- ○ Excessive Personal Calls or Visitors
- ○ (Other) _____

Supervisor's Comments:

Has employee been counseled before on this matter?　　○Yes　○No

If Yes, Date: _____

Employee's Response (his or her view of the situation; reasons for why the situation exists):

ACTION PLAN: State here any agreements made between supervisor and employee that will improve or eliminate the situation.

It is understood that this counseling record will be placed in the employee's file.

Supervisor's Signature _____　　Date: _____

Employee's Signature _____　　Date: _____

If it walks like a duck, quacks like a duck and looks like a duck...it must be a duck. —Proverb

Level Three Counseling: The Meeting

So far, we're celebrating the success we've had with Joe and Mary, but alas, all seems to be lost with Ronnie. Not only is he coming up with feeble reasons for the quality problem (the vendor's raw material is subpar, the quality inspector has it in for him, etc.), but you've overheard him complaining to other employees about not being appreciated and being dealt an unfair hand by management. He's not only become a member of the Victim's Unit Club in your company, he's running for its presidency.

Prior to this meeting with Ronnie, you have hopefully gone back and re-read the sections of this book on *Fundamental No. 6: The 11 percent Solution* and *Fundamental No. 7: Life is Just One Big Cost-Benefit Analysis.* In doing so, you have now fortified yourself for the unpleasant task ahead. You now know that Ronnie is in the Victim's Unit category of 11 percenters and that there is likely no way this will ever work out unless you want to work on it until your retirement. You also know that the cost of keeping Ronnie far outweighs any benefits you might derive by letting him remain in your employ. Finally, the chances of his leaving on his own are right up there with your winning the lottery.

By the time the meeting is actually held, your mind is made up that the termination is going to take place. Therefore, the suggested script is pretty much a one-way presentation, and you can leave this book on the shelf. I personally prefer the meeting to be a one-on-one, but certainly understand, especially in the litigious times in which we now try to maneuver, that it's a good idea to have a witness sit in, either another manager or a pro from HR.

While on the subject of protecting yourself and the company in this extraordinarily stressful situation, a few other consistent practices you should have in place – and if they apply to your enterprise – are: Having a final paycheck in hand (including vacation and earned sick time pay), COBRA form, life insurance conversion and 401(k) information. If your state requires an unemployment compensation form be given to the employee, provide that as well. In short, have on hand all the information and material you will need to be able to make this meeting the last contact between you. I hope it goes without saying that while you may be providing a person two weeks' severance pay, you never, never give them two weeks' notice and have them hanging around for the next 10 days. Talk about asking for trouble! (Note the words "consistent practices" above. I've seen too many instances where bosses have given two weeks' severance to one person, three weeks to another, and none to a third. Attorneys representing terminated employees love this stuff. Talk about asking for *real* trouble!)

- **Describe** the history of the problem and the situation as it now stands: "Ronnie, we've gone 'round and 'round on this work quality problem. I've asked you to identify a cause and solution, and made myself available for your questions and ideas. I think I've been more than fair. You haven't done your part. Your unwillingness or inability to work on this problem leaves me no choice but to let you go."

- **Ask** Ronnie if there's anything he'd like to say. However, I'm raising a big red flag here. Asking the person if he wants to say anything is an optional step and should be used only if you've rehearsed a lot with a study buddy, or mastered *Fundamental No. 3: It's Strictly Business, Nothing Personal,* and are thus able to completely detach yourself emotionally from the dialogue. When I'm doing live training on this subject, most workshop participants turn white when I suggest this step. So if you're feeling I'm way out there for suggesting it, I can't argue with you. I still think it's a good idea, because inviting questions shows you to be secure in your decision. But again, I would avoid doing it if you're not fully prepared to manage the comments you might get about you not being fair, the company being too cheap to buy good equipment, other people getting away with the same behavior, all the good things he did in the past, and on and on. The trick to it is not to get caught up in an argument, and rather stay with responses like, "I understand you feel you weren't treated fairly." "I understand you disagree with my assessment." Whatever they say, *understand* without getting baited into a discussion. Throw in a head nod or two and a few "uh-huhs," and you'll look and sound like a pro. Gaetana is an HR professional whom I respect a lot. She's one of the rare ones who can equally represent the feelings and position of management and employees. The exit line she has used over the years when conducting a termination meeting is: "We gave it a good run." Gaetana claims the line came from Jack Welch's time at GE. What I especially like about the sentence is that it doesn't assess blame, simply expresses a reality, and implies that all parties can now move on (not so different from Dave Mason's song line about *"no good guys...no bad guys...just you and me and we just disagree"*).

- **Don't back down.** You've put lots of time and energy into this relationship and situation, and even though you're tempted to change your mind, you should feel confident that you've done all you can to save the situation. Tell yourself that backing down will only prolong the agony; that you would not be helping the enterprise, the employee, or yourself.

To further buttress your resolve in closing the book on Ronnie, you should remind yourself that in not taking action, you're running a high risk of losing some of your best performers (the 17 percent). Don't think for a minute that your "A" players aren't watching to see what you do about *Ronnie.* I mentioned much earlier that anecdotal research suggests that a high toleration of 11 percenters can serve to drive out your "A" players. Like the *Off* switch being flipped on a giant turbine engine, they slowly whirr themselves down from peak performance, then rather quickly exit your enterprise and go somewhere else, because "A" players can only perform at high levels and are able to dumb down only temporarily.

I want to provide you here with some counsel on how to end the meeting, but because of the variables involved (as examples: Is the person mild-mannered and reasonable, or temperamental; are you operating in a union environment [you have my sympathies]; are there hard and fast termination procedures in place), the best I can do is offer some general guidelines or considerations. To every extent possible, treat the person respectfully and courteously. If they appear they want to shake hands, shake hands. Be sure to get their keys, security cards and such but in a kind manner ("I will need your keys and laptop. Is there a way you can get them for me without it being embarrassing?"). These days, it seems to be a preferred practice to escort people to clear their desks then out of the building. If that's your practice, try to be subtle about it. Try thinking in these terms: *Am I sorry about this? Of course I am. However, I'm not sorry I'm doing it, only that it has to happen.*

Termination meetings drain everybody. Unfortunately, most bosses postpone them for way too long, hoping the situation or the employee will just go away. But neither of those things ever happens. And as time goes on, the bitterness grows on both sides. One of the downsides in terminating someone is that you'll probably be seen by that person as an *Unforgettable Boss*...in a *bad* way. That's not such a terrible deal. The number of the people who will still love you is about 89 percent.

Summary: Here's what I hope you learned in this chapter.

- Personnel policy manuals have their place in the enterprise, but they are not a substitute for good management. As organizations grow in size, new people get added and the way things get done become more complex. During this growth period, there is a strong tendency to manage the day-to-day ambiguities of work-life through a set of written rules that can actually stymie the enterprise's forward movement, because of the energy and effort required to develop and enforce them. Ruling with a combination of your head and heart rather than a volume of written rules calls for a bit more courage, but the payoffs of a healthy, more vibrant enterprise are worth the effort. Guidelines requiring individual judgment are great, but when it comes to written policy and procedures, less is more.

- Similarly, having a *Progressive Discipline* procedure in place can quite often serve to cause more alienation and conflict than cure. In theory, progressive discipline makes a lot of sense, because it lays out the steps to take in hopefully improving the relationship between the employee and the boss or the employee and the workplace in general. In practice, however, completing the usually four-step process can take months. Some of the delay occurs because paper is used as a correspondence tool rather than the spoken word (People get written up with a note in their file, but very little dialogue with the boss about the cause of and solution for the problem). Then the boss waits and hopes that the problem will go away by itself, but it doesn't, and more time goes by. Progressive discipline also has built into it a step where the employee is suspended without pay in the hope that he or she will "get religion" while at home. When there is a need for counseling, do it *in the moment*, when the infraction occurs. Waiting until performance review or until some other future date after you've accumulated more evidence is not a good idea.

- *Level One Counseling* is a formal but not rigid dialogue with the employee being counseled, and the objective is to determine awareness and cause of the infraction, plus a plan for improvement. Employing the *Describe and Ask* technique is a useful and non-threatening way to do this, mostly because it keeps the *ownership* of the problem and *authorship* of the solution with the employee where it belongs (*Fundamental No. 4*). All counseling meetings should be held in private. The boss should express confidence the plan will work, and provide *attaboys* for all signs of improvement.

- *Level Two Counseling* turns up the heat a little bit because the employee hasn't kept to the commitment made at Level One. Here, the boss becomes more directive and clearly states improvement expectations within explicit time frames. The boss is still interested in hearing the employee's thoughts and ideas, but a little less so. The results of this meeting should be documented and placed in the employee's file. Finally, if Level One and Level Two counseling is managed effectively, you're more than likely able to preempt Level Three.

- *Level Three Counseling* is really the endgame and is more about putting into effect a decision to terminate than actual *counseling*. Using a study buddy or executive coach to help you write and practice scripts for any kind of counseling meeting with an employee is extremely valuable, but especially so for the termination meeting. It's essential to keep *Fundamental No. 3: It's Strictly Business, Nothing Personal* in your mind, script and tone.

If you have a hero, look again; you have diminished yourself in some way   -Sheldon Kopp

A Few Closing Thoughts

Over this 35-year career, I've had the good fortune to know and work with a lot of *Unforgettable Bosses*, and the one thing they all have in common is what can be best described as a split personality – but it's a healthy one. In one lane of their mental parkway, there is self-doubt, concern about doing the right thing on behalf of the people they manage, to a point of regularly seeking feedback from their employees and colleagues. They then take that feedback and keep trying to work it into their daily management efforts. Traveling in the other lane is self-confidence, the courage to take risks with people-based decisions. They have a sense about people that says, "I'll trust you until you show me I can't," rather than the other way around. (They're the kind of people who while driving and stopping at an intersection will ask their passenger in the jump seat if it's safe to pull out to make a left turn. If they get a "yes," they do it without looking to the right, even a little bit.) In my view, it's this almost paradoxical combination of traits that make them so successful in the boss role.

Becoming an *Unforgettable Boss* is certainly not an easy task. It requires almost a pre-occupation with the welfare and morale of everyone in the enterprise, and that includes yourself. I mentioned the concept of exaggerated learning several times, striving to apply a new skill at the 100 percent effort level, knowing you'll only get half-way there. It's a good way to learn something new, but it can also make you feel like you're failing more than you actually are.

They say there are two things you don't want to see being made: sausages and legislation. Now you can probably add a third: bosses. Becoming any kind of a boss is a flawed process. There is no one straight road to get there; too many confounding variables get in the way. As a result, your enterprise and the people in it need constant tinkering. I smile when I hear people talk about dysfunctional families. I'm thinking, show me a *functional* one! Similarly, show me a functional enterprise. In the end, be a little easy on yourself. Sheldon Kopp also said as part of his Register of the 927 Eternal Truths: *How strange, that so often, it all seems worth it.*

REFERENCES

A League of Their Own (1992), *Imbd.com*/title/tt0104694/quotes, Retrieved April, 2012.

Berne, Eric (1964), *Games People Play-The Basic Handbook of Transactional Analysis*. New York: Ballantine Books.

Blanchard, K.H. & Hersey, P. (1977). *Management of Organizational Behavior, 3rd Ed-Utilizing Human Resources*. New Jersey: Prentice Hall

Briggs, P., & Myers, K.(1998). *Myers-Briggs type indicator Form M* [Booklet].

Drucker, Peter F. (2006). *The Practice of Management* (2nd Ed.), N.Y.: Harper Business

DISC, *Wikipedia.org*/wiki/DISC assessment, Retrieved April, 2012

Enneagram, *Enneagram worldwide.com*/explore_the_anneagram, Retrieved April 2012

Hogan Assessments, *Hoganassessments.com*/Hogan-personality-inventory?/ Retrieved April, 2012

Kavanaugh, James (1972), *There Are Men Too Gentle to Live Among Wolves*, N.Y.;E.P. Dutton

Kohn, Alfie (2005). *Unconditional Parenting, Moving From Rewards and Punishments to Love and Reason*, N.Y., Atria Books

Rosemond, John. *Wikipedia.org*/wiki/John_Rosemond

Skinner, B.F. (1948), *Walden Two*. Ind.,Hackett Publishing Company

Welch, Suzy & Welch, Jack (2005), *Straight From The Gut*. Harper Business

See what **Bob, Kelly** and company excel in
by visiting <u>delisagroup.com</u>

Made in the USA
Middletown, DE
12 April 2016